Screen Saviors

Screen Saviors

Hollywood Fictions of Whiteness

HERNÁN VERA AND ANDREW M. GORDON

ROWMAN & LITTLEFIELD PUBLISHERS, INC.
Lanham • Boulder • New York • Oxford

To our brothers Rodrigo Vera, Cristián Vera, and Phillip H. Gordon

ROWMAN & LITTLEFIELD PUBLISHERS, INC.

Published in the United States of America
by Rowman & Littlefield Publishers, Inc.
A Member of the Rowman & Littlefield Publishing Group
4720 Boston Way, Lanham, Maryland 20706
www.rowmanlittlefield.com

PO Box 317, Oxford, OX2 9RU, United Kingdom

British Library Cataloguing in Publication Information Available

Library of Congress Cataloging-in-Publication Data

Vera, Hernan, 1937–
  Screen saviors : Hollywood fictions of whiteness / Hernan Vera &
Andrew M. Gordon.
    p. cm.
Includes bibliographical references and index.
  ISBN 0-8476-9946-3 (cloth : alk. paper)—ISBN 0-8476-9947-1 (pbk. :
alk. paper)
  1. Whites in motion pictures. 2. African Americans in motion
pictures. 3. Race relations in motion pictures. 4. Motion
pictures—United States. I. Gordon, Andrew, 1945– II. Title.
  PN1995.9.W45 V47 2003
  791.43'655—dc21

                                                    2002010037

Printed in the United States of America

♾™ The paper used in this publication meets the minimum requirements of American
National Standard for Information Sciences—Permanence of Paper for Printed Library
Materials, ANSI/NISO Z39.48-1992.

Contents

Foreword: A Nation of Sheep

Joe R. Feagin

In this pioneering and highly original book, Hernán Vera and Andrew Gordon analyze popular Hollywood movies made since 1915. They choose movies made by white directors and producers to examine how whites present themselves and their history. In a consistently insightful and provocative analysis, Vera and Gordon explore how these major movies celebrate the reality and power of whiteness and thereby disguise or distort the country's long racist history.

Hollywood movies are much more than a matter of entertainment. Hollywood has become a major educational institution. For the majority of Americans, Hollywood's movies are a constant source of images, ideas, and "data" about the social world. Indeed, the average citizen spends about 13 hours a year at movie theaters, and half of all adults go to the movies at least once a month. Even more significant, given the country's multiracial future, is the fact that a majority of younger Americans view going to movies as very important in their lives, and more than six in ten watch at least one movie video a week. Almost all U.S. families now have a VCR, and watching movies is the top leisure-time activity. Americans spend a large portion of their waking time watching movies in theaters and on television, far more time than they spend on other sources of information such as magazines and books.[1]

Some social commentators view this media-drenched situation as a great achievement in human communication, as a major enlightenment of humanity and a support for democracy. Yet, moviemaking and the other mass media are today controlled by a very small and quite undemocratic elite, one that is substantially concerned with maintaining current class, racial, and gender arrangements. This media elite is a major generator and reinforcer of the ideologies that rationalize the social hierarchies of this very unequal society. This elite has long dominated the creation and dissemination of system-rationalizing ideas by means of the mass media, politics, the schools, and the churches. Today, the mass media, including movie theaters and television, provide powerful tools to disseminate this system-rationalizing ideology in its many subtle and blatant forms.

Who are the members of the U.S. moviemaking elite? Today, just a few dozen people, almost all of them white men, run the movie business. All are at the helm of companies that are part of very large media conglomerates. Women and people of color have, at best, a marginal presence in the shaping of moviemaking and most other media enterprises.[2] Many of the white male moviemakers are relatively liberal in their personal politics; yet when it comes to racial matters—as Vera and Gordon show well— they still offer up a mostly sanitized and whitewashed view of the racial and other social history of the United States. There are, of course, few actors, writers, and directors of color in their midst to counter white prejudices and stereotypes about social worlds. Indeed, over the years many white, male movie executives have participated in limiting the role of, or discriminating against, African American actors, directors, and writers. Other than a few token black stars such as Halle Berry or Denzel Washington, most of Hollywood's productions today employ few African Americans or other Americans of color in influential positions.[3] Given the absence of Americans of color in key positions, it is not surprising that the views offered by Hollywood are often misinformed or thoroughly whitewashed.

Vera and Gordon provide much evidence for how this whitewashed world was created and how it has evolved over the decades. They show that the central elements of this racially stereotyped world have been created by the world's most prominent moviemakers, many of them men of high intelligence and much creative imagination. Examining major movies since the first decades of the 20th century, Vera and Gordon demonstrate and explain the many negative images of African Americans that appear there, images that were communicated to countless millions of viewers over numerous generations.

In some early films, such as the much-heralded *Birth of a Nation* (1915) celebrating the Ku Klux Klan, images of African Americans are viciously racist caricatures. Early white moviemakers made no attempt to portray African Americans or their lives realistically. In these movies, white Americans are always the heroes and African Americans are portrayed as villains, cheerleaders, or bystanders to white history-making.

In regard to racial imaging, perhaps the most influential Hollywood film ever made is *Gone with the Wind* (1939), an extraordinarily popular and still money-making film. It is today shown many times a day and in countless countries around the world. This movie has played a central role in communicating to Americans of many different backgrounds, as well as to people in other countries, what U.S. history (the Civil War) and U.S. racial relations are supposed to be about, from a white perspective. Vera and Gordon quote one woman who says that *Gone with the Wind* has taught "three generations [of whites] how to be Southerners." All the heroes in this racist film are white, whereas the black characters are mostly stereotyped as loyal servants or mammies. Vera and Gordon present a clear argument for how this movie has, for many decades, helped to shape basic images of white and black Americans. Although these early racist movies purport to tell U.S. history, they are basically social propaganda films for the white supremacist view of U.S. history. Their racist fantasies have often been taken for the real world. As the movie critic James Snead put it, film making can, "governed by the film maker's will, imagination, and ideological slant, present a fantasy or ideal world that has nothing to do with the real world, but present it *as if it were the real world.*"[4]

Moving on to more recent movies, Vera and Gordon demonstrate, in a highly original analysis, that there has been a significant decline in crudely racist images of African Americans in Hollywood movies since the late 1950s. Yet this shift in images of African Americans has for the most part *not* been accompanied by a changed image of white society and white institutions. In more recent movies such as *Guess Who's Coming to Dinner* (1967) and *Glory* (1990), the images of African Americans have changed very significantly from those of *Birth of a Nation* and *Gone with the Wind.* Recent, more liberal movie portraits do now encompass the intelligence, bravery, seriousness, and commitment of African Americans. Of course, this major change has not come mainly as the result of generosity on the part of the moviemaking elite but rather from the pressures of African American and other civil rights demonstrators who have protested racial discrimination in the United States since the 1950s.

In contrast to the changing images of African Americans over the course of nearly a century of movies, Hollywood images of whites—and especially white institutions— have stayed much the same. In the late 1900s and early 2000s, as in the early 1900s, the movie image of the ideal white self is always pushed to the center, and it is consistently a white self that is good, brave, generous, and powerful. In *Guess Who's Coming to Dinner*, for example, it is the white patriarch (Spencer Tracy) who dominates the tension in the picture and who, in the end, chooses the racially tolerant option he earlier rejected, thereby upholding the "sincere fiction" of the good white man yet one more time in the movies.

In addition, a number of major Hollywood movies have shown a heroic white self that is a type of "messiah" figure for people of color, a white figure that saves the latter from misfortune. This is true of *Glory*, which centers disproportionately on the white commander of a black military unit. When racial matters appear in Hollywood films, the images of white superiority and virtue almost always remain central.

Even in the pathbreaking Hollywood movie about a revolt by enslaved Africans, *Amistad* (1997), as Vera and Gordon demonstrate well, the central hero is still a white male messiah, in this case U.S. president John Quincy Adams. Although the movie presents the horrors of the slave ships for the first time in a mainstream movie, and has an admirable black hero in Cinqué, the leader of the enslaved Africans, it deals with the brutality of slavery by focusing on a rare event when U.S. legal institutions supported the freeing of enslaved Africans. The only reason this Supreme Court decision went the way it did was because the Africans concerned were *not* owned by U.S. slaveholders but by foreign slaveholders. In fact, virtually all *those same white-controlled institutions* worked hard to keep African *Americans* fully enslaved in this period. It is Adams whose speech to the Supreme Court is seen as the messiah-like moment in the film that results in the Court's freeing the Africans. Although slavery is no longer romanticized, U.S. legal institutions are indeed romanticized, and major aspects of U.S. racism are once again swept under the rug.

Over the course of several other innovative chapters, Vera and Gordon also discuss an array of related motifs that are used in Hollywood films involving racial matters. These include the motif of romance across lines of civilization (e.g., the three *Mutiny on the Bounty* films), the motif of white women being served by black women (e.g., *Gone with the Wind*), the motif of the racial masquerade where whites attempt to pass as not white (e.g., *Soul Man*), and the motif of white and black buddies (e.g., *The Defiant Ones*). Whatever the motif used to channel the film, these movies either have attempted to buttress the racist system (prior to about 1958 and the beginnings of the Civil Rights movement) or have tried to show that once-troubled institutions have changed since earlier periods and are now healthy and non-racist. From the *Birth of a Nation* to the latest Hollywood films, whites as a group have almost always been portrayed as morally and intellectually superior and as meritorious. In recent movies, a few white bigots may appear, yet contemporary society is not shown to be institutionally racist. In few movies is there a serious acknowledgment of the seamy racist side of contemporary society.

Significantly, there is much unity of approach in Hollywood on these racial matters. Vera and Gordon describe and critically analyze Hollywood movies made by dozens of different white directors, producers, and writers, people with different imaginations and styles. Yet virtually all the movies they have made fit the same mold of not challenging white privilege and the racist character of U.S. institutions. Some recent Hollywood movies do question the actions of some racist white individuals, but only a *very* few (*Little Big Man, Bulworth, Lone Star*) try to raise questions about the institutional character of racism in U.S. society.

Unfortunately, recent survey data continue to show that the majority of white Americans still buy into some negative images of African Americans and into the positive view of the United States as not institutionally racist. In addition, most Americans, including most white Americans, are not well informed about important aspects of U.S. history and society. For this reason, the white-male elite can continue to misinform the general population on racial matters. Starting when they are young children, most whites come to adopt the stereotyped and prejudiced views of racial matters held by previous generations and still circulated by established authorities. Among the white authorities, since at least the 1910s and 1920s, have been the moviemakers. Today, as in the past, Hollywood movies communicate much misinformation about U.S. society. For most movie watchers, the movies still teach major lessons about class, racial, and gender understandings; reinforce and support racial and other social hierarchies; and help to perpetuate the deeply inegalitarian foundation of U.S. society.

Like sheep following their leader everywhere, most white Americans accept much of what they see in the mass media as real and use this misinformation to make judgments about the society around them. The movies have had a profound effect on the minds of many people, to the extent that many accept movie fantasies as historical reality. Even prominent Americans have demonstrated an inability to tell the fictional accounts of the movies from real life. For example, in his 1980 campaign for the presidency, Ronald Reagan often described a "true" story about a heroic bomber pilot in World War II. According to Reagan, the pilot decided to land his badly damaged bomber because one of his men was severely injured and said the emotional words, "We'll ride it down together." Yet the account was not from historical reality but from a film, *A Wing and a Prayer*, in which Reagan had been an actor.[5]

Is there hope for change in white attitudes and actions? Are more moviemakers following the lead of the few moviemakers who have occasionally challenged the racist histories, portraits, and images of this society? Sadly, there is little sign of such a change. Conformity to anti-black and other racist imaging persists today and is even becoming a global trend that is creating or reinforcing white-racist images across the world. Every minute of every day, somewhere on this planet, television stations broadcast and movie theaters show many of the most blatantly racist Hollywood movies, such *Gone with the Wind, The Little Rascals*, the many Tarzan movies, the many cowboy-and-Indian movies, and even Disney cartoon classics such as *Song of the South*. They also show the latest movies, those that continue to celebrate white Americans and white-controlled institutions. For nearly a century now, U.S. movie corporations have not only generated and reinforced racist images of Americans of color and stereotyped positive images of white Americans for those who live in the United States but also circulated these racist images in most other countries. The corporations that now control Hollywood's moviemaking and the other U.S. mass media are increasingly in charge of global education. Something like half of Europe's entertainment programs (other than sports) are based on U.S. sources. Growing billions of the world's peoples now get their entertainment from U.S. movies, television programs, and videos, as well as directly from the U.S. Armed Forces' television broadcasts and cable channels.[6]

The consequences of this are negative for African Americans wherever they may be. And there are boomerang effects when those who have watched U.S. movies come to the United States as immigrants. Thus, one study interviewed rural Taiwanese who had never been in the United States. While they sometimes realized that the U.S. mass media were engaged in stereotyping, most still accepted racist views of African Americans.[7] These negative images were gleaned from U.S. movies, television shows, and music videos seen in Taiwan. Similarly, other researchers have reported that recent Latin American immigrants to the United States often have anti-black attitudes when they arrive because they have seen so many U.S. movies.[8] Anti-black images are carried by the new immigrants into the United States and become the basis for negative attitudes toward and negative interactions with black Americans.

The U.S. movie industry is thus heavily implicated in the globalization of racism, and it has been thus implicated for several decades. As Vera and Gordon make clear, a number of reform strategies are now very much in order, if the United States and the world are to counteract this globe-circling reinforcement of racism directed at African Americans and other dark-skinned peoples. At the center of these strategies must be teaching all viewers of the movies a critical approach, one that enables them to see through and behind the creations of those moviemakers who would control our minds, imaginations, values, and practices.

Notes

1. Mediascope, "Media Use in America: 2000," www.mediascope.org/pubs/ibriefs/mua.htm (Ret: May 10, 2002).

2. Entman, Robert M., et al. 1998. *Mass Media and Reconciliation: A Report to the Advisory Board and Staff, The President's Initiative on Race.* Washington, D.C.

3. Lambert, Pam, et al. 1996. "What's Wrong with This Picture? Exclusion of Minorities Has Been Way of Life in Hollywood," *People,* March 18, 1996, 42.

4. Snead, James. 1994. *White Screens, Black Images.* New York: Routledge, p. 134. (His italics.)

5. Carroll, Robert T. 2001. "Memory," skepdic.com/memory.html (December, 3, 2001). This commentary cites Schacter, Daniel L. 1996. *Searching for Memory—The Brain, the Mind, and the Past.* New York: Basic Books, p. 287.

6. Barnet, Richard J. and John Cavanagh. 1994. *Global Dreams: Imperial Corporations and the New World Order.* New York: Touchstone, p. 138; I draw here on Feagin, Joe R. 2000. *Racist America: Roots, Current Realities, and Future Reparations.* New York: Routledge, chapter 3.

7. Hsia-Chuan Hsia. 1994. "Imported Racism and Indigenous Biases: The Impacts of the U.S. Media on Taiwanese Images of African Americans," presented at the annual meeting of the American Sociological Association, August 5–9, 1994, Los Angeles, California.

8. Rodriguez, Nestor. Personal communication, March 1996.

Acknowledgments

We wish to acknowledge Joe R. Feagin, Daniel Bernardi, Malini Schueller, Louise Newman, Robert E. Fox, Norman Holland, Robert Silhol, Felix Berardo, María Inés Vera, Raul Santoyo-Gamio, and Christine Camacho de Santoyo for reviewing and commenting on early chapters of the manuscript. An early version of chapter 2 appeared in *Classic Hollywood, Classic Whiteness* and is reprinted by permission of University of Minnesota Press. We also want to thank Mark Reid, Debra King, and Maude Hines for valuable insights. Dean Birkenkamp provided strong editorial support and patience. John J. Smith gave us valuable technical support. Mary Corliss, of the Museum of Modern Art Film Stills Archive, helped locate many of the photos. The Institute for the Psychological Study of the Arts at the University of Florida and its program assistant, Sonja Moreno, also provided help. The members of the Group for the Application of Psychology and the American Civilization Seminar at the University of Florida as well as the International Conference on Literature and Psychology allowed us to present our work in progress. Sheila Dickison, of the University of Florida honors program, enabled us to team-teach the undergraduate honors course "Sincere Fiction of the White Self in the American Cinema." The students in that class taught us a great deal about the way movies shape what we know of race and race relations. We also wish to thank the graduate students in the "Race and Film" seminar in the fall of 2000 at the University of Florida for expanding our research horizons.

Introduction

Our movies and television shows often do not portray the values of
the real America I know.

—President George W. Bush, on February 21, 2002, in China

Hollywood movies are one of the main instruments for establishing the apartheid
mind-set that leads people of all colors to automatically consider white to be superior.
Hollywood spreads the fictions of whiteness around the world.

Years before I (Hernán Vera) ever set foot in the United States, I had viewed hundreds of American movies in Chile that taught me about the superior qualities of white
Americans and their victories over evil Mexican *bandidos*, savage Sioux and Apache, im-
moral Italian gangsters, and inscrutable, backstabbing "Orientals." I had also learned
about the wonderful friendships between whites and their dark-skinned "inferiors" and
the loyalty and admiration that people of color felt toward whites. These movies gave
me a broad reservoir of images, situations, and behavioral templates to draw on when I
came to live in the United States. Yet I was surprised to learn, when I arrived, that I was
not considered white but Latino and was stereotyped with the consequential contempt.

I (Andrew Gordon) am the grandson of Russian Jewish immigrants who were not
considered whites. Because I grew up after World War II, after the Jews were admitted
into the exclusive American club of whiteness, I have been able to "pass" for white. As
Daniel Bernardi remarks, "There are no whites, only those who pass for white."[1]

In the wake of the catastrophe of September 11, 2001, commentators noted that
American films were perhaps not entirely superfluous in understanding the terrorist attack. The terrorists were recruited from Islamic fundamentalists who see American films
"as infecting their world, influencing their children's attitudes in ways they find abhor-
rent."[2] According to Azmi Bishara, an Arab Israeli member of the Israeli parliament,
America is tearing apart the fabric of Arab society in numerous ways. First is that, "with
its cultural hegemony, it fosters a huge industry of negative Arab images."[3] In the news
about Pakistani reaction to the first American and British air attacks on Afghanistan, it
was reported that a theater showing an American movie had been burned by a crowd of
demonstrators.

In this book we examine almost a century's worth of movies to look at images of
the white self in Hollywood movies by white directors featuring white protagonists and

1

people of another color. We consider the white self to be a fiction. In films, as in real life, a considerable effort of the imagination is necessary to "see" a person. We call these fictions "sincere" because those who construct them are seldom aware of the alternative images they could have portrayed. Films are part of a broader project that leads us to misrecognize the nature of the racial divide in which Americans live. Because the white self is still endowed in today's world with much of the privilege achieved during the colonial era, the way in which white people are presented in the media is important for everyone, not just for whites.

The image that whites have of themselves is acquired by contrast to the images of others; the image these "others" have of themselves is acquired by contrast to the image of whites. Nelson Mandela, who led South Africans out of apartheid, relates in his autobiography "a strange sensation" he had during one of his trips after a change of airplanes. "As I was boarding the plane I saw that the pilot was black. I had never seen a black pilot before, and the instant I did I had to quell my panic. How could a black man fly an airplane? But a moment later I caught myself: I had fallen into the apartheid mind-set, thinking Africans were inferior and that flying was a white man's job. I sat back in my seat, and chided myself for such thoughts."[4]

We are the result of the images, stereotypes, and knowledge that define us and constitute us as human beings.[5] The white self is an invention, a fiction that we take for real and rarely question. In chapter 1 we introduce our conceptual starting point. Subsequent chapters, in a cumulative fashion, develop a theory of the sincere fictions of the white self in Hollywood movies of the twentieth century.

In chapter 1, we provide a series of provisional definitions. In the study of race relations it is crucial to examine the widely shared images that produce and reproduce the way we feel and behave toward others. That is why we study how white directors have represented the white self. Most psychologists believe that these mental images of ourselves and others constitute "a residue within the mind" of relationships we had with important people throughout our lives.[6] As adults we bring to all our relations modes of relating to different people, that is, separate and articulate concepts of whom we and others are. These are referred to as object-relations. The portrayal of characters and situations in film, we believe, leaves "residues within the mind" that are comparable to those left behind by our important relations.

Chapter 2, "The Divided White Self," discusses a series of films about the Civil War from across the decades of the twentieth century: *Birth of a Nation* (1915), *The Littlest Rebel* (1935), *Gone with the Wind* (1939), *Raintree County* (1957), and *Glory* (1990). Each of these films is a landmark of its particular era in the representation of whites interacting with blacks. The image of blacks changes with the passing of time from the gross, vicious stereotypes in *Birth of a Nation* to the heroic rectitude, faithfulness, and valor of the black soldiers in *Glory*. However, the African Americans remain secondary characters coded to enhance the white self. In contrast to this changing representation of blacks, there is a persistence across time in the representation of the ideal white American self, which is constructed as good-looking, powerful, brave, cordial, kind, firm, and generous: a natural-born leader worthy of the loyalty of slaves or subordinates of another color.

The American Civil War has been used in these movies to dramatize a split in the white self. All the movie plots lead to a final reconciliation or reunification of the split white self through marriage or family reunion in the first four films and through sacrificial death in battle in *Glory*.

In chapter 3, "The Beautiful White American: Sincere Fictions of the Savior," we look at a series of Hollywood films about the messianic white self, the redeemer of the weak, the great leader who saves blacks from slavery or oppression, rescues people of color from poverty and disease, or leads Indians in battle for their dignity and survival. The messiah is marked by charisma, the extraordinary quality that legitimizes his role as leader and that of the foreign population as followers. The messiah fantasies are essentially grandiose, exhibitionistic, and narcissistic. In the white mind, racial others do not exist on their own terms but only as "self-objects" bound up with the white self.[7]

In chapter 4, "White Civilization and Its Contentments," we examine *Amistad* (1997), a film that represents the state of the neoliberal agenda on race relations in contemporary America. The film is praiseworthy in many respects. Nevertheless, we argue that *Amistad*, ostensibly the story of the quest of enslaved Africans for freedom, becomes in the Spielberg version yet another sincere fiction of the white self. *Amistad* seems to be on the side of enslaved Africans, but it actually validates white civilization and the American legal institutions that enforced slavery.

Chapter 5, "*Mutiny on the Bounty:* Civilization and Its Discontents," examines three film versions of *Mutiny on the Bounty:* from 1935, 1962, and 1984. We argue that this drama links two powerful themes about which white Americans remain profoundly ambivalent: romance with a racial other and revolution. It provides us, as critics, with a way of talking about racism, sex, imperialism, and rebellion—in other words, of talking about "civilization and its discontents" in different decades of the twentieth century.

Chapter 6, "Racism as a Project: *Guess Who's Coming to Dinner*," introduces Sartre's concept of the project: we examine what films want to bring into being in the future. We argue that, on the surface, the project of this film appears to be anti-racist. It tackles the ultimate American racial taboo of black-white romance. But the actual project of *Guess Who's Coming to Dinner* is to expand the white self by announcing, "Look how tolerant we are!" *Guess Who's Coming to Dinner* plays not only on the objective situation—the audience's knowledge of the historical conditions—but also on the audience's subjective racism.

Chapter 7, "Scarlett and Mammy Revisited: White Women and Black Women in Hollywood Films," argues that the prototype for the relationship between white and black women in American film can be found in *Gone with the Wind* (1939). The relationship of Scarlett and Mammy, rich white mistress and her black maid who functions as mother substitute, superego, and servant, persists in American film melodramas about women since World War II, although modified and, in films of the 1990s, sometimes radically revised.

Chapters 8 and 9, "White Out: Racial Masquerade by Whites in American Film," study films in which a white person attempts to pass as someone of another race. There is a long tradition in American popular culture of blackface minstrelsy. However, only since World War II has the white masquerade been self-consciously incorporated in the plots of movies. Behind most of the white race-switching plots there is a post–World War II dissatisfaction with the limitations of the white bourgeois self—a white self-loathing—and a romanticization of the racial other.

Chapters 10 and 11 concern black-white buddy films. *The Defiant Ones* (1958) established the pattern for the Hollywood interracial buddy film, a formula easily incorporated into many genres that continues today. Although the emergence of the Hollywood biracial buddy film in *The Defiant Ones* coincides with the emergence of the Civil

Rights movement, it may paradoxically work as a way to assert the white self and to contain black aspirations.

Chapter 12 is our conclusion, "The Crisis of Whiteness." We summarize our main finding: the image of the white self has remained essentially unchanged in American films across the twentieth century even as the images of the racial other have changed. Despite the Civil Rights revolution of the 1950s and 1960s, white privilege still dominates American society. The improved representation of racial others is a device to maintain the status quo of white privilege against the recognition earned by these previously suppressed others.

Notes

1. Bernardi, Daniel, ed. 2001. *Classic Hollywood, Classic Whiteness.* Minneapolis: University of Minnesota Press, p. xxii.

2. Turan, Kenneth. 2001. "Seeing Movies Can Offer Relief and a Chance to Escape." National Public Radio (NPR), *Morning Edition,* September 24.

3. Bishara, Azmi. 2001. Quoted in David Remnick, et al. "From Our Correspondents: September 11, 2001," *New Yorker,* September 24, 54–74.

4. Mandela, Nelson. 1995. *Long Walk to Freedom: The Autobiography of Nelson Mandela.* Boston: Little, Brown, p. 292.

5. Foucault, Michel. 1977. *Discipline and Punish: The Birth of the Prison.* New York: Pantheon, pp. 27–28.

6. Greenberg, Jay R., and Stephen A. Mitchell. 1983. *Object Relations in Psychoanalytic Theory.* Cambridge, Mass.: Harvard University Press, p. 11.

7. Kohut, Heinz, and Paul H. Ornstein. 1978. *The Search for the Self.* New York: International Universities Press.

CHAPTER 1

Learning to Be White through the Movies

Why does *Gone with the Wind* touch such deep chords inside me? Maybe because it put those chords there in the first place. This is the movie that taught me and three generations how to be Southerners. It doesn't move us because we are Southern; we are Southern because we have taken this movie to heart.

—Susan Stewart[1]

I was the only Negro in the theater, and when Butterfly McQueen went into her act, I felt like crawling under the rug.

—Malcolm X[2]

Learning to Be White through *Lethal Weapon 4*

The opening scene of a recent popular movie, *Lethal Weapon 4* (1998), teaches its audience about race relations in the United States. Riggs (Mel Gibson) is a white Los Angeles Police Department (LAPD) cop, and Murtaugh (Danny Glover) is his black partner. Through the first three films in the series, they had been established as inseparable friends who would willingly die for each other. They are so close that Riggs for a while even lived in Murtaugh's home. Theirs is a utopian male bonding in which race is never an issue. Their common gender and their mutual devotion to their risky occupation apparently make race irrelevant—for them and, so the movie's unspoken assumption goes, for the rest of America as well.

As the movie opens, Riggs and Murtaugh are the first to arrive in their car on the scene of a crime. A psychotic criminal who is protected by armor and armed with an assault rifle and a flame thrower is destroying an entire city block in downtown L.A. As the partners are pinned down under fire, they exchange secrets about their families. In the midst of the flames and gunfire, Murtaugh, the black cop, tells his partner, Riggs, the white cop, that Riggs's live-in companion Lorna is pregnant. Riggs responds by revealing that Murtaugh's daughter Riane is also pregnant. The implication is that the

Gone with the Wind *has taught three generations how to be white Southerners.*
Copyright 1939 Metro-Goldwyn-Mayer.

partners share such familiarity and intimacy that they are privy to each other's family secrets. These are policemen in a life-or-death situation in which, like soldiers in combat, they must cooperate to survive. The policemen, however, appear to be impervious to the havoc in the background. This is truly a friendship under fire that blossoms through humor and the exchange of embarrassing secrets.

Murtaugh is more shocked by the revelation than is Riggs. His shock is understandable because he and the audience believe that his daughter is unmarried. So Murtaugh's question, "Is he black?" meaning the unknown father, which Riggs comically misconstrues as referring to the flame-throwing criminal, has the black partner introducing the issue of race difference between the partners for the first time in this movie. In the previous film, we had seen that Murtaugh was so possessive of his daughter that he even feared that Riggs had slept with her.

Considering this opening scene, for the film to conclude happily, the following conditions must be met: both Riggs and Murtaugh must survive and remain friends; both the black and the white child must be born healthy; and both Riggs and Riane must be married—Riggs to his pregnant girlfriend Lorna and Riane to the father of her child, who must be a black man. For a happy ending, there must be a restoration of middle-class American family norms, which include not only marriage but also a guarantee against miscegenation. Because all the previous films in the series ended happily, the audience can safely assume from the beginning that all these conditions will be met by the end of the film.

Although the two men are partners, the white hero Riggs is bolder and less afraid than Murtaugh and always takes the lead in any violent confrontation. Thus the scene ends with Murtaugh, at Riggs's suggestion, stripping to his undershorts and flapping his arms like a chicken to distract the criminal while Riggs shoots. The humor throughout the scene, and throughout the *Lethal Weapon* movies, is at Murtaugh's expense, never at Riggs's.

In the previous movies in this series, we had seen the partners progress to this level of intimate friendship. The scene tells us that these men are more intimate with each other than they are with their respective, secret-keeping family members. They are married to each other more than to their respective spouses. The nakedness of the black cop and Riggs's teasing Murtaugh about the little hearts on his undershorts suggest anxiety about a homoerotic involvement between the partners, which is both acknowledged and quickly denied through jokes.

Entertainment seekers will readily recognize the fictional nature of the action comedy. However, recognizing the fictional nature of the race relations portrayed requires a more critical attitude toward the film, an attitude that few filmgoers bring to the movie theater. The relationship between the cop buddies in this scene presents American life upside down. The fact that the concern over race comes from the black cop confirms the white stereotype that blacks are the only ones concerned about race. Furthermore, the fear of miscegenation is placed on the black partner, when historically this has been much more of a white obsession. The level of intimacy in the symbolic marriage between the partners, like that of Huck Finn and Jim, is one of the notions that the audience must accept to consider the human relations portrayed as believable. In a movie in which almost everything else is unbelievable, the idealized white-black closeness must be among the most believable elements.

Lethal Weapon 4: *The idealized closeness of white and black. Copyright 1998 Warner Bros.*

Finally, an American audience in 1998 would be well aware that the LAPD faced chaos in the streets during the 1992 riots, and the violence here might be disturbingly reminiscent of that event. But the presence in the scene of black and white cop partners who love each other, the racelessness of the person committing the havoc (because of the armor we cannot tell if it is male or female, white, black, or any other color), and the total lack of motivation or social context for the violence carefully neutralize all these possible negative associations.

Although the films are targeted to both white and minority audiences, the writers and director of the *Lethal Weapon* series are white men. If we consider this opening scene as the dream of an American white man, it is a fantasy about utopian interracial bonding, a symbolic marriage between a white man and a black man and between their respective families. The white man's identity is dependent on the love and loyalty of the black partner. As fellow policemen, they defend the law in the public realm of the urban jungle while also defending the law in the private realm of the family. The white man would never dream of sleeping with his black partner or with his black partner's daughter. Or would he? Why must these possibilities be raised at all, only to be denied through comedy?

The *Lethal Weapon* movies are preposterous fantasies. It is easy to dismiss them as mere entertainment, a blend of spectacular action and comedy. Yet, in this brief, very strong scene the audience has been treated to a black-white relationship as preposterous and fantastic as the action in the movie, a relationship that the audience has to misrecognize and accept as plausible or real to enjoy the film. The cruelty and inequity of race relations in the United States are thus removed from view and from awareness.

Why Study Movies?

This book examines the way in which the white self is fictionalized in the American cinema throughout the twentieth century in popular Hollywood films with white protagonists interacting with people of another color. And the vast majority of Hollywood films have been made and continue to be made by and about white Americans.

We need to study movies because ordinarily we do not want to think about the influence that they have on us and on our society. We tend to dismiss the cinema as mere entertainment; yet it has profound effects, shaping our thinking and our behavior. As Susan Stewart proposed at the beginning of this chapter, movies can teach us who we are: what our identity is and what it should be. "Radio, television, film and the other products of the culture industries," Douglas Kellner argues, "provide the models of what it means to be male or female, successful or a failure, powerful or powerless. Media culture also provides the materials out of which many people construct their sense of class, of ethnicity and race, of nationality, of sexuality, of 'us' and 'them.' Movies manufacture the way we see, think of, feel, and act towards others."[3]

We need to study movies not only because of what they tell us about the world we live in but also, and most importantly, because movies are a crucial part of that world. In the simulations of the moving pictures we learn who has the power and who is powerless, who is good and who is evil. "Media spectacles," Kellner writes, "dramatize and legitimate the power of the forces that be and demonstrate to the powerless that if they fail to conform, they risk incarceration or death."[4]

We live in a cinematic society, one that presents and represents itself through movie and television screens.[5] By 1930 the movies had become a weekly pastime for a majority of Americans. After 1950, with the advent of television, watching moving pictures became a daily activity, even an addiction, in the United States and other countries in the industrialized world. One report projected that for the year 2001, the average American spent 1577 hours in front of the TV set, 13 hours in movie theaters, and 55 hours watching prerecorded videos at home.[6] This represents 28 percent of our waking time. It is also five times the number of hours the average American spent in 2001 reading books, newspapers, and magazines.

In the same way that literate societies are dramatically different from illiterate societies, the social organization of cinematic societies is dramatically different from that of noncinematic ones. Without taking into account the impact that the moving pictures in television and cinema screens have on the people of a country, we could no more understand contemporary society than we could understand it without realizing the impact of literacy. The daily rhythms of our lives, what we know and what we ignore, are set by the rhythm of and the information contained in the screens of cinema and television.[7] Countries without a film industry can be considered colonies for foreign filmmakers.[8] Within countries, one can, of course, speak of diversely cinematized segments of the population because the time, energy, and money spent on media consumption vary greatly by age, class, religion, income, race, geography, and other such sociodemographic variables.

The Hollywood film industry does not portray all the segments of society and the world populations equally, with the same frequency, accuracy, or with the same respect. Consider that Latinos, who according to the 2000 U.S. Census constitute one of the largest U.S. minority groups, have seldom been represented as the protagonists of Hollywood films. The *Video Hound Golden Movie Retriever Index*, for example, lists only 17 films under the category of "Hispanic America," roughly half of which are Hollywood main releases. In contrast, the same index lists 69 films in the category "Ireland," 151 under "Judaism," 45 under "British Royalty," and even 119 under "Zombies"![9]

Allan G. Johnson notes that of the films that have won the Academy Award in the category Best Picture from 1965 through 1999, "none set in the United States places people of color at the center of the story without their having to share it with white characters of equal importance" (e.g., *In the Heat of the Night* [1967] or *Driving Miss Daisy* [1989]). "Anglo, heterosexual males, even though they are less than twenty percent of the U.S. population," he proposes, "represent ninety percent of the characters in the most important movies ever made."[10] Until recently, most minority characters in Hollywood movies have usually been caricatured and portrayed with disrespect.[11]

Much of what we know about people we consider to be "others" we learn through the movies. The moving pictures allow access to private spaces, scenes that would normally be out of the reach of our eyes. Through the film media we learn what life supposedly is like or used to be like and what it is in distant lands and in private places.

Films also represent us, the spectators, who find enjoyment and solace in them. The streets we walk; the landmarks in our cities we go by; the appliances, furniture, and gadgets we use every day; the cars and buses we ride; and the music we listen to all appear in the movies. The social roles we play—as children, parents, workers, and lovers—are also recognizable in films. The words and the jargon the characters use in the movies are part of the language we speak. In this sense, we, the audience, watch ourselves. Much of the attraction and power of film, its ability to make us laugh or cry and to teach us about the world and about ourselves, rests on our being, simultaneously, spectators and subjects being gazed on.

The cinematic viewing experience, in our opinion, is one of recognizing and misrecognizing ourselves in the moving pictures. Watching a movie is the experience of sharing—or sometimes, of resisting—the way of seeing, the ideology, and the values of the filmmakers, their gaze, and their imagination. Through their technology and their language, films implement ways of looking at class, gender, and race differences. Filmmakers can make us see these differences, but they can also hide them from our sight by creating pleasing fictions. This way of seeing carries the individual and social biases of the filmmakers but also the biases and standpoints of the culture of the people for which films are produced, the culture to which the film belongs.

Political leaders, film critics, social scientists, and filmmakers have all recognized the pedagogical aims of movies. Lenin thought that the cinema was the most influential of the arts, a great teacher that could be shown to huge numbers all over Russia with portable projectors.[12] Thus, while American film was born as an amusing novelty, Russian film was born as a pedagogical tool.[13] German filmmaking reached a peak as a propaganda device in Leni Riefenstahl's documentaries for Hitler's regime.[14] The contributions of the film industry to the propaganda effort in the United States during the World War II and the Cold War are well documented.[15]

Dialectics of Race in Film

In this book, we regard films in a dialectical fashion, considering them in two opposed ways. First, we consider them as a means to celebrate whiteness, to teach what it is like to be white and to enjoy the privilege of being white. Second, we consider movies as social therapeutic devices to help us cope with the unjust racial divide by denying or obscuring white privilege and the practices on which it depends. Our analyses will be informed by this double view. We believe that unless we capture the tension and contradictions between these two intentions and the central need of Hollywood to entertain and to be profitable, we would miss critical elements of the role films play in the production and reproduction of racism in the United States and around the world.

Consider that in Susan Stewart's earlier remark about *Gone with the Wind,* although she recognizes that the film taught her how to be "Southern," she fails to recognize that it only taught her how to be a *white* Southerner: white becomes so normative and universal a category that she does not even need to mention it. She does not notice the ways the film forces African Americans into the background and occludes their story. Recall Malcolm X's humiliation, when he was the sole black patron in a white theater, at seeing how blacks were portrayed in *Gone with the Wind.* Lorraine Hansberry, the black playwright, confirms Malcolm X's response when she writes that *Gone with the Wind* did not teach blacks to be blacks.[16] The fact that in the United States white "goes without saying" in statements such as Susan Stewart's is an important trait of what in this book we call "the white self."

How did we select the films? The vast majority of Hollywood films are by, for, and about white people. We are therefore interested in twentieth-century Hollywood film written, produced, and directed by whites and featuring white protagonists interacting with people of another color. For that reason, we have excluded films by African American directors such as Spike Lee or John Singleton. Although they are excellent filmmakers, we are interested in how whites present themselves to wide audiences. Most of the films meet one or more of the following criteria: they are regarded as classics, have been nominated for Academy Awards, are popular video rentals, or have received much critical attention. The exceptions are lesser films that help us elaborate a particular theme. For the most part, the films we study are easily available through video outlets.

Theory in This Book

We are attempting to map out a territory that until recently has been largely neglected. Although there have been several fine recent books on critical white studies and on particular aspects of the white self in cinema,[17] what distinguishes our study is its comprehensiveness—the wide selection of films from across the twentieth century (in the final chapter, we also consider a few films released in 2000 or 2001) and the attempt to show how the representations of the white self in Hollywood films are part of a project that wants to extend white privilege into the future. The collaboration between a sociologist and a film critic is also new. We do not wish to present here definitive analyses but to open analytical fields and to invite readers to perform their own critical examination of whiteness in these and other films.

In our exploration, we are guided by a series of assumptions and concepts that we will introduce and develop as our analysis of specific movies progresses throughout the book. At this stage, we introduce only some key concepts to outline the standpoint from which we undertake this research. The concept of self, of the white self—the portrayal of which we will be examining—is used by scholars to designate who and what we are. The self is the human person, the place in which all experience—our memories, our pain and pleasure, our emotions—is organized. By self, we mean the sense of being a person, the experience of existing as an individual contained in the space of a body over time. As universal as this notion might be, it is highly culture specific. In the United States, the fundamental entries on our birth certificates are name, birth date, gender, and race. These constitute our legal sense of self. Race is also crucial to our psychological sense of self. Without it we would be fatally disoriented, like Joe Christmas in Faulkner's *Light in August,* who goes mad and is destroyed because he never knows whether he is white or black.

Whiteness

The key element to understanding racial thinking in the United States and in much of the world today is white supremacy. The modern concept of race and the notion of whiteness were invented during the period of European colonization of the Americas and Africa. The stock of knowledge we call racism has been developed in the past five hundred years precisely to establish the superiority of whites and to contribute a veneer of legitimacy to colonial domination, exploitation, or extermination of people of color, both domestically and internationally, by whites.

One difficulty in studying "whiteness" is that, until recently, it was an empty or invisible category, not perceived as a distinctive racial identity. Richard Dyer writes, "As long as race is something only applied to non-white peoples, as long as white people are not racially seen and named, they/we function as a human norm. Other people are raced, we are just people."[18] Thus, most white Americans either do not think of their "whiteness" or think of it as neutral. The power of whiteness rests in its apparent universality and invisibility, in the way it has gone unexamined. Nevertheless, the images of film, especially of films in which whites interact with persons of another color, offer a way to study white self-representation across the twentieth century. As has often been said, "Whites don't have a color until a person of color enters the room."

Until recently, sociologists and culture critics concentrated on prejudice, that is, on the distorted images that we construct of others we perceive as different. For example, Bogle (1997), Cripps (1977), Snead (1994), and Guerrero (1993), among others, have studied the prejudicial images of African Americans in American films.[19] We want to shift the focus to the representation of the white self-concept.

Whiteness as we understand it today in the United States is a construct, a public fic- /
tion that has evolved throughout American history in response to changing political and |
economic needs and conditions. Whiteness has always been a shifting category used to \
police class and sexual privilege. At the beginning, only "free white persons" could become American citizens. White privilege depended on the exclusion of "others," but the
definition of who was non-white constantly changed. Thus, previous historic categories
such as Celt, Slav, Alpine, Hebrew, Iberic, Anglo-Saxon, and Nordic have been incorporated into the contemporary concept of "white" or "Caucasian." "Caucasians are made
and not born."[20] We argue that the notion of whiteness has become so integral to the
American identity that it is embedded in the national unconscious.

Race

In practice, the term "race" designates one or more biological traits (e.g., skin color)
from which a sociopolitical hierarchy is derived and the assumption that some races are
superior and therefore deserve to be more powerful than others. In spite of the concentrated efforts by scientists over the past one hundred years, the concept of "race" has
become progressively more elusive, to the extent that today we can say that race is an il-
lusion, a fiction that no longer leads to a meaningful classification of humans in the biological or social sciences. It is not an objective or fixed category. Race, according to Omi
and Winant, is "an unstable and 'decentered' complex of social meanings constantly being transformed by political struggle." Although the concept of race may be a fiction, we
cannot simply jettison it because it "continues to be central to everyone's identity and
understanding of the social world."[21]

Today the vast majority of humans across the globe still think, feel, and act as if "race"
were real, as if it pointed to true, useful differences among people. Furthermore, no one
alive today has lived in a world in which race did not matter.[22] In the United States, race
matters in the chance each of us had of being born alive and healthy. Race matters in the
neighborhoods where we grow up, the quality of the education we obtain, the persons we
choose as friends, spouses, or lovers, the careers we pursue, the health and opportunities
of the children we are going to have, and the churches we attend. Race matters in the
length of our life span. Finally, race matters even in the cemetery where we lie after death.

At the beginning of the twenty-first century, the memories of the horrors in which race
was the operative concept are still fresh. Among others, the horror of racial segregation and
lynching in the United States, of the Nazi Holocaust in Europe, of apartheid in South
Africa, and of the "ethnic cleansing" in Bosnia and Kosovo cannot be ignored. One can also
not deny that members of oppressed groups find identity, self-expression, and solidarity in
racial and ethnic categories. Historically and today, race and the violent or subtle practices
we call racism shape both the structures of our societies and the daily rhythms of our lives.

We cannot begin to explain the contradiction between the scientific uselessness of
the concept of race and the real consequences the application of racial categories bring
about. At the interpersonal level, the biological trait or set of traits thought to reveal
"race" are used as assumptions about other physical, intellectual, emotional, or spiritual
traits of persons with those characteristics. In the United States, for example, those who
are not considered white are often automatically assumed to be smelly, "greasy," less in-

telligent, lazy, dirty, not in control of their emotions, unreliable, and so on.[23] The category of race, however fictional, is taken for real and is real in its consequences.

Today, white supremacy still dominates America.[24] Consider that the Constitution of the United States of 1789, the fundamental document of the first democratic society, accepted the slavery of Africans and African Americans within its borders and gave Congress the authority to suppress slave insurrections. For tax distribution purposes, a slave was counted as three-fifths of a person. In 1861, both houses of the U.S. Congress passed a bill that would have made slavery a permanent feature of the American legal system. Today, decades after the Civil Rights revolution of the 1960s, the enforcement of civil rights laws is very weak, at best. Film production is one of the resources through which power is wielded by the classes that benefit from the racial status quo.

In chapter 2, "The Divided White Self," we explain what we mean by sincere fictions. In subsequent chapters we develop the concept of racism as a project and of object relations as they relate to the pedagogy of the cinema.

Notes

1. Stewart, Susan. 2000. "Lessons Learned: The Enduring Truths of *Gone with the Wind*," *TV Guide*, December 23–29, 26.

2. Malcolm X, with Alex Haley. 1965. *The Autobiography of Malcolm X*. New York: Grove, p. 42.

3. Kellner, Douglas. 1995. *Media Culture: Cultural Studies, Identity, and Politics between the Modern and the Postmodern*. New York: Routledge, p. 1.

4. Ibid, p. 2.

5. Denzin, Norman K. 1995. *The Cinematic Society: The Voyeur's Gaze*. London: Sage, p. 1.

6. Veronis, Suhler & Associates. 1999. "Table 920. Media Usage and Consumer Spending: 1992 to 2002: Communications Industry Report." New York.

7. Operators of a public utility plant discovered that the peaks in water consumption in the evening coincided with the commercial breaks in prime-time TV shows.

8. Mast, Gerald. 1976. *A Short History of the Movies*. Indianapolis, Ind.: Bobbs-Merrill, p. 181.

9. Craddock, Jim, ed. 2001. *VideoHound's Golden Movie Retriever 2001: The Complete Guide to Movies on Videocassette, DVD, and Laserdisc*. Detroit, Mich.: Visible Ink.

10. Johnson, Alan G. 2001. *Privilege, Power and Difference*. Mountain View, Calif.: Mayfield, p. 108.

11. Powers, Rothman, and Rothman studied social and political themes in motion pictures, including an examination of white and minority representation through content analysis of a random sample of 394 top-grossing movies released between 1946 and 1985. They found that "in the past twenty-five years, minorities are substantially more likely to be rated positively and less likely to receive negative character ratings than whites in popular movies." Unfortunately, the authors do not report the race, gender, or age of the judges who performed the ratings, describing them merely as "college students." Thus, the intersubjective reliability testing they performed cannot be evaluated on issues of race and ethnicity. What whites judge to be "positive" or negative" representations can differ widely from what blacks perceive, as the O. J. Simpson trial showed. In *Bamboozled* (2000), Spike Lee illustrates how different the perspectives of black and white can be in the portrayal of blacks. To get himself fired, a black TV producer creates a very bad "New Millenium Minstrel Show" filled with negative stereotypes and insulting characterizations of blacks. But the program is embraced by the station's white manager and white writers. The program also becomes a ratings success despite black protest. See Powers, Stephen, David J. Rothman, and Stanley Rothman. 1996. *Hollywood's America: Social and Political Themes in Motion Pictures*. Boulder, Colo.: Westview, p. 177.

12. Mast, *A Short History of the Movies*, p. 181.

13. Ibid., pp. 181–82.

14. Ibid., p. 179.

15. Vanderwood, Paul J. 1988. "An American Cold Warrior: *Viva Zapata!* (1952)," in *American History/American Film: Interpreting the Hollywood Image*, eds. John E. O'Connor and Martin A. Jackson. New York: Continuum, p. 184.

16. Lorraine Hansberry is best known for *Raisin in the Sun* (1959), the first play by an African American woman produced on Broadway and winner of the Drama Critics' Circle Award. She also wrote the screenplay for the successful film adaptation of the play (1961).

17. Bernardi, Daniel. 1996. *The Birth of Whiteness: Race and the Emergence of U.S. Cinema*. New Brunswick, N.J.: Rutgers University Press; Bernardi, Daniel. 2001. *Classic Hollywood, Classic Whiteness*. Minneapolis: University of Minnesota Press; Frankenberg, Ruth. 1993. *White Women, Race Matters: The Social Construction of Whiteness*. Minneapolis: University of Minnesota Press; Dyer, Richard. 1997. *White*. London: Routledge; Frankenberg, Ruth. 1997. *Displacing Whiteness: Essays in Social and Cultural Criticism*. Durham, N.C.: Duke University Press; Gabriel, John. 1998. *Whitewash: Racialized Politics and the Media*. London: Routledge; Hill, Mike. 1997. *Whiteness: A Critical Reader*. New York: New York University Press; Kincheloe, Joe L. 1998. *White Reign: Deploying Whiteness in America*. New York: St. Martin's; Lipsitz, George. 1998. *The Possessive Investment in Whiteness: How White People Profit from Identity Politics*. Philadelphia: Temple University Press; Morrison, Toni. 1992. *Playing in the Dark: Whiteness and the Literary Imagination*. Cambridge, Mass.: Harvard University Press; Nakayama, Thomas K., and Judith N. Martin. 1999. *Whiteness: The Communication of Social Identity*. Thousand Oaks, Calif.: Sage Publications; Pfeil, Fred. 1995. *White Guys: Studies in Postmodern Domination and Difference*. London: Verso.

18. Dyer, Richard. 1997. *White*. New York: Routledge, p. 1.

19. Bogle, Donald. 1997. *Toms, Coons, Mulattoes, Mammies, and Bucks*. New York: Continuum; Cripps, Thomas. 1977. *Slow Fade to Black: The Negro in American Film, 1900–1942*. New York: Oxford University Press; Guerrero, Ed. 1993. *Framing Blackness: The African American Image in Film*. Philadelphia: Temple University Press; Snead, James A., Colin MacCabe, and Cornel West. 1994. *White Screens, Black Images: Hollywood from the Dark Side*. New York: Routledge.

20. Jacobson, Mathew Frye. 1998. *Whiteness of a Different Color: European Immigrants and the Alchemy of Race*. Cambridge, Mass.: Harvard University Press, p. 4. See also Roediger, David. 1991. *The Wages of Whiteness: Race and the Making of the American Working Class*. London: Verso; Allen, Theodore. 1994. *The Invention of the White Race*. London: Verso; Ignatiev, Noel. 1995. *How the Irish Became White*. New York: Routledge; Brodkin, Karen. 1998. *How Jews Became White Folks & What that Says About Race in America*. New Brunswick, N.J.: Rutgers University Press.

21. Omi, Michael, and Howard Winant. 1994. *Racial Formation in the United States: From the 1960s to the 1990s*. 2d ed. New York: Routledge, p. 55.

22. Morrison, Toni. 1997. "Home," in *The House that Race Built*, ed. Wahneema Lubiano. New York: Vintage Books, pp. 3–12 (p. 3).

23. Over the past thirty years I (Hernán Vera) have been conducting in my classes an exercise that illustrates this point. Students are asked to mention, out loud, traits of different racial/ethnic groups, which are then written on the blackboard in respective columns. Usually, "Spics" is the first column, followed by "Niggers," "Wops," "Micks," "Polacks," "Kikes," and "Chinks." These terms of abuse are used to emphasize the fact that these are stereotypes and not real people. The traits listed—smelly, "greasy," less intelligent, lazy, dirty, not in control of their emotions, and unreliable—form part of the stereotype of all groups, with the exception of the two last ones, whose stereotypes differ considerably from the rest. The length of the list of traits varies from one class to the next, but not in the stereotypical similarity attributed to all the groups. Other stereotypical traits attributed to minority groups in this exercise are being musical, oversexed, having a tendency to commit crime, funny accents, and greasy hair.

24. West, Cornel. 1997. "Afterword," in *The House that Race Built*, ed. Wahneema Lubiano. New York: Vintage, pp. 301–3. See also, Feagin, Joe R. 2000. *Racist America: Roots, Current Realities, and Future Reparations*. New York: Routledge, p. 2.

CHAPTER 2

The Divided White Self

> A good deal of time and attention has been invested in the exposure of racism and the horrific results on its objects.... But that well-established study should be joined with another, equally important one: the impact of racism on those who perpetuate it.
>
> —Toni Morrison[1]

Films Analyzed:
Birth of a Nation (1915)
The Littlest Rebel (1935)
Gone with the Wind (1939)
Raintree County (1957)
Glory (1990)

Sincere Fictions

Prejudices are representations of others that apparently say nothing about how persons see themselves in their encounters with others. However, images of oneself are inseparable from images of others.

Our identity, the sense of who we are, is formed over time by selectively appropriating or rejecting aspects of the people with whom we have interacted. What we call "sincere fictions of the white self"[2] are deliberately constructed images of what it means to be white. These images bring about the "misrecognition" of the true bases of the social relations being fictionalized. White privilege can only be exercised without guilt by denying its existence and by ignoring its historical origins and continuing injustice. In the United States, white privilege originated in conquest, slavery, and brute force. It persists today largely through the symbolic labor of sincere fictions that attempt to efface the memory of the origins of white privilege and to deny its continuing existence and its appalling results.

Our use of the term "sincere fictions" assumes that humans are constantly producing and consuming stories—some fantasized, others based on real events—about themselves and the world in which they live. We call these fictions sincere because they are

Birth of a Nation: *When D. W. Griffith was asked why he called his film* Birth of a Nation, *he replied, "The birth of a nation began . . . with the Ku Klux Klans, and we have shown that." Courtesy Museum of Modern Art Film Stills Archive.*

rooted in the self-concept that we seldom examine, that we take for granted. Sincerity refers to our remaining unaware of alternative aspects we could have incorporated into these fictions. To be sincere implies honestly believing in something, although one could also be sincere out of repression, denial, naïveté, or simple ignorance.

Race is not an array of physical and mental traits; race is a way of relating to others, a way of conceiving ourselves. It rests on images learned at our parents' knees and in our communities and culturally reinforced through religion, education, the workplace, and the media.

Because we are talking about the identity not simply of individuals but of the majority group in U.S. culture, it is appropriate to examine Hollywood movies to learn about the white self. In addition to the fact that most Hollywood film makers are white, movies aim to address a mass audience through sound and image narratives that will reverberate among the largest possible number of viewers. Most of these narratives deal with the way whites feel, think, and act. But also, in the United States and worldwide, generations who may have never seen Native Americans, blacks, Latinos, or Asians can effortlessly acquire the prejudices of the dominant group through the images presented in film. As these films extol the white self, they diminish the selves of people of color, who also internalize the representations on the screen. The movies are sincere fictions of American culture, made by a major American industry, and for American (and, ultimately, worldwide) consumption. To cite Toni Morrison: "the subject of the dream is the dreamer."[3]

The Divided White Self

In this chapter, we look at "the sincere fictions of the white self" as they can be seen in the images of Hollywood movies that deal with one of the crucial periods in American history and in American race relations: the Civil War and the Reconstruction. We have chosen five films spanning most of the twentieth century, from 1915 to 1990: *Birth of a Nation* (1915), *The Littlest Rebel* (1935), *Gone with the Wind* (1939), *Raintree County* (1957), and *Glory* (1990). In these films, the image of blacks changes with the passing of time from the gross, vicious stereotypes in *Birth of a Nation* (1915) to the heroic rectitude, faithfulness, and valor of the black soldiers in *Glory* (1990). In these films, however, African Americans are always secondary characters coded to enhance the white self.

All five films have protagonists presented as ideal white Americans. We find in these movies a persistence across the century in representations of the ideal white American self, which is constructed as powerful, beautiful, brave, cordial, kind, firm, and generous: a natural-born leader. Such stereotyping is to be expected in the notorious *Birth of a Nation,* a hymn of praise to the Ku Klux Klan, but it is surprising to encounter the same stereotypes 75 years later in *Glory,* a supposedly liberal film about the first black regiment to fight in the Civil War. This persistence suggests that the sincere fictions of the white self maintained themselves throughout the twentieth century despite decades of struggle and apparent change in American race relations.

We also find that the Civil War is used as a means to dramatize a split in the white self. These movies are not about white versus black but white versus white. The conflict in *Birth of a Nation, The Littlest Rebel,* and *Raintree County* is North versus South, in *Gone with the Wind,* antebellum South versus post–Civil War South, and in *Glory,* white liberal Northerners versus white bigoted Northerners. All the movies work toward a final reconciliation or reunification of the split white self through marriage or family reunion in the first four films and through sacrificial death in battle in *Glory.*

Birth of a Nation: A White Nation Is Born

D. W. Griffith's silent film *Birth of a Nation,* based on Thomas Dixon's 1905 novel *The Clansman,* is one of the seminal American films of the twentieth century in terms of codifying the sincere fictions of the white self on the screen. This notorious film had an enormous impact in its day: said to have inspired a new wave of terror by the Ku Klux Klan, it was also denounced by the NAACP. *Birth of a Nation* made more money than any other silent film. It was also the first film ever screened at the White House. President Woodrow Wilson, a Southerner and a historian, reportedly said of *Birth of a Nation,* "It is like writing history with lightning. And my only regret is that it is all so terribly true."[4]

This film "represents two historical landmarks: an incomparable racial assault and a major breakthrough for subsequent filmmaking technique."[5] *Birth of a Nation's* aesthetic accomplishments have been praised as if they could be separated from its white supremacist goals. We agree with those critics who consider the film to be the "most negative racial characterization in U.S. film history" and "the most massive racist assault in the history of mass communications."[6] *Birth of a Nation* is an epic of white supremacy and propaganda for the Ku Klux Klan, the oldest, most notorious terrorist organization in the United States. James Baldwin writes, "*Birth of Nation* is really an elaborate justification of mass murder. The film cannot possibly admit this."[7]

Nonetheless, its vicious portrayal of blacks has been excused by alleging that Griffith tried to be "fair to Negroes" as he, a Southerner, understood them.[8] Thus, the blame for the Negrophobic images is shifted from Griffith to the culture to which he belonged. In our terminology, D. W. Griffith's fictional images are "sincere," that is, they are part of a much broader ideological system that he took for granted. As James Baldwin says, "The film cannot be called dishonest: it has the Niagara force of an obsession."[9] The aim of the film, to present what was apparently a historical pageant to produce a misrecognition of history and of reality, was well characterized by the sociologist Thorstein Veblen, who commented, "Never before have I seen such concise misinformation."[10]

The movie is divided into three parts—the antebellum South, the Civil War, and the Reconstruction—an epic structure repeated in *Gone with the Wind*. These stages could be said to correspond to the construction of a national, white identity through splitting of introjected objects, identification with social roles, the creation of an ego ideal, and the final exclusion of unwelcome aspects of the self. *Birth of a Nation* elaborates a myth about the South that was repeated in many later movies. First we see the grace and charm of the plantation South (like Camelot before the fall). In the second stage, gallant Southerners fight nobly to the end for a lost cause and vicious Northerners loot and destroy Southern homes. The third and final stage of the Reconstruction is represented by scenes of predatory Northern carpetbaggers inciting Southern blacks to lawlessness and riot, until order is finally restored by the rise of the Ku Klux Klan in *Birth of a Nation* and of Southern capitalism in *Gone with the Wind*.

In the opening antebellum sequence of *Birth of a Nation,* we are introduced to two families, the Stonemans in the North and the Camerons in the South. Both are aristocrats and natural leaders, honorable, noble, and gallant representatives of the best of the white self. The brothers of the two families are good friends, and there is a romantic attraction between one Stoneman brother and one Cameron sister and one Cameron brother and one Stoneman sister. These families are mirror images of each other and seem destined to unite.

There is, however, one "bad object" among these idealized representations of the white self; Congressman Austin Stoneman, father of the Northern family, is a fierce abolitionist with a scheming mulatto mistress. Stoneman, a caricature of an actual historical figure, the Northern congressman Thaddeus Stevens, is the film's main villain, represented as a vindictive and power-hungry demagogue who is blamed for the conflict between North and South and the division of the two families. Michael Rogin claims that "Griffith wanted to demonize blacks and keep them under control at the same time. . . . If blacks were not to have minds of their own, however, the film required a bad white father."[11] Stoneman is a caricature of the white Northerner as "outside agitator," who wants to exact revenge against the South by inciting blacks to anarchy, a view that persisted in the South through the Civil Rights movement of the 1950s and 1960s. In the Southern view, blacks were incapable of organizing themselves but always required white leadership.

The fact that Stoneman's sons are blameless is part of the simplistic pattern of binary oppositions in the film: whites are either noble and selfless or base and self-serving; blacks are either faithful servants or vicious upstarts. Both self and other are split into good and evil, and the splitting accounts for the conflict in the film and the need for a reunification of the white self.

The movie takes a Southern point of view of American history. The antebellum South is represented as Edenic. The Camerons, wealthy plantation owners, are introduced as they greet each other with hugs and kisses on the front porch of Cameron Hall. The father is the kindly master, everyone dotes on the little sister, and puppies frolic at their feet. We get an idyllic, sentimentalized version of familial bliss.

There is one other idyllic fantasy: a visit by the family to the cotton fields, where blacks pick cotton in the background, and to the slave quarters, where happy blacks dance in the presence of the white masters. The slaves are presented as suited to their position and contented with their lot, yet at the same time they are blamed for the war. A title card tells us, "The bringing of the African to America planted the first seeds of dis-Union."

The war splits the Stonemans from the Camerons, since they fight on opposite sides. Both families lose sons. Ben Cameron demonstrates his courage and nobility at the battle of Petersburg. The title card reads: "The Little Colonel pauses before the last charge to succor a fallen foe" as he gives water to a wounded Union soldier. The implication is that these whites do not really hate each other; war is just something they must do, an inevitable process that simply happens. Nevertheless, at this stage the white self is split and alternates uneasily between the wish to destroy the object and the desire to nurture it.

Ben Cameron is captured and due to be executed on a false charge, but his mother successfully pleads for clemency to "the Great Heart," President Lincoln. *The Littlest Rebel* contains a similar scene; in both films, noble, good-hearted Northern officers are exempt from Southern animosity. Also in both films, Lincoln is the ultimate good father, the Great White Saint, the epitome of the best of the white self, the man who, if he had survived, would have effected the reconciliation of North and South—or, to put it another way, would have healed the split white self. Lincoln serves as an iconic figure, an embodiment of the ego ideal in the sincere fiction of the white self.

Congressman Stoneman, a rival to Lincoln, argues against Lincoln's postwar policy of clemency for the South, saying, "The leaders must be hanged and their states treated as conquered provinces." Lincoln wants to treat them like errant children who can return to the family: "I shall deal with them as if they had never been away." If Stoneman is the father who rules by force, then Lincoln is the father who rules by love.

With the assassination of Lincoln, Stoneman becomes uncrowned king. Proclaiming, "We shall crush the white South under the heel of the black South," he sets up in power in the South his protege, the mulatto Silas Lynch.

Lynch, who is as power hungry as his white mentor, is a caricature of the Southern view of the "uppity nigger" who desires miscegenation. Lynch is the second mulatto character in the film, after Stoneman's mistress. James Baldwin writes, "All of the energy of the film is siphoned into these two dreadful and improbable creatures. . . . they are like creatures in a nightmare someone is having. . . . But how did so ungodly a creature as the mulatto enter this Eden, and where did he come from? The film cannot concern itself with this inconvenient and impertinent question. . . ."[12] The mulatto is such a nightmarish figure to the white man for two reasons: first, because he defies the strict binary opposition between black and white on which white America relies; and second, because he is evidence of white men's rape of black women. Thus the film must force a misrecognition of historical reality by inverting this criminal desire and projecting it instead onto not one but two black rapists.

A second war commences, in which the Ku Klux Klan, led by white Southern aristocrat Ben Cameron, and their allies, the "faithful blacks," defend the old social order against invading white Northerners and their proxies, crazed Northern blacks who want to seize power and rape white women. Both families are threatened. The black soldier

Gus, described as a "renegade, product of vicious doctrines," tries to rape the Camerons' young daughter. She chooses death before dishonor, and the KKK kills Gus. (In the film as originally screened, they castrate him.) Next, the ironically named black leader, Silas Lynch, tries to force himself on Elsie Stoneman. The KKK is seen as the defender of Southern rights, property, and honor—especially of the sexual purity of white women. Griffith said that one aim of the film was "to create a feeling of abhorrence in white people, especially white women, against colored men."[13] The film aimed to keep in line not only blacks but also white women.

Birth of a Nation presents an upside-down version of American history in which blacks oppressed whites. The Ku Klux Klan did not originate during Reconstruction to protect white women from black Union soldiers, as the movie proposes, but was a continuation of the slave patrols of the antebellum South. Adult, propertied, white males throughout the South were required to participate in the violent racial enforcement of these patrols.[14]

Ironically, the conventions of screen narrative and representation transform the KKK into heroes with whom we are expected to sympathize. In the final battle, "The former enemies of North and South unite to resist the mad results of the carpetbaggers' political folly." The director D. W. Griffith tacked on a patriotic coda for the sound re-release of *Birth of a Nation* in 1930: the singing of the national anthem and a color shot of the Star-Spangled Banner waving in the breeze. This addition suggested that the film celebrated the birth of a new, unified nation, rather than the rise of the KKK.

Despite its "vituperativeness," *Birth of a Nation* "is, in fact, a conciliatory film, and one of the more puzzling of its missions is both to castigate the behavior of some Northerners after the war, while at the same time offering a symbolic reunification of North and South (at the expense, it should be added, of black claims to justice)."[15] One way to account for this puzzling, contradictory aspect of the film is to see it as a narrative about the need for the reconciliation of the divided white self. Thus, race relations are really secondary in the film and the rebellious blacks only a device to force the Northern and Southern whites to reunite as they recognize that they are brothers under the skin—or rather, brothers because of their skin. As one of the movie's title cards reads: "The former enemies of North and South reunited again in defense of their Aryan birthright." It also helps to explain another puzzling aspect of the film: the fact that all the principal black roles are played by whites in blackface; the "blacks" are whites in minstrel disguise. As Michael Rogin notes, "The climax of *Birth* does not pit whites against blacks, but some white actors against others. . . . White actors switched back and forth from playing Klansmen to playing blacks."[16] In *Birth of a Nation*, blacks simply do not matter: they are only counters in the struggle of a split white self to reunite.

The Littlest Rebel: The Redeemer Child

The Littlest Rebel replays *Birth of a Nation* twenty years later in the form not of an epic but of a children's story and a minstrel show. *The Littlest Rebel* is the Civil War reenacted as a *Lassie* movie, with Shirley Temple as the brave youngster and Bill "Bojangles" Robinson as the faithful pet who comes to the rescue of his child master. The co-optation of black song and dance in the musical numbers of Temple and Robinson turns the film into a vaudeville or minstrel show; in one scene, Temple actually wears blackface. Like *Birth of a Nation, The*

Littlest Rebel is a masquerade, featuring imaginary whites and imaginary blacks. Convoluted levels of misrecognition and self-delusion mark this sincere fiction of the white self: the adult white self is disguised as a little girl, and the little girl pretends to be black.

Once again, we see the agony of a split white self, symbolized by the war between the North and the South. In the 1930s, however, the fear was not of a Civil War but of a class war. Shirley Temple functions as a redeemer child who can heal the divisions of the Civil War, or, symbolically, of the Depression. The iconic figure of Lincoln, the Great White Father, now takes on overtones of Franklin D. Roosevelt.

Like *Birth of a Nation, The Littlest Rebel* is sympathetic to the South but ultimately conciliatory in an effort to reconcile the divided white self. Temple plays Virgie Carey, only child of a perfect Southern family, lords of a plantation and slaveholders, like the Camerons in *Birth of a Nation*. Once again, the family is rich, handsome, loving, brave, and chivalrous, and their black slaves are totally devoted to them. (We wonder what it is in the white American self that expects and demands unswerving love and loyalty from those it oppresses.) The child protagonist of *The Littlest Rebel* makes the film less rabidly racist than *Birth of a Nation*. Offensive stereotypes can thereby be presented innocently by focusing on the friendship of the charming little Virgie and the faithful family retainer, the resourceful Uncle Billy.

SHIRLEY TEMPLE in THE LITTLEST REBEL with John Boles, Jack Holt, Karen Morley, Bill Robinson. A Fox Picture

The Littlest Rebel: *The pairing of Shirley Temple and Bill Robinson is an attempt to bridge opposites. Copyright 1935 Fox Film Corp. Courtesy Museum of Modern Art Film Stills Archive.*

The pairing of Shirley Temple and Bill Robinson bridges opposites—young and old, female and male, white and black—to defuse the tensions between these rigid social categories. The historical remove makes the union of the two possible. James Snead writes, "Only the strictly defined conditions and prohibitions of Southern plantation life could furnish the sensibilities of the thirties with acceptable insulation for what we get on screen: the warmth, even heat, of an extremely intimate relationship between an older black man and a younger white girl, on the surface at least a violation of strict racial and sexual decorum."[17] Uncle Billy, however, is presented as an unthreatening character: clever but loyal, affectionate, childlike and asexual, and eager to serve and to entertain his white masters. He is as much family dog as family retainer. Just as Lassie makes her master, Timmy, seem worthwhile and sympathetic, so Bill Robinson provides the perfect foil for Shirley Temple, always at her service. His love and devotion to the family, whom he repeatedly rescues, are simply taken for granted: the white self deserves no less.

The film opens with a party scene; there are also parties early in *Gone with the Wind* and *Glory.* These social gatherings showcase the white self at its best: rich, charming, and gracious. Little Virgie hosts her birthday party, acting the perfect Southern belle, imitating her mother. As the ideal white self, she is kind, gentle, condescending, and powerful, attentive to all the rules of etiquette as she commands the slaves who are serving the children. This white self, even as a child, plays her role adeptly. Virgie asks, "How would you like to see Uncle Billy dance?" and Billy smilingly complies.

The Littlest Rebel: *Shirley Temple as a redeemer child who heals the divisions of the Civil War. Copyright 1935 Fox Film Corp. Courtesy Museum of Modern Art Film Stills Archive.*

The serenity and grace of the birthday party—the antebellum idyll—is abruptly shattered by the announcement that war has broken out. (Similarly, the declaration of war disrupts the ball at the Wilkes's plantation in *Gone with the Wind.*) The Carey family, like the Camerons in *Birth of a Nation* or the O'Haras in *Gone with the Wind,* are Southern gentry brought low by the war: the father away, serving as a Confederate scout; the mansion invaded by brutal Union troops; the family reduced to living in the slave quarters; the mother taken ill and dying (like Scarlett's mother in *Gone with the Wind*); and, finally, the father arrested and sentenced to hang as a spy. Despite all these melodramatic events, this remains a child's version of the Civil War: we see no battles and nobody dies except the mother.

In the climax, Virgie emerges as the child savior, the mediator who reconciles North and South. Both her father and Colonel Morrison—the kind Northern officer who took pity on Captain Carey and little Virgie after Mrs. Carey died and gave them a pass—await execution in prison. Uncle Billy and Virgie dance in the street to earn train fare to Washington, where Virgie pleads to Lincoln for clemency for her father and the Colonel (in yet another scene borrowed from *Birth of a Nation*). She, of course, charms him, as she charms every authority figure in the film, for they all have hearts of gold that melt before the power of this little girl. She sits on Lincoln's lap as he peels an apple, which he shares with her (but not, we note, with Uncle Billy, who is also present).

In the end, Virgie reunites with her two loving fathers—Captain Carey and Colonel Morrison—and also has a black father figure in Uncle Billy. Through Shirley Temple, the white self is mythically presented to itself as a redeemer child, Virgie the virginal, innocent yet powerful, able by virtue of her goodness and charm to dissolve all opposites—North and South, black and white—and to reunite the split white self.

Gone with the Wind: The Great White American Melodrama

One of the favorite movies of all time, *Gone with the Wind* is the great white American melodrama, an epic, picture-book-pretty, operatic fiction of the white self. It has many parallels to the movies we have discussed: many similar scenes of the Edenic antebellum South (here shown as a world out of Arthurian romance), the War and the suffering of the South (a paradise lost), and the Reconstruction, with further suffering of the South.

There is a direct line of descent between *Birth of a Nation* and *Gone with the Wind.* Although separated by 24 years, both films are domestic melodramas based on the most popular Southern novels of their respective generations. Thomas Dixon, author of *The Clansman* (1905), the novel on which *Birth of a Nation* was based, wrote a letter of extravagant praise to Margaret Mitchell, author of the novel *Gone with the Wind* (1936). He said that Mitchell had written a novel based on authentic Southern history, like his own, and praised *Gone with the Wind* as "the greatest story of the South ever put down on paper, you have given the world THE GREAT AMERICAN NOVEL [sic]." Mitchell replied, "Your letter of praise about *Gone with the Wind* was very exciting. . . . I was practically raised on your books and love them very much."[18] In truth, the film of *Gone with the Wind* is *Birth of a Nation* without the bedsheets and hoods of the Klan.

The film is not as Negrophobic as *Birth of a Nation* because David O. Selznick, the producer of *Gone with the Wind,* carefully "excised all references to the Ku Klux Klan, renegade Negroes, and other Southern legends" to bring this Southern novel "into the center of American popular opinion" during the second term of President Franklin D. Roosevelt, whose wife Eleanor Roosevelt was liberal on race. Hattie McDaniel won an Academy Award as Best Supporting Actress, the first Oscar for an African American, for her portrayal of Mammy. Nevertheless, *Gone with the Wind* is tinged with nostalgia for the antebellum South and portrays an antiseptic slavery without whips, chains, or rape.[19]

The film presents a divided white self, but here the division is coded not so much as North versus South but rather as Old South versus New South. The movie narrates the transformation from the antebellum plantation South to the modern industrial South. We follow the story of Scarlett O'Hara (Vivien Leigh), who changes from an empty-headed young Southern belle before the war into a tough capitalist entrepreneur during Reconstruction.

Ideologically, *Gone with the Wind* could be said to be an apology for capitalism during the revival of capitalism at the end of the Depression. In 1939, the country had been devastated and was struggling to recover, a situation similar to that of the South during Reconstruction. *Gone with the Wind* represents the peak of the "plantation genre," which flourished in such Hollywood films of the 1930s as *Dixiana* (1930), *Mississippi* (1935), and *Jezebel* (1938). As the Depression continued, the antebellum mansions swelled in size and scale, culminating in the fantasy palace of Twelve Oaks in *Gone with the Wind.* The opulence of the settings serves as an apology not only for capitalism but also for racism. "The mansion and its grounds are used to legitimate the rule, and masked terror, of the plantation system in the cinematic Old South," writes Ed Guerrero.[20]

In the movie, two contrasting couples represent the split in the white self. Melanie (Olivia de Havilland) and Ashley Wilkes (Leslie Howard) are the epitome of the old white Southern self or, rather, of the sincere fiction of the white plantation owner: generous, honorable, courteous, kind, calm, monogamous, sedate in their lovemaking, but also rather passive and sickly. Their opposites in every respect, Scarlett O'Hara and Rhett Butler (Clark Gable) embody the new white Southern self: selfish, dishonorable, rule breakers, ruthless, lively, polygamous, passionate, and active and healthy. Scarlett and Rhett are profiteers, perfect capitalists, although Scarlett is far more childish and narcissistic and less self-aware than Rhett. So we are presented with two sincere fictions of the white Southern self: the old cavalier versus the new entrepreneur.

Behind the story is a yearning for an impossible reunification of the fantasy Old South and the New, for a blend of the supposed grace and charm of the vanished plantation society with the spirit and enterprise of the rising industrial South. The keynote of nostalgia for a lost world of fairy tale or Arthurian romance is struck in the opening: "There was a land of Cavaliers and cotton fields called the Old South. . . . Here in this pretty world gallantry took its last bow. . . . Here was the last ever to be seen of Knights and their Ladies Fair, of Master and of Slave. . . . Look for it only in books, for it is no more than a dream remembered. A Civilization gone with the wind." This explains both Scarlett's yearning throughout the film for Ashley, the epitome of the Old Southern cavalier, and Rhett's farewell speech to Scarlett: "I'm going to Charleston, back where I belong. . . . I want peace. I want to see if somewhere there isn't something left in life of charm and grace." Rhett, too, misses the order of the old world; he is tired of the turmoil of this New South, represented by Scarlett. In psychological terms, this longing for a lost, mythical world of unmitigated happiness and wholeness could represent a desire to return to a stage of preoedipal bliss before there was any difference between self and objects, before the splitting of the white self.

Although Melanie and Ashley represent the best of the Old South, of the white propertied classes, of the idealized white self, they are victims and losers, unsuited to survive in the postwar South. They lose their land and their home and become dependent on Scarlett, who is tough enough to make it in the New South: she marries a store-owner to save her land, builds a sawmill, runs it with convict labor, and rebuilds Tara, the O'Hara family mansion.

The movie justifies the creation of the modern white self, the capitalist entrepreneur, but it tries to reconcile itself to the contradictions of capitalism by having it both ways. Scarlett, a survivor, uses any means to come out on top: she is manipulative, venal, ruthless, and driven. Yet it is difficult to hate her because she constantly suffers. She adapts successfully to the new order of capitalism but pays a terrible emotional price. The audience can applaud itself for not being as selfish as Scarlett and, at the same time, sympathize with her sufferings and see her as a lost little orphan girl. The movie is a melodrama about the sufferings of the white race (we never see blacks suffering).

In terms of cinematic genres, *Gone with the Wind* follows the conventions of the woman's romance. In the course of the movie, Scarlet suffers because of her love for Ashley, who is a married man, and because of the devastating war and its aftermath. As melodrama, this movie throws in everything: war, violence, serious wounds, bloody amputations, explosions, fire, difficult childbirth, starvation, poverty, loss of home, madness, death of a friend, death of parents, death of husbands, death of a child, murder, attempted robbery and attempted rape, prostitution, adulterous longings, and unrequited love. What more could an audience want?

All the characters in *Gone with the Wind* are types, but the film allows a much greater range of types and human qualities among the whites than among the blacks. Reduced to background figures, blacks appear mostly as slaves: loyal servants like Mammy (Hattie McDaniel), stupid and cowardly servants like Prissy (Butterfly McQueen), or clownish servants. Whites are seen as worthy of the subservience, loyalty, and love of the faithful servants. The blacks are no more than conveniences, psychic extensions of the whites, intended to prop them up. Mammy serves three generations of O'Haras, identifies totally with them, and seems to have no family of her own, no name other than her functional one as surrogate mother to her white masters, and no life outside that white household. She upholds aristocratic white family tradition and honor and often scolds and upbraids Scarlett. She is like an externalized, walking superego, but as a comically obese black slave, she is unthreatening: bossy but powerless, loving, and eternally loyal.

Autonomous blacks—those who are not servants and who mix freely with "white trash"—are represented, as in *Birth of a Nation,* as dangerous and lawless. First we see the unholy alliance of Northern white and Northern black carpetbagger invade Georgia. Next we see the attempted rape of Scarlett by a poor black and a poor white. Scarlett is naturally rescued from this assault by her faithful former slave. The subsequent nighttime revenge raid on a shantytown by the propertied whites resembles a Klan raid in *Birth of a Nation,* minus only the white robes. The dangerous black characters, however, quickly disappear from view, and this is only a minor episode in a busy movie, not the central concern it is in *Birth of a Nation.*

Because the black servants never change, they act as comforting figures in a turbulent world where everything constantly changes. A beacon of stability, Mammy never alters her behavior or her attitude toward the family, whether she serves them as a slave before the war or a supposedly free housekeeper after it. The blacks are remnants of the Old South. As Ashley expresses it in a nostalgic speech to Scarlett: "Oh, the lazy days! The warm still country twilight. The high, soft negro laughter from the quarters. The warmth and security of those days."

In the end of the movie, the blacks remain the same but the whites change. Scarlett survives and soldiers on, but she has lost both Ashley and Rhett. The reconciliation between the Old South and the New never takes place, and the white self remains irremediably split, symbolized by the isolated figure of Scarlett. All she has left is Tara, the symbol of the Old South and of family continuity, but it is an empty symbol now that both the old world and the family are lost. Although the longing to return may persist, the "warmth and security" of preoedipal bliss is gone with the wind.

Raintree County: The Insane South

Raintree County (1957) is another Civil War epic, based, like *Birth of a Nation* and *Gone with the Wind,* on a popular novel. Again, like *Gone with the Wind,* it is a long movie that begins with an orchestral overture and includes an intermission in the middle. However,

Raintree County could not emulate the box-office success of *Gone with the Wind* because it is an uncomfortable blend of 1950s, Tennessee Williams–style psychodrama with *Gone with the Wind*'s melodrama.

Raintree County simply reverses the polarity of *Gone with the Wind*. Here, the antebellum North, instead of the antebellum South, is the idyllic, utopian land of grace, beauty, and charm. The film opens with beautiful scenes of a lush green landscape in Indiana in the summer of 1859, echoing the opening scenes of Georgia in *Gone with the Wind*.

The hero is an impossibly noble young white Indianan, John Shawnessy (Montgomery Clift), the fastest runner in Raintree County and valedictorian of his class. Groomed for greatness, he is a poet, a seeker after the mythical raintree of the title. John's plans are derailed when a conniving Southern belle, Susannah (Elizabeth Taylor), tricks him into marriage by falsely claiming she is pregnant. They honeymoon in the South and return to Indiana, where John becomes a teacher. Eventually she bears him a son. During the Civil War, Susannah runs away to the South with their child, and John joins the Union Army to find them, risking his life in battle many times, devoted to his crazy wife.

Raintree County: *Susannah and servant in a pose reminiscent of Scarlett and Mammy. Copyright 1957 Metro-Goldwyn-Mayer. Courtesy Museum of Modern Art Film Stills Archive.*

Susannah is tormented because of her family legacy. Her crazy mother killed her husband and the black maid Henrietta when she found them in bed together and then set fire to the house. Only the child Susannah survived, but she feels guilty for having told her mother about the affair, assumes Henrietta was her real mother, and hates herself, mistakenly believing she has black blood. Susannah is psychotic, a Scarlett too much in love with her black mammy. She wages her own internal civil war because she is divided against herself on the race issue.

In this narcissistic fantasy, the Northern white self, represented by John, is a noble abolitionist, but the Southern white self, represented by Susannah, is an insane slaveholder. The two are joined in an unstable marriage. The movie moves from North to South several times. The North is idyllic, and the antebellum South, like Susannah, has great surface charm and beauty (represented by a river boat and a cotillion ball) but is ultimately a gothic horror of ruined mansions that conceal terrible family secrets, whorehouses with mulatto prostitutes, and madhouses. The North must rid itself of the burden of the perverted South, and the movie ends when the Civil War is over and Susannah kills herself, freeing John to marry his long-suffering hometown sweetheart, who has waited for him patiently.

Despite the 1950s liberal pretensions of the film, blacks appear only as minor characters, background figures, docile servants loyal to their white masters. The focus is on the melodrama of the whites, especially on the impossibly good, heroic John.

Glory: White Liberal Agony

Over fifty years separate *Gone with the Wind* from *Glory*. In the interim, the plantation genre withered, the Civil Rights movement occurred, and the New South prospered. Nevertheless, despite the apparent progress, racial divisions were still deep and wide: America moved from the age of Martin Luther King to the age of Rodney King. A new myth took root in the post–Civil Rights era: that institutionalized racism no longer exists and that the United States is now an egalitarian society.[21] That is the message of *Glory,* a self-congratulatory film meant to reassure whites and blacks about how far America has come in race relations. In 1990, as in 1915, 1935, 1939, or 1957, Hollywood movies about the Civil War still promulgated sincere fictions of the white self.

Glory is one of a spate of 1990s films on the Civil War, such as Ken Burns' massive documentary *The Civil War* (1990); *Gettysburg* (1993); and *The Oldest Living Confederate Widow Tells All* (1994). On the surface, *Glory* presents a very different take on the war than that of earlier Hollywood films, offering a Northern liberal point of view and telling a story previously untold in the movies, about black soldiers' service to the Union. It can also lay claim to a greater degree of realism and historical veracity because it is a biopic, or docudrama, based on the exploits of a white hero, Colonel Robert Gould Shaw (Matthew Broderick), a Boston Brahmin and abolitionist who commanded the first black regiment to fight in the Civil War. Shaw and his regiment are commemorated in a monument in Boston (which inspired Bostonian Robert Lowell's 1964 poem about the Civil Rights movement, "For the Union Dead"). Of course, the question of "realism" and "historical authenticity" in Hollywood films is always problematic—even D. W. Griffith considered his *Birth of a Nation* the first "realistic" filmic depiction of the Civil War and included historical figures, such as Lincoln, and tableaus recreating historical events with painstaking care.

Glory follows Shaw's military career from his wounding at the battle of Antietam, through his return to Boston, to the formation and training of the regiment and their first skirmish in the South and ends with the valiant but futile suicide charge on Fort Wagner in South Carolina, in which Shaw dies along with half the regiment.

Besides its supposed historical authenticity, the film also offers a greater variety of black characters. It differs from previous Civil War films by showing blacks as heroic combatants and as more realistic figures who grow and develop rather than remaining static stereotypes, docile or comic servants. There is Thomas, an educated Bostonian, born free and raised alongside Shaw, who now works for Shaw's father. The first to volunteer to serve in the regiment, the educated but soft Thomas is a poor soldier during training, but he finally shows his mettle under fire, when he demands to be allowed to fight after he is wounded. Next is Rawlins (Morgan Freeman), known as "Gravedigger," an escaped slave, the oldest and wisest of the recruits, who becomes a leader and is promoted to sergeant. Third is Jupiter, an illiterate field hand who stammers but is a crack shot. Finally, there is Tripp (Denzel Washington), another escaped slave, embittered, alienated from his fellow blacks, and full of hatred for whites. By the end of the film, Tripp has bonded with the regiment and is loyal to the Colonel. The screen time devoted to such a variety of realistic black heroes, portrayed by distinguished black dramatic actors, shows an advance in Hollywood's treatment of African Americans, although it may also be seen as a marketing strategy to draw a large black audience as well as a white one. One critic, though, dismisses the black characters as "an ensemble of stereotypes," some old and some new: Thomas is "the Buppie," Rawlins "the Uncle Tom," Jupiter "the rural hick," and Tripp "the Wild Tom." They are fictional types whereas Shaw is a complex historical figure.[22]

Apart from the racial issue, *Glory* follows the conventions of a standard Hollywood war movie: the training of the eager, raw recruits through harsh methods to make them ready for battle; the sadistic, foul-mouthed Irish top sergeant who bullies the men for their own good; the commanding officer, stern but kindly, who cannot afford to fraternize with the men but disciplines and really loves them. The audience sympathizes with the grave responsibility and loneliness of his command. We follow the men as they grow into real soldiers, bond, become loyal to the commander, and, in the final combat, prove their heroism even at the cost of their lives. Although *Glory* could be seen as an anti-war film because of the realistic blood and gore, it also glorifies war as a male proving ground. Moreover, it justifies the Civil War as a brutal but necessary conflict fought for the noble cause of black freedom. This ignores the complicated nexus of economic and political reasons for which the war was actually fought.

Moreover, despite the obvious differences of *Glory* from *Birth of a Nation, The Littlest Rebel, Gone with the Wind,* and *Raintree County,* it purveys some of the same sincere fictions about the white self as these earlier films. *Glory* centers on the heroism of Shaw, the great white savior who dared to take command of the first black regiment, built them into a strong fighting force, and gave his life on their behalf. The focus throughout stays on Shaw, whose voice-over narration in the form of letters home controls the narrative, and the black characters remain secondary. Shaw grows from the tentative and baffled captain at Antietam to the brave, self-assertive colonel of the final charge. The view of the black man may have changed in this film, but the view of the white man has not: the ideal white American self is still constructed as powerful, brave, cordial, kind, firm, and generous—a leader. There are no autonomous blacks in this film, only blacks led by whites. The blacks are forged into an efficient fighting machine because of their loyalty to the white colonel, who deserves their loyalty because he is the noblest character in the film, so that their heroism and sacrifice serve then to validate and glorify Shaw. The death of Shaw—when the men are pinned down, he stands up and charges, seeming to offer himself as a human sacrifice to embolden them—is the climax of the film. It resembles a crucifixion. "Shaw died for our racial sins," writes Mark Golub.[23]

The existence of blatant racism among the white Union enlisted men and officers, such as the brutal Irish sergeant and the cruel Colonel Montgomery, also serves to confirm Shaw's nobility, just as in *Birth of a Nation, The Littlest Rebel,* and *Gone with the Wind,* the mean Northern carpetbaggers or predatory Union soldiers serve as foils to the virtue of the Southern heroes or heroines. Once again, we could also view this division as aspects of the split white self. Robert Burgoyne reads *Glory* as a post-Vietnam narrative about purging white guilt: "Shaw is constructed principally as a redemptive image of whiteness, a sacrificial figure who counteracts or 'cleanses' the racial bias among the whites detailed throughout the film."[24]

The treatment of Tripp demonstrates how the black characters reinforce the sincere fictions of the white self in *Glory.* Tripp starts out hating whites, but he eventually converts from a "bad black" to a good one who loves the colonel, proving that the whites deserve the loyalty of the blacks. In one scene, Shaw orders Tripp flogged for desertion (Shaw later learns that Tripp was looking for shoes because the men were so poorly equipped). The scene is deliberately filled with painful reminders of slavery: the white

Glory: *The agony of the white liberal witnessing the flogging of a black soldier.*
Copyright 1990 Tristar Pictures.

master ordering the disobedient black whipped as a lesson to the others. When Tripp's shirt is stripped, his bare back is crisscrossed with the scars of previous whippings he endured as a slave. As the flogging proceeds, the shots alternate between extreme closeups of Tripp's face as he defiantly stares down Shaw and of Shaw's face as he reacts to the flogging. Tripp's expression never changes, even as tears of pain roll down his face, but Shaw flinches. In other words, Tripp's scene of pain turns into the agony of the great white liberal caught in a bind between his abolitionist beliefs and his duty as a commander to maintain discipline for the good of the men.

In a later scene, Shaw congratulates Tripp for fighting well in their first skirmish and asks him to bear the regimental colors into battle. Tripp refuses, saying, "I ain't fighting this war for you, sir." Nevertheless, Shaw is trying to make up for his previous treatment of Tripp and the two at least are talking. During the final charge, after several flag bearers fall, Tripp retrieves the flag before he, too, is cut down. In the last scene, as the Confederates toss the bodies of the dead Union soldiers into a mass grave, Tripp winds up with his head resting on the bosom of the Colonel. This sentimental image seems to suggest that even the surliest black will eventually come to love the kind and noble white master. In *Birth of a Nation,* the threat of the renegade black Gus had to be neutralized by killing him; in *Glory,* the bad black is neutralized by converting him into a loyal follower of the white leader before killing him. This is scarcely progress.

As Robert Burgoyne says, "*Glory* comes to the same conclusion as D. W. Griffith's *Birth of a Nation*: white identity is defined and clarified by black identity, which forces 'whiteness' into the open and compels it to speak in a language of its own."[25]

Glory: *Even the surliest black will eventually come to love the kind and noble white master. Copyright 1990 Tristar Pictures.*

Conclusion

How is one to understand the persistence of such stereotypes across time in Hollywood movies, despite the changes in race relations in American society? One could say that Hollywood cinema is an economically conservative medium that tends to rely on proven formulas for storytelling. We know, however, that cinematic formulas change over time. A more likely explanation is that, even as fashions in storytelling change, the deep structure of white American identity persists over time, and the changes in American race relations have done little to undermine white privilege.

Identity is a construct, a fiction, but it is a deeply embedded, remarkably persistent, and necessary fiction. Sometimes people prefer to die rather than to relinquish their identity. Race is another fiction, preserved in the United States because the arbitrary division between white and black helps maintain white privilege. The fictions of race intersect with the constructions of identity to create the sincere fictions of the white self. These sincere fictions, incorporated on the level of object relations and therefore largely unconscious, sustain a white ego ideal and preserve the notion of the black as the "other," preventing us from recognizing the brutal reality of the racial oppression on which American society has always been based and from recognizing our own internalized racist notions. Until we confront the psychological underpinnings of racism and expose the sincere fictions of the white self, any changes in American race relations will continue to be superficial.

Notes

1. Morrison, Toni. 1992. *Playing in the Dark: Whiteness and the Literary Imagination.* Cambridge, Mass.: Harvard University Press, p. 11.

2. We borrow the concept of "sincere fiction" from the sociologist Pierre Bourdieu, who elaborated on an idea of the sociologist Marcel Mauss. In *The Gift,* Mauss claims we engage in a gigantic social lie when we pretend that gifts are voluntary, when most gifts are obligatory. (See Mauss, Marcel. 1967. *The Gift.* trans. E. E. Evans-Pritchard. New York: Norton.) Bourdieu extends this notion to suggest that almost all social relations depend on "the sincere fiction of disinterested exchange:"

> *the institutionally organized and guaranteed misrecognition* which is the basis of gift exchange and, perhaps, of all the symbolic labor intended to transmute, by the sincere fiction of disinterested exchange, the inevitable, and inevitably interested relations imposed by kinship, neighborhood, or work, into elective relations of reciprocity. . . . the labor required to conceal the function of the exchanges is as important an element as the labor needed to carry out the function. (Bourdieu, Pierre. 1990. *The Logic of Practice.* Stanford, Calif: Stanford University Press, p. 112.)

3. Morrison, *Playing in the Dark,* p. 17.

4. Rogin, Michael Paul. 1987. *Ronald Reagan, the Movie, and Other Episodes in Political Demonology.* Berkeley: University of California Press, p. 192.

5. Taylor, Clyde. 1996. "The Rebirth of the Aesthetic in Cinema," in *The Birth of Whiteness: Race and the Emergence of U.S. Cinema,* ed. Daniel Bernardi. New Brunswick, N.J.: Rutgers University Press, pp. 15–37 (p. 15).

6. Ibid., p. 17.

7. Baldwin, James. 1985. *The Price of the Ticket: Collected Nonfiction, 1948–1985.* New York: St. Martin's, p. 584.

8. Agee, James. 1971. "David Wark Griffith," in *Focus on The Birth of a Nation,* ed. Fred Silva. Englewood, N.J.: Prentice Hall, quoted in Taylor, "The Rebirth of the Aesthetic in Cinema," p. 19.

9. Baldwin, *The Price of the Ticket,* p. 583.

10. Quoted in Taylor, "The Rebirth of the Aesthetic in Cinema," p. 19.

11. Rogin, Michael Paul, *Ronald Reagan, the Movie, and Other Episodes in Political Demonology,* pp. 208–9.

12. Baldwin, *The Price of the Ticket,* pp. 586–87.

13. Rogin, *Ronald Reagan, the Movie, and Other Episodes in Political Demonology,* p. 219.

14. Hadden, Sally E. 2001. *Slave Patrols: Law and Violence in Virginia and the Carolinas.* Cambridge, Mass.: Harvard University Press.

15. Snead, James. 1994. *White Screens/Black Images: Hollywood from the Dark Side,* ed. Colin MacCabe and Cornel West. New York: Routledge, p.18.

16. Rogin, *Ronald Reagan, the Movie, and Other Episodes in Political Demonology,* p. 223.

17. Snead, *White Screens/Black Images,* p. 44.

18. Wood, Gerald. 1983. "From *The Clansman* and *Birth of a Nation* to *Gone with the Wind,*" in *Recasting: Gone with the Wind in American Culture,* ed. Darden Asbury Pyron. Miami: University Presses of Florida/Florida International University, pp 123–36 (p. 123).

19. Cripps, Thomas. 1983. "Winds of Change: *Gone with the Wind* and Racism as a National Issue," in *Recasting: Gone with the Wind in American Culture,* ed. Darden Asbury Pyron. Miami: University Presses of Florida/Florida International University, pp. 137–38, 141.

20. Guerrero, Ed. 1993. *Framing Blackness: The African American Image in Film.* Philadelphia, Pa.: Temple University Press, p. 23.

21. Bonilla-Silva, Eduardo. 2001. *White Supremacy & Racism in the Post–Civil Rights Era.* Boulder, Colo.: Lynne Rienner, p. 89.

22. Ibid.

23. Golub, Mark. 1998. "History Died for Our Sins: Guilt and Responsibility in Hollywood Redemption Histories." *Journal of American Culture* 21 (no. 3): 23–45 (p. 36).

24. Burgoyne, Robert. 1997. *Film Nation: Hollywood Looks at U.S. History.* Minneapolis: University of Minnesota Press, p. 23.

25. Ibid.

CHAPTER 3

The Beautiful White American: Sincere Fictions of the Savior

Films Analyzed:
Stargate (1994)
Indiana Jones and the Temple of Doom (1984)
The Man Who Would be King (1975)
City of Joy (1992)
The Green Berets (1968)
To Kill a Mockingbird (1962)
Mississippi Burning (1988)
One Flew Over the Cuckoo's Nest (1975)
The Matrix (1999)
Three Kings (1999)

Stargate: *The white messiah strikes a Lawrence of Arabia pose. Copyright 1994 Metro-Goldwyn-Mayer.*

In this chapter, we extend our investigation of the sincere fictions of the white self by looking at a series of Hollywood films about the white savior. The messianic white self is the redeemer of the weak, the great leader who saves blacks from slavery or oppression, rescues people of color from poverty and disease, or leads Indians in battle for their dignity and survival. This is a narcissistic fantasy found in many Hollywood movies. Often the white messiah is an alienated hero, a misfit within his own society, mocked and rejected until he becomes a leader of a minority group or of foreigners. He finds himself by self-sacrifice to liberate the natives. White messiahs are overwhelmingly male; women do not seem to qualify for this exalted status. Often the white outsider is instantly worshiped by the natives, treated like visiting royalty or a god. This is presented as to be expected, as no less than he deserves. The messiah is marked by charisma, the extraordinary quality that legitimizes his role as leader and that of the foreign population as followers.

The image of the white messiah is ubiquitous in recent American action-adventure movies, especially hit series such as *Die Hard, Superman, Batman, Indiana Jones, Rocky, Rambo, Terminator, Alien,* and *The Matrix.* Such films typically concern a white hero or superhero (only in *Alien* and *Terminator* is it a heroine) who triumphs despite impossible odds against archvillains and saves the city, the nation, or the world. Often he defeats megalomaniac "others": foreigners, Nazis, or extraterrestrials who want to rule the world. This is a reflection of American civic religion, which transforms collective endeavors into the battle of a lone individual against the forces of organized evil. It is reinforced by Hollywood, which favors narratives about strong individuals. The white action messiah reaffirms modern, individual subjectivity. The action hero is typically a loner. But in more recent films, such as *Die Hard 3, The Matrix,* and *Three Kings,* the white hero has a multicultural team of helpers.

We focus on white messiahs who lead people of another color. This is such a powerful cultural myth because it presents whites with pleasing images of themselves as saviors rather than oppressors of those of other races. The adventure of a white messiah is an ideal vehicle for propaganda movies such as *Glory,* a story about a white hero leading blacks into battle in the Civil War, which we discussed in chapter 2. The messiah fantasies are essentially grandiose, exhibitionistic, and narcissistic. In the white mind, racial others do not exist on their own terms but only as what Kohut calls "a self-object," bound up with the white self.[1]

There are many such films, but for the purposes of this argument we have limited ourselves to a sample from the 1960s through the 1990s. First is a series of stories about Americans encountering the exotic East or a facsimile of Asia: *Stargate* (1994), *Indiana Jones and the Temple of Doom* (1984), *The Man Who Would be King* (1975), *City of Joy* (1992), and *The Green Berets* (1968). Next we look at two movies about white men battling racism in the American South: *To Kill a Mockingbird* (1962), and *Mississippi Burning* (1988). We then consider a popular movie about a white man who helps a native American: *One Flew Over the Cuckoo's Nest* (1975). Finally, we consider two recent movies—*The Matrix* (1999) and *Three Kings* (1999)—that update the white messiah's myth by providing him with a racially diverse team of helpers.

What we discover in movies about the white messiah reconfirms what we found in the films about the Civil War. First, the ideal white self is constructed as powerful, brave, cordial, kind, firm, and generous: a natural-born leader. Other racial and ethnic groups exist as dependent, faithful followers to bolster the grandiose white self-image. And second, in many of these movies, there is a split in the white self, similar to the one we uncovered in the Civil War movies, which can only be resolved through violence. The sincere fictions encoded in the white messiah movies enable the white self to live with itself and to absolve the guilt of racism by portraying whites as noble and self-sacrificing on behalf of other racial and ethnic groups, innocent victims who badly need rescue by white Americans.

In myths such as *Stargate* and *Indiana Jones and the Temple of Doom,* imperialism justifies itself in the name of religious, democratic, or humanitarian goals. White Americans are in foreign lands not to get wealthy from the natural resources or to exploit the population but to liberate them from slavery. The oppressors are an extraterrestrial tyrant in *Stargate* and Indian aristocrats in *Temple of Doom*. Two critics write, "*Indiana Jones* is a cinematic variant on the theme of the 'white man's burden.' It seeks to represent imperialism as a civilizing, socially progressive force and so to legitimize Western domination of others. It does so by identifying oppression with the indigenous system of rule."[2]

Stargate: The Gulf War in Outer Space

Stargate, one of the most popular films of 1994, is a good starting point because it presents an almost pure mythic paradigm. Its hero possesses the entire inventory of messianic traits. The film borrows from a wealth of myths, including the legends of Moses and of Christ, and from previous science fiction films using the hero myth, such as *Star Wars* (1977) and *Dune* (1984). But its myth making really pertains to American foreign policy in the 1990s, particularly to the relationship of white Americans to Middle Eastern peoples.

Stargate begins with the discovery of an ancient, giant metal ring during an archaeological excavation in Egypt. Decades later, an American government project activates the ring, aided by Dr. Daniel Jackson, an Egyptologist and linguist, who decodes the symbols on its face. Apparently the ring serves as a gateway to distant stars. They send a military team, led by Colonel Jack O'Neill, to investigate the planet on the other side of the portal, at the other end of the universe. Jackson accompanies them. The men discover a desert planet with a population of dark-skinned slaves dressed in Arab garb who labor in the mines. The slaves have forgotten their own history, inscribed in the walls of caves in what turn out to be Egyptian hieroglyphs. They are kept in ignorance and ruled by terror by an alien being who calls himself Ra, the Egyptian sun god. Ra created the ancient Egyptian civilization and also built the pyramids on Earth as landing sites for his spaceship. Jackson, able to read the hieroglyphs, reveals the truth to the people and persuades them to revolt, in which they are aided by Colonel O'Neill and his men. They finally defeat Ra with an atomic bomb, blowing up his spaceship in a climax similar to that of *Star Wars*.

The mythic elements in *Stargate* are obvious. Jackson is an orphan and an outcast, mocked and scorned by the scientific community. The only one with faith in him is a wise old woman, a mother figure who recognizes his talent. He quickly shows his extraordinary ability by decoding the symbols. Jackson is next scorned by the soldiers as an outsider and a hopeless "dweeb." But the natives immediately bow down before him, believing him to be the chosen one because he wears an amulet with the sign of Ra, which was given him as a good luck charm by the old woman. Jackson is tested by various ordeals: he maintains his chastity in the face of sexual temptation; he descends into the underworld (the pyramid); he dies and is resurrected (in one of Ra's machines); he refuses to kill his comrades when ordered by Ra; he brings his slain lover back to life; he is almost killed again by Ra, but he escapes; and, after he decodes the hieroglyphs, he leads the people in their fight for freedom. The animated feature *Atlantis* (2001) duplicates the plot of a linguist who decides to stay with the natives after he deciphers their forgotten writing.

The split in the white self occurs between the two heroes of the film, who are foils. Jackson represents knowledge but O'Neill represents military might. Jackson has faith, but O'Neill is embittered, suicidally depressed over the death of his son. Jackson is the mythic hero, the man of an extraordinary destiny, but O'Neill is a conventional action hero. The two initially have nothing in common, and they clash, but later they unite to liberate the natives, and both are redeemed by the experience. At the end, Jackson stays, having found a wife and a place as leader of the tribe. O'Neill returns home, but he has found a substitute son in one of the native boys and has overcome his suicidal grief. The explicit message seems to be that white men can overcome their differences and find themselves by fighting together to liberate the natives from slavery in a foreign land. The natives exist for the white men to realize their own potential, and immersion in the exotic other will heal the split in the white self.

But *Stargate* has a quite different implicit message. The indigenous population is portrayed as credulous, ignorant, and superstitious. If you wear the right amulet, they will bow down and treat you like a god. Like the natives in Hollywood jungle movies of the 1930s and 1940s, they are amazed by a pocket lighter and can be won over with a candy bar. The natives on this planet, who are descendants of the Egyptians, have been slaves for thousands of years, and, without the coming of white men, would have remained slaves for thousands more. All it takes is one smart, white American to lead them to freedom. According to the logic of *Stargate*, if Columbus had been an American, he would have come to the New World not to exploit, enslave, convert, or exterminate the indigenous population but as a humanitarian to liberate the enslaved masses from the yoke of tyranny. These white Americans are portrayed as good guys, even though they carry an atomic bomb.

Stargate uses a mythic plot to convey its ideological message. The film, which appeared in 1994, is a thinly disguised allegory about the Gulf War of 1990–1991, in which the American government sent its armed forces to liberate desert people from a tyrannical invader. The evil Ra, who is a monstrous, androgynous alien—played by Jaye Davidson, who portrayed a transvestite in *The Crying Game* (1992)—is a version of Saddam Hussein. Saddam is again mocked as gay in the animated feature *South Park* (2000). *Stargate* was so popular that it led to a television series and a made-for-television movie.

Indiana Jones: The White Messiah Defeats Evil Religion

Indiana Jones and the Temple of Doom is similar to *Stargate*: another myth about the white messiah who liberates the slaves in an Eastern land. *Temple of Doom* indulges in even more blatant stereotyping and caricaturing, justifying this by setting the action in the 1930s, using 1930s movie conventions from the action-adventure and cliffhanger genres, and playing the clichés larger than life and close to preposterous. The tongue-in-cheek, retro mode is established in the opening sequence, an elaborate, Busby Berkeley style song-and-dance sequence set in a Shanghai nightclub in 1936. A blonde American woman sings "Anything Goes" in Chinese. We are signaled that "anything goes" in this movie, including old movie clichés and outdated racist and sexist stereotypes. On his adventures, "Indy drags with him an oriental orphan (the only male his equal) and a screeching, hysterical woman."[3]

In *Temple of Doom*, we are in *Gunga Din* (1939) territory, in which the natives are either loyal subjects of the British Crown or rebellious, blood-crazed Thuggee cultists. The division of racial others into the good—faithful helpers of the white man—and the bad—murderous thugs—is introduced in the opening sequence, in which Indy's life is threatened by Chinese gangsters, who try to poison and shoot him, while he is aided by a loyal Chinese partner, who dies saving him, and by a Chinese street kid whom he has adopted.

In the next sequence, Indy shows up in an impoverished Indian village. As in *Stargate*, the natives treat him as their savior and put on a feast in his honor. In both movies,

Indiana Jones and the Temple of Doom: *Indy frees the children.*
Copyright 1984 Lucasfilm, Ltd. Courtesy Museum of Modern
Art Film Stills Archive.

the hero shows his respect by eating the native cuisine, even though his companions find the food repulsive.

There are in fact many similarities between Daniel Jackson in *Stargate* and Indiana Jones, who both represent the mythic white American hero, the best of the white American self. Both are learned men, with doctorates in linguistics or archaeology, who respect other cultures. Both know languages, so they can communicate with the natives, and both put their learning to use to free the slaves (the whites are not the oppressors—extraterrestrials or other natives are the villains). Both are scientists but also men of action willing to use violence to defend themselves or the innocent. Both are tested by the same series of ordeals: they maintain their chastity in the face of temptation, descend into the underworld, die and are resurrected (Indy becomes a zombie slave of the Thuggee cult until he returns to normal), refuse to execute their comrades when ordered to by the villain, rescue a lover, and finally escape and lead the people to freedom. Most important, both these fictional characters are kind, fearless mythic heroes who risk their lives for people of an oppressed race, the polar opposite of real-life colonial masters.

Jackson, however, is selflessly pure, whereas Indy is an ambivalent character who seems to include both sides of the split white self. Indy is both a scientist and a soldier of fortune, an archaeologist who respects other cultures and a grave-robber and thief of valuable antiquities. In the opening sequence, he attempts to sell for profit an urn containing the remains of a Chinese emperor. When the Indian villagers ask him to return a sacred stone to their village, one is never quite sure whether he wants the stone for their sake or for the "fortune and glory" to which he refers. The greedy, self-serving side of Indy is caricatured in Willie Scott, the gold-digging American woman who accompanies him. Yet she, too, later helps free the slaves.

The white American self, torn between serving himself and serving others, embodies the contradictions of capitalism. He is the classic American hero seen in such characters as Rick in *Casablanca* (1941) and Han Solo in *Star Wars* (1977). And in movies such as *Stargate* and *Temple of Doom,* although white Americans may initially have a profit motive in going to foreign lands, they soon abandon it to free the oppressed masses.

As in *Stargate,* the natives are helpless to liberate themselves. There seem to be no strong men in the Indian village, only women and old men. All it takes is one enterprising American, the great white God sent by destiny, to free the people. Near the end of the movie, when Indy confronts the villainous Mola Ram, high priest of the Thuggees, Indy accuses him: "You betrayed Shiva!" The white American has now appropriated the Indian identity and speaks with the voice of Hindu orthodoxy to denounce the heretic.

In elevating the white American self to the stature of a mythic superhero, both movies distort history and, while seeming to respect other cultures, actually insult them, implying, for example, that the ancient Egyptians were incapable of building the pyramids or that twentieth-century Indians eat monkey brains; indulge in devil worship, unspeakable rituals, and human sacrifice; and exploit children as slave labor.

The Man Who Would Be King:
The Messiah Plays God

The Man Who Would Be King is a similar story of a mythic superhero, a great white god come to enlighten the ignorant heathen. But director John Huston's version of a Rudyard Kipling story presents the myth ironically, as a cautionary tale about the disaster that ensues when a white imperialist starts believing that he is a god. Among the movies we consider about the white messiah, *The Man Who Would Be King* seems at first to demonstrate the delusive nature of the sincere fictions of the white self. Unfortunately, it ends up reaffirming them by glorifying its roguish heroes and stereotyping the natives.

Huston's movie is framed as a tale told to Kipling by his acquaintance "Peachy" Carnahan. Carnahan and his best friend Daniel Dravitt (another Biblical Daniel, like Jackson in *Stargate*) are former British soldiers who remain in late nineteenth-century India rather than return to dull, working-class lives in England. Carnahan and Dravitt are soldiers of fortune, not ambivalent ones like Indiana Jones, but rogues out to steal whatever they can. They retain audience sympathy because they are loveable scoundrels, loyal to each other, fun-loving play actors, and bold adventurers. After trying various scams, they decide to pull their boldest con job: they undertake an expedition to the remote land of "Kaffiristan," a country no white man has seen since Alexander the Great. They intend to awe the natives with firepower, set themselves up as kings, and return rich with loot. No one in the movie ever questions the morality of such a conquest, exploitation, and theft.

Kipling first meets them when Carnahan steals his watch and returns it because the watch bears a Masonic emblem. Their membership in this secret society forms a bond between these two white men, even though they are of different social classes. Later, the Masonic emblem serves Dravitt well when the natives take it as the sign of his godhood, just as the natives in *Stargate* bow down because Jackson wears the emblem of Ra. According to the movie, the conqueror Alexander the Great was the founder of the Masons, forming a secret fraternity of white men that has lasted throughout Western civilization. Huston says, "I used a Masonic emblem to symbolize a universal connection between men."[4] Nevertheless, in the plot, the native recognition of a supposedly universal symbol only serves the purposes of Western imperialists.

At first, all goes according to plan. Dravitt is set up as king and god, and even serves the people well, dispensing justice and improving conditions. But things go awry when Dravitt suffers delusions of grandeur. He starts to think he really is a god and the reincarnation of Alexander and that events have been determined by destiny. When his terrified bride bites him during the marriage ceremony, he bleeds, revealing he is not a god. The angry natives turn against the Englishmen. Dravitt falls to his doom when they cut a rope bridge over a chasm. (There is a similar scene in *Temple of Doom*, except that Indy survives the cutting of the bridge.) Carnahan is crucified but lives to tell the tale, although he is crippled and half crazy.

Unfortunately, despite its irony about the white savior, *The Man Who Would Be King* is as condescending in its view of the natives as *Stargate* and *Temple of Doom*. Indians and other Asians are seen in clichés: as exotic others, comic buffoons, or ignorant primitives. The main Indian character is a Ghurka soldier comically nicknamed "Billy Fish," as if his real name were unimportant. Although he knows the two Englishmen are con artists, he serves them loyally, finally dying on their behalf, like Gunga Din. Because of the childlike portrayal of the natives, Afghanistan (where the action is supposedly set) refused to allow the movie to be shown in its theaters.

One critic claims the racism in the film is due to Huston's attempt to be faithful to Kipling and not to impose contemporary attitudes on the film.[5] But according to another critic, "Huston has traditionally viewed . . . natives as amoral, entertaining creatures who need to be taken care of, admired, amused, and used but never trusted or treated as equals."[6] If Huston is faithful to Kipling, it is probably because he shares Kipling's racism.

The Man Who Would Be King resembles Huston's earlier film *The Treasure of the Sierra Madre* (1948), in which a group of white American men dig for gold in Mexico. Both films are cautionary tales about the corruption caused by excessive greed or power, but they both see racial others as childlike primitives or barbarians and never question the logic of white supremacy or of imperialism. For all its irony, *The Man Who Would Be King* is a narcissistic fantasy, like *Stargate* and *Indiana Jones,* in which the natives have been waiting for a white savior. The difference is that Huston portrays ironically what happens when narcissism goes to the extreme of megalomania. The plot of *The Man Who Would Be King* was borrowed for the recent, sentimentalized animated feature *The Road to El Dorado* (2000).

City of Joy: The White Messiah Reborn in India

City of Joy is a more realistic portrait of Indian culture than *The Man Who Would Be King,* showing a wide variety of Indian characters of more than one dimension. Unlike the previous three movies, it is not about a mythic superhero. The protagonist, Max, is a disillusioned white American doctor who comes to India to find enlightenment. But an ashram cannot help him. Instead, he realizes himself by serving the poor and the lepers in a free clinic in "the City of Joy," a ghetto in Calcutta. Max begins as a reluctant messiah, but by the end he has become committed to the people and decides to stay.

City of Joy: *The messiah is popular with the children. Copyright 1992 TriStar Pictures, Inc. Courtesy Museum of Modern Art Film Stills Archive.*

The story of Max is paralleled by the story of Hasari, a poor farmer driven off the land, who comes to Calcutta with his family to start a new life. At first, the family is swindled and forced to sleep in the streets. But eventually Hasari finds work as a rickshaw driver and the family finds a home in the City of Joy. The lives of these two displaced people, the American and the Indian, become intertwined, and each helps the other. Max gives Hasari courage to stand up to the gangsters who control the rickshaw business and terrorize the community. And Hasari gives Max a family to which he can belong. At the end, Max sits in a place of honor at the wedding of Hasari's daughter. Max and Hasari have both found a home in the City of Joy and become leaders of the community.

Unlike the two male protagonists, women are consigned to conventional, secondary roles in *City of Joy,* except for the Irish nurse, a tough, admirable woman who runs the clinic alone until she recruits Max. But her function is really a maternal one: to prop up the hero. Like the wise old woman in *Stargate,* she recognizes and nurtures the messiah's potential.

City of Joy is exceptional for a Hollywood film in giving equal time to an American and an Indian and in showing respect for Indian culture. Nevertheless, it shares the same arrogant assumption as the other movies discussed, the notion that all it takes is one white man to rescue or transform a foreign community. Max will save the City of Joy by inspiring the people with American ideals, helping the Indians to overcome their cultural passivity and to stand up for their rights.

Despite their colonialist assumptions and cultural arrogance, there is an opposite notion often implied in the white messiah movies: that white American culture is incomplete and that exotic foreigners have more soul, so that you can realize yourself in another country in a way you never could in America. Thus what happens in the white messiah movies is usually a two-way process: not only does the messiah influence the community, but he too is changed by contact with the people. Jackson in *Stargate* and Max in *City of Joy* are American outcasts who decide to stay in a foreign culture because they have become identified with it. Jackson is an orphan who never really had a father and Max always resented his; in fleeing America, he is trying to escape his father. What happens to both Jackson and Max is a kind of rebirth through entry into a substitute family of another race.

The Green Berets: The Messiah Saves Vietnam

In contrast, *The Green Berets,* the weakest movie of the lot, presents us with a cardboard white messiah who never changes. It is pro-war propaganda, released in 1968, during the height of the Vietnam War. The movie failed, perhaps because it is a vanity production of John Wayne, by John Wayne, and for John Wayne, who codirects and stars, and because the American public was divided at the time about the war. Wayne plays Colonel Kirby, the usual invincible John Wayne military commander, a Green Beret who leads all the operations and never suffers a scratch. Unlike the other white messiahs in the movies, Kirby is never tempted, never doubts, and never develops. *The Green Berets* is static, with many battle scenes but no dramatic tension.

It opens with a press conference in which the Army explains that the United States is fighting for the South Vietnamese, who need and want Americans to protect them from brutal Communists. The sole black character in the film is a spokesman for the U.S. government position. A cynical, anti-war reporter accompanies Colonel Kirby to Vietnam, where he undergoes a change of heart when he sees how the Green Berets offer free medical assistance to poor villagers, adopt a cute little war orphan (a stock character, like Short Round, the Chinese orphan in *Temple of Doom*), and fight valiantly against the evil Viet Cong, who slaughter civilians. The Vietnamese are either loyal allies or treacherous enemies who must be killed. Like Kirby, everyone in this movie is constructed of cardboard.

In the final scene, Kirby comforts the cute little Vietnamese war orphan, giving him his green beret and saying, "You're what this war is all about." And they walk off hand in

The Green Berets: *"You're what this war is all about." Copyright 1968 Warner Brothers/Seven Arts. Courtesy Museum of Modern Art Film Stills Archive.*

hand to the tune of "The Green Berets," a song in which this elite force of Cold Warriors is called "America's best." Rarely has the sincere fiction of the white messiah been presented so crudely: the Vietnamese population is reduced to a grateful little boy who must be protected by John Wayne. How can Americans be wrong or be racist, when "the best" of the white American self is fighting to protect innocent foreign children of color against aggression? (Indiana Jones is also a kind American warrior, the liberator of children, although *Temple of Doom* is not such naked propaganda.)

Green Berets uses sentimentality to disguise the fact that the Vietnam War was a narcissistic conflict for the United States. As the recent memoir of Robert S. McNamara reaffirms, U.S. involvement had little to do with the welfare of the Vietnamese but a lot to do with the ideological struggles of the Cold War and with American self-esteem.[7] American intervention in fact produced millions of war orphans, both North and South Vietnamese and American as well. But to recognize that would cause intense psychological discomfort to the white self-image as the savior of people of color.

The South Gets Saved

Next we consider two movies that take place in the exotic American South and invent white messiahs as heroes of the Civil Rights Movement: *To Kill a Mockingbird* and *Mississippi Burning*. The black characters in the two movies are, with few exceptions, docile and passive. The active figures are the white saviors and their antitheses, the hostile rednecks.

The villains in these southern melodramas, stereotypical hostile rednecks or southern sheriffs, are stock characters who entered American popular culture with the Civil Rights movement and proliferated in movies of the 1960s and 1970s such as *Easy Rider* (1969) and *Deliverance* (1972).[8] Smoldering with irrational hatred of anyone different from himself—blacks, women, the middle class, hippies, and northerners—the redneck is an American primitive "whose basic plot function in popular film is to provide the threat or the occasion of random violence."[9] The redneck, "like the abusive southern sheriff, is portrayed as a defender of the worst traditional American values—jingoist patriotism, racism, and sexism."[10]

In terms of the sincere fictions of the white American self, the hostile redneck is a lower-class character on whom racism and sexism can be projected. The members of the audience can reassure themselves that they do not resemble this brute, so therefore they must not be racists. This ignores the fact that racism is not necessarily a factor of education or class but permeates all levels of white American society. Racism comes in many forms, some violent and overt, and therefore highly visible and useful for the purposes of movie melodrama, but most subtle and covert, often institutionalized, and therefore largely invisible.

To Kill a Mockingbird: The Messiah as Attorney for the Defense

To Kill a Mockingbird, a faithful adaptation of Harper Lee's Pulitzer Prize–winning novel, was released in 1962, during the height of the Civil Rights movement. Although it is a nostalgia film, set in the Depression-era South thirty years in the past, it was obviously intended to have contemporary relevance. The effect of the movie is to soothe white consciences by suggesting that race prejudice was worse in the past, that such bigotry is largely restricted to ignorant Southern rednecks, and that there will always be a white saint willing to fight for justice and equality for blacks. The unintentional irony of the movie lies in the fact that the liberal white saint is ineffectual.

To Kill a Mockingbird deals with the explosive subject matter of race prejudice indirectly, by distancing it in time and showing it through the eyes of a little girl. There is much humor and tenderness in her memories. The voice-over narrator is a grown woman, Jean Louise "Scout" Finch, looking back on an event in her childhood. Her father, the lawyer Atticus Finch, defended the black sharecropper Tom Robinson, who was unjustly accused of raping a white woman. The movie places us in the position of an innocent, curious child spying on a corrupt, prejudiced, violent society. Scout is more naïve observer than participant in the central action. Through identification with Scout, the adult audience is also rendered innocent, absolved of blame for racism.

Scout and her brother Jem idolize their father, Atticus, who is a liberal messiah and the ideal patriarch. Atticus is played by Gregory Peck, a handsome actor who portrayed a paragon of anti-racist virtue and dignity in other Hollywood movies, such as *Gentleman's Agreement* (1947) (see chapter 8).

Opposed to Atticus is Bob Ewell, a white farmer and father of the woman who accused Tom of rape. Ewell can't understand how Atticus could defend a black man. He begins to stalk the lawyer and in the film's climax tries to kill Scout and Jem. Thus we once again see a split white self. Both Atticus and Ewell are widowers with daughters, but there the similarity ends. Where Atticus is middle-class, educated, liberal, brave, peaceful, sober, and a kind father, Ewell is working class, ignorant, bigoted, cowardly, violent, a drunkard, and a child abuser. Atticus is the idealized white self, and Ewell, the hostile redneck, is the white anti-self. The narrative needs the brutish Ewell to ennoble Atticus by contrast. In a prophetic scene, Atticus shoots a rabid dog, foreshadowing the eventual fate of Ewell.

Another series of parallels is created by the introduction of Boo Radley, a retarded white neighbor of the Finches. Boo serves as a double for Tom Robinson. Although Boo is white, as a victim of prejudice he is symbolically black. His name also suggests his blackness: "boo" suggests a ghost and blacks are also referred to in racial slurs as "spooks" or "boogie men." Tom and Boo are both pariahs within the community, unjustly accused of being violent brutes and feared, although they are kind men. Both are much gossiped about but unseen until late in the story. Both are disabled: Tom is crippled in his left arm and Boo is retarded. Both are prisoners: Tom is in jail and Boo is confined to his house by his father. Finally, the children spy on the trial of Tom just as they spy on Boo. A critic writes: "Just as the townspeople stereotype Tom Robinson due to their fear of blacks, Scout, Jem, and Dill [a neighbor child] stereotype Boo Radley as a bogeyman extraordinaire."[11] The positive outcome for Boo—he saves the children's lives and becomes a part of the family—balances the tragedy of Tom Robinson and suggests the possibility of overcoming prejudice.

Boo is not only a surrogate black but also a double for Atticus, a childlike surrogate father. Boo is a guardian angel, watching over the children, secretly giving them gifts, and killing Ewell when he attacks Scout and Jem. Ewell must be exterminated as the white mad dog, although not by Atticus, for that would taint the white messiah in the eyes of his children and of the audience.

This suggests a curiously contradictory aspect of this sincere fiction of the white liberal father. The film reveals Atticus to be principled, dignified, and noble but powerless. When Atticus stands guard outside the jail during the night to protect Tom from a lynch mob, it is instead Scout who saves Tom. By innocently greeting members of the mob by name as neighbors, she shames them into leaving. Atticus cannot successfully defend Tom in the courtroom either, because Tom is found guilty and then killed (supposedly while attempting to escape), and he cannot defend his children against Ewell; instead Boo saves them.

To Kill a Mockingbird: *"Miss Jean Louise, stand up. Your father's passing."* Copyright 1962 *Universal International Pictures.*

So Atticus is actually a failed white messiah, but the film applauds him for his integrity. In a crucial scene, after Tom is found guilty by the all-white jury, the blacks in the balcony stand up to honor Atticus and the black minister tells Scout, "Miss Jean Louise, stand up. Your father's passing." Atticus does not speak to them, maintaining his distance. The blacks in the film are all powerless victims, as docile and dependent on white people as Tom Robinson. A critic writes, "The scene here is a white fantasy of black behavior, in which the black community pays homage to the failed but noble efforts of a liberal white southerner."[12]

To Kill a Mockingbird, for all its good intentions, is another narcissistic fantasy about the white self congratulating itself for overcoming racism, at the same time that it turns blacks into passive, secondary characters.

Mississippi Burning: History Rewritten

Mississippi Burning, released in 1988, 26 years after *To Kill a Mockingbird,* also looks back on the Southern past, to the Civil Rights movement of the mid 1960s. It is loosely based on events that took place after the murder of three Civil Rights workers near Philadelphia, Mississippi, in 1964, but it fictionalizes these events greatly. Unlike the gentle,

sometimes humorous *To Kill a Mockingbird,* it is a violent, often brutal film about violent times, filled with shootings, beatings, explosions, burnings, and lynchings, reflect-
ing the increasing sensationalism of contemporary Hollywood film. But like *To Kill a
Mockingbird,* the movie alleviates white guilt by suggesting that race prejudice is a thing
of the past, restricted to ignorant southern rednecks, and that fearless white saints will
always emerge to fight for justice and equality for blacks. Again, as in *To Kill a Mockingbird,* the blacks are depicted primarily as passive, suffering victims, incapable of fighting
for themselves. Not much has changed in Hollywood films over the decades, and we get
another self-congratulatory, narcissistic fantasy about the white messiah.

The messiahs in this film are two FBI men. In actuality, the heroes of the Civil
Rights movement were black ministers such as the Reverend Martin Luther King Jr.,
many black Southerners, both workers and students, a few white Southerners, along
with black and white Northern volunteers from churches and campuses. People like
Chaney, Goodman, and Schwerner, the slain Civil Rights workers, were heroic. Their
story would have been worth telling. In the movie, we learn nothing about them because
they are killed in the opening scene.

In fact, the FBI at the time was a bastion of white privilege, a club consisting almost exclusively of white males, and it systematically impeded the Civil Rights movement. FBI chief J. Edgar Hoover, no friend to minorities, suspected the Civil Rights
movement of being infiltrated or led by Communists and terrorists, and he had Martin Luther King Jr. closely monitored and harassed. *Mississippi Burning* grossly distorts
history to reinforce faith in white patriarchy by glorifying the FBI. Writes the film critic
Jonathan Rosenbaum, "in terms of its own deranged emotional-ideological agenda, the
FBI *is* the civil rights movement."[13]

British director Alan Parker defended his film by saying, "our film cannot be the definitive film of the Civil Rights struggle. Our heroes are still white. And in truth, the film
would probably never have been made if they weren't." He knew "the movie's primary
audience was going to be whites (both in the United States and abroad)."[14]

Coretta Scott King, Martin Luther King's widow, asked, "How long will we have to wait
before Hollywood finds the courage and the integrity to tell the stories of some of the many
thousands of black men, women, and children who put their lives on the line for equality?"[15] And Rosenbaum complained that "the film's indifference to the truth of the situation is indicative of where its real interest lies: with the good or evil intentions of whites, not
with the everyday experience of blacks."[16] The same Hollywood strategy is evident in *Ghosts
of Mississippi* (1996), which focuses on the white lawyer as the savior rather than on the historical figure of Medgar Evers, a black martyr of the Civil Rights movement.

As in *Stargate,* there are two heroes, two FBI agents representing split aspects of the
white American self who at first quarrel but later cooperate to defeat a common enemy.
The historian Harvard Sitkoff commented sarcastically that the movie implies that southern blacks won their civil rights because "two white guys learned to work together."[17]

The screenwriter Chris Gerolmo said he based the relationship between Ward and
Anderson on that between the peaceful lawyer and the tough cowboy who battle the
outlaw in John Ford's western *The Man Who Shot Liberty Valance* (1962).[18] Ward
(Willem Dafoe) is a tightly buttoned Northern liberal, one of Kennedy's best and bright-
est, an agent who goes by the book. His heroic liberal credentials are established by the
fact that he took a bullet protecting James Meredith at the University of Mississippi. But
in this situation he is an outsider. Anderson (Gene Hackman) is an insider, looser than

Ward, a good old boy and former small-town Mississippi sheriff. He seems included in the movie to suggest that not all white Southerners or Southern sheriffs are redneck racists. Anderson understands these people, so he relies on winning their confidence and getting them to talk. Later he resorts to unorthodox methods—seduction of a woman witness and brutal intimidation—to get results. Ward at first strongly disapproves of Anderson's methods but later goes along with him. The movie allows us to applaud Anderson's illegal tactics, which are seen as the only way to break the silence of a sealed, segregated community where whites are too loyal to talk and blacks too frightened to testify. In actuality, the FBI solved the case by bribing Klan informants.

Like *Stargate,* the movie also introduces a brave woman. In *Stargate,* she was the native woman who fell in love with Jackson and helped lead the revolt. In *Mississippi Burning,* she is a beautician married to the deputy sheriff. The deputy is a suspect in the disappearance of the three young men, and his wife at first supports his alibi. She doesn't hate blacks because she is victimized by the same white male violence that oppresses them. Anderson is certain she knows the truth and will talk. Although their relationship never becomes physical, Anderson takes advantage of their mutual attraction until she trusts Anderson enough to reveal where the bodies are buried, which cracks the case. Her husband brutally beats her for talking, sending her to the hospital, but Anderson later beats the husband in retaliation.

But in both *Stargate* and *Mississippi Burning,* women are secondary characters, and the heroine must be brought to consciousness through a white male. Only the romantic interest of the hero allows her to be brave, and he must rescue her when she is in danger.

As in *To Kill a Mockingbird,* blacks are secondary characters, kept in the background, even though *Mississippi Burning* uses black gospel music throughout the soundtrack. With few exceptions, blacks suffer passively, kept silent through beatings, bombings, and lynchings. Once again, they are dependent on the largesse of white liberals to defend them, which belies the black political activism of the 1960s.

The villains are again stereotyped rednecks, brutes like Bob Ewell in *To Kill a Mockingbird.* Here the violent bigots include members of the sheriff's department and working-class members of the Ku Klux Klan, depicted as overweight, foul-mouthed thugs and cowardly predators who operate in packs under the cover of night. There are also television interviews with average Mississippians, who are represented as mostly bigoted and hostile to outsiders. "Director Alan Parker had chosen many of the extras for the movie himself, seeking people with ugly, stereotypically redneck features. Virtually all the individuals representing common folk and segregationists in the movie reflect popular images of the southern 'cracker.'"[19] Ward, Anderson, and the beautician are the only sympathetic white liberals around, and thus made to seem all the more heroic.

The movie at first appears to promote white guilt. Even though no charges are brought against him, the mayor of the small Mississippi town hangs himself—a patently false contrivance because no Southern mayor ever committed suicide from contrition over racism. Ward pontificates: "He was guilty. Anyone's guilty who watches this happen and pretends it isn't. No, he was guilty all right. Just as guilty as the fanatics who pulled the trigger. Maybe we all are."

Nevertheless, while it claims that we are all guilty, the movie absolves us by making it clear that these events happened many decades in the past, by showing that justice triumphed and the guilty were punished, and by splitting the white self, allowing us to identity with noble, heroic FBI agents and to disidentify with stereotyped racist rednecks. "'We're all guilty,'" says Rosenbaum, is "a nifty little formula that lets everyone off the hook."[20]

One Flew Over the Cuckoo's Nest: The Messiah Gives His Life

The movie *One Flew Over the Cuckoo's Nest* is an instance of the complete white messiah myth. Ken Kesey's best-selling 1962 novel was later made into a play and a hit movie. The protagonist, McMurphy, is an individualist in the American grain, one of the most recognizable archetypes in contemporary American popular culture: a rebel and an outlaw, a totally free spirit who stands up to the establishment on behalf of the oppressed (the inmates of a mental hospital), even though it costs him his life. McMurphy's popularity might also be explained by the fact that he is the only hero in the movies under discussion who fulfills the entire myth of the messiah. One critic writes, "*Cuckoo's Nest* the movie portrays the typical adventures of Joseph Campbell's monomythic hero who is called to adventure, who engages the forces of darkness, who struggles with doubt and temptation, and who triumphs in the end . . . by transferring his virtues to others through sacrifice."[21] McMurphy is a cowboy Christ who dies so that we may live.[22] In particular, he is the cowboy who sacrifices himself for his Indian buddy.

The conflict in the movie is allegorical and highly schematic in its dichotomies: McMurphy represents male sexuality, freedom, the cowboy, the outlaw, the human, and nature; the Big Nurse represents sexual repression, control, the schoolmarm, the law, the machine, and civilization. But the allegory is conceived in individualistic, white American male terms, and the deck is stacked in favor of the messiah, the good McMurphy versus the evil Nurse Ratched. Leslie Fiedler describes Kesey's novel as a new version of "the old, old fable of the White outcast and the noble Red Man joined together against home and mother, against the female world of civilization."[23] The film is much the same fable.

The struggle between McMurphy and Nurse Ratched is a struggle for the Chief's soul in which the cowboy frees the Indian. The Chief begins as the perfect institutionalized person: docile and apparently deaf and dumb. He ends as a strong, autonomous Indian brave who escapes from the hospital.

Nevertheless, the liberation of the Indian here is not done for the sake of Native Americans. Consider a turning point in the movie, when McMurphy needs one more vote so he and the men can watch the World Series on television. In desperation, he turns to the chronic patients. Finally, he gets the Chief to hold up his hand. McMurphy enlists his Indian buddy to help him battle a woman (the Big Nurse) and some blacks (her aides) on behalf of himself and a group of white men. The Chief acts as a surrogate for McMurphy and the white inmates, a stand-in for the white self.

The final scene of the movie can also be considered in terms of the white self. When the Chief lifts the machinery to smash the window and escape from the hospital, he seems like the aboriginal American breaking out of the reservation and back into the freedom of nature. But in terms of the plot, he is doing it to fulfill the legacy of McMurphy (who had tried but failed to do the same thing) and to act as a surrogate for the imprisoned white inmates.

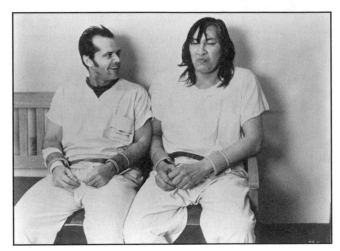

One Flew Over the Cuckoo's Nest: *McMurphy and the Chief. Copyright 1975 Fantasy Films and United Artists. Courtesy Museum of Modern Art Films Stills Archive.*

The real conflict in the movie is a civil war taking place within the white self that is enacted through the medium of the Indian. Despite their antagonism, McMurphy and Nurse Ratched are similar characters. Both see themselves as generous, kind, self-sacrificing, natural leaders. Both are extremely stubborn control freaks seeking a following, Nurse Ratched through a therapeutic regime and McMurphy through his program of countertherapy (in one scene, he impersonates a doctor). The civil war is between two versions of the white self, one bureaucratic and the other charismatic.

The Matrix: The White Messiah and His Multicultural Disciples

Finally, two recent films, *The Matrix* (1999) and *Three Kings* (1999) demonstrate how the myth of the white messiah persists in Hollywood cinema, except that now the white hero has a racially diverse team of helpers.

The Matrix presents an unambiguous tale of a white messiah. Like *Star Wars* or *Stargate*, it is a science-fiction action adventure that borrows from a wealth of myths. *The Matrix* alludes to the legends of Jesus and Orpheus and to a host of popular culture fantasies and fairy tales, including *Alice in Wonderland, The Wizard of Oz, Twenty Thousand Leagues under the Sea,* and *Sleeping Beauty.*

The premise is similar to that of other recent dystopian science fiction films such as *The Terminator* (1984) and T*erminator 2: Judgment Day* (1991): the machines have taken over and the remaining humans must fight for survival. In *The Matrix,* it is 2199 and the surface of the Earth has been destroyed in the war with the machines. Deep underground, humans are bred as a source of energy for the machines and kept lifelong in an embryonic state, dreaming that they are living in an American city in 1999. This dream world, called the Matrix, is a computer simulation intended to keep the populace docile. A few people from Zion, the last human city, insert themselves via computer into the Matrix to disrupt it, but they are endangered by the agents, extremely powerful sentient programs who destroy anyone who threatens their control.

Morpheus, the rebel leader, cruises the underworld in a hovercraft, like Jules Verne's Captain Nemo. Morpheus and his crew rescue from the Matrix Thomas Anderson, by day a computer programmer for a large corporation, by night an outlaw hacker known as "Neo." Morpheus is convinced Anderson may be "the One" foretold by "the Oracle": the man who can defeat the agents. Neo, whose name is an anagram of "One," is unaware he is living in a simulated reality. First he must be extracted from the Matrix, reborn in the real world, reeducated, and trained.

The Matrix seems to favor racial and gender diversity through its casting. Morpheus is black, and his crew are both black and white, men and women. In contrast, the agents, all called "Smith," are unemotional, identical-looking white men who dress uniformly in black suits like the FBI. The movie thus implies that the real, human world in which the good guys live is multicultural and multigendered whereas the computer simulation world of the Matrix is dominated by white men. When Morpheus battles one of the "Smiths," he tells the agent, "You all look alike to me," an ironic reversal of the stereotype whites apply to blacks. Here the white oppressors are uniform and indistinguishable: indeed, they are not even human. This message is underscored when Morpheus is captured by the head agent, who turns him over to a gang of white cops who beat Morpheus savagely with their batons in a scene strikingly reminiscent of the Rodney King video.

Nevertheless, the movie's potential critique of white racism is contradicted by the mythic plot, in which the black characters—Morpheus, the Oracle, and Morpheus's crew members Tank and Dozer—are disciples who serve the white Messiah Neo.

Three Kings: Revising the Gulf War

Three Kings (1999), released the same year as *The Matrix*, also depends on an updated white messiah, once again aided by a racially mixed team. Although the film is harshly critical of the confused messianism of American foreign policy in the Gulf War, it nevertheless creates another American hero who risks his life to rescue people of color.

The question the film raises is: What was the purpose of the Gulf War? This same question is voiced by two characters: Special Forces Major Archie Gates and the television journalist Adriana Cruz. Was the war fought to liberate the people of Kuwait, to teach a lesson to Saddam Hussein, or simply to protect the oil reserves? The war liberated Kuwait but stopped short of liberating Iraq, leaving the anti-Saddam rebels twisting in the wind, at Saddam's mercy without American military assistance.

Movies often rewrite history, expressing ideological wish fulfillment. *Mississippi Burning*, as we saw, rewrites the Civil Rights movement to make white FBI agents the biggest heroes of the movement. And *Stargate* and *Three Kings* both rewrite the Gulf War: in *Stargate* the U.S. Army uses an atomic bomb to blow up an evil dictator who oppresses Arabs (a stand-in for Saddam Hussein), and in *Three Kings* the U.S. Army aids the Iraqi rebels after the war ends.

Unlike these other movies, however, *Three Kings* is thoughtful, distinguished by its pointed political contradictions and deliberate moral ironies. For example, a captured

American soldier is tortured by an Iraqi officer who was trained in interrogation by the American military when Iraq was at war with Iran.

The film also criticizes the racism of the American troops, who show ignorance about and contempt for Arabs. Although a black American sergeant objects to the terms "dune coon" and "sand nigger," he has no objection when a white comrade suggests they use instead the more acceptable alternatives of "towel head" and "camel jockey." The movie opens with the shooting of an Iraqi soldier. We see the man get hit and die in painful close-up, which induces sympathy for him, yet the American troops call him a "raghead" and snap photos of the corpse as victory trophies.

But the film also shows the conversion of a group of American soldiers, who come to sympathize with the plight of a group of Iraqi refugees and decide to rescue them. The white messiah here is Major Archie Gates, who begins as a cynical opportunist who, to cushion his imminent retirement from the U.S. Army, sets out to steal for himself and his men the Kuwaiti gold held by Saddam's troops (a plot device borrowed from *Kelly's Heroes* [1970]). But when the Major witnesses the killing of an unarmed Iraqi woman in front of her husband and little daughter, he suddenly changes his mission to rescuing these Iraqi rebels from Saddam's Republican Guards. It is as if the soldiers of fortune in *The Man Who Would Be King* were suddenly transformed from self-serving thieves into champions of oppressed peoples. Thus, despite its acid critique of American foreign policy in the Gulf War and its persistent black humor, the film is at heart a sentimental story about an American good guy standing up to absolute evil (in contemporary American popular mythology, Saddam Hussein is linked with Satan—see for example the satiric *South Park* movie [2000]), giving up the gold and risking his life to save Iraqi refugees.

As a nod to diversity, the film includes a range of white, black, and Latino characters. The two television journalists are a Latina and a blonde woman. Major Gates' team consists of three young working-class men: one uneducated white Southerner, one naïve white store clerk from California, and one black baggage handler. There is also a black colonel in command. Nevertheless, the leader of the mission and the hero of the film is Major Gates, the white messiah who commands the loyalty and respect of his team and of the Iraqi rebels.

The same pattern, in which the goal of the white protagonist changes from greed to rescuing oppressed ethnic or racial others, is seen as well in *Stargate* and in the animated features *Pocahontas* (1995), *The Road to El Dorado* (2000), and *Atlantis* (2001).

Conclusion: The World Revolves Around the White Messiah

In the movies about the white messiah we have discussed, with the exception perhaps of *City of Joy* and *Three Kings*, we do not see real Indians, Iraqis, Vietnamese, African Americans, or Native Americans. Instead we see projections, fantasies created by the white filmmakers. The foreigners and minority characters are usually docile and grateful. If they are active, they are either loyal disciples of the white messiah or evil heathen. The white messiah movies tell us little about those of other races but much about the desire of the white self to avoid guilt and to see itself as charismatic and minorities as needing white leadership and rescue. None of the Hollywood messiahs resembles leaders such as Martin Luther King Jr., Cesar Chavez, Saul Alinsky, and many other real-life leaders.

In the language of object relations, "the central meaning of narcissistic libido is an erotic or libidinal attachment with oneself, even if an object is the vehicle for such involvement."[24] As Erich Fromm puts it, "for the narcissistically involved person, there is only one reality, that of his own thought processes, feelings and needs. The world outside is not experienced or perceived objectively, i.e., as existing in its own terms, conditions and needs"[25]

Notes

1. Kohut, Heinz. 1977. *The Restoration of the Self.* New York: International Universities Press.

2. Postone, Moishe and Elizabeth Traube. 1985. "*Indiana Jones and the Temple of Doom*: The Return of the Repressed," in *Jump Cut* 30: 12–14 (p. 12).

3. White, Armond. 1984. "Temple of Gremlins," *Films in Review*, August/September, 411–13 (p. 413).

4. Kaminsky, Stuart. 1978. *John Huston: Maker of Magic.* Boston: Houghton Mifflin, p. 199.

5. Hammen, Scott. 1985. *John Huston.* Boston: Twayne, p. 130.

6. Kaminsky, *John Huston,* p. 202.

7. McNamara, Robert S. and Brian VanDeMark. 1995. *In Retrospect: The Tragedy and Lessons of Vietnam.* New York: Times Books.

8. Loukides, Paul, and Linda K. Fuller. 1990. *Beyond the Stars: Stock Characters in American Popular Film.* Bowling Green, Ohio: Bowling Green University Popular Press, p. 95.

9. Ibid, p. 91.

10. Ibid, p. 93.

11. Abernathy, Jeff. 1991. "'I Knowed He Was White Inside': *Huckleberry Finn* and Stereotype in the Twentieth Century Southern Novel." Ph.D. Dissertation in English. Gainesville: University of Florida, p. 91.

12. Ibid., p. 101.

13. Rosenbaum, Jonathan. 1997. *Movies as Politics.* Berkeley: University of California Press, p. 123.

14. Toplin, Robert Brent. 1996. *History by Hollywood: The Use and Abuse of the American Past.* Urbana: University of Illinois Press, p. 36.

15. Ibid., p. 35.

16. Rosenbaum, *Movies as Politics,* p. 123.

17. Sitkoff, Harvard. 1989. "*Mississippi Burning,*" *Journal of American History* 76 (3): 1019–20 (p. 1020).

18. Toplin, *History by Hollywood,* p. 31.

19. Ibid, p. 43.

20. Rosenbaum, *Movies as Politics,* p.124.

21. Zubizarreta, J. 1984. "The Disparity of Point of View in *One Flew Over the Cuckoo's Nest,*" *Literature/Film Quarterly* 22 (no.1): 62–9 (p. 63).

22. See Hauck, R. B. 1970. "The Comic Christ and the Modern Reader." *College English* 31: 498–506; Pearson, C. 1974. "The Cowboy Saint and the Indian Poet: The Comic Hero in Ken Kesey's *One Flew Over the Cuckoo's Nest,*" *Studies in American Humor,* 1: 91–8; Wallis, B. 1972. "Christ in the Cuckoo's Nest: Or, the Gospel According to Ken Kesey." *Cithara* 12 (no.1): 52–8.

23. Fiedler, Leslie. 1968. *The Return of the Vanishing American.* New York: Stein & Day, p. 177.

24. Eagle, Morris N. 1984. *Recent Developments in Psychoanalysis: A Critical Evaluation.* Cambridge, Mass.: Harvard University Press, p. 59.

25. Fromm, Erich. 1956. *The Art of Loving.* New York: Harper, pp. 35–6.

CHAPTER 4

Amistad: Civilization and Its Contentments

Film Analyzed:
Amistad (1997)

The White Liberal Agenda on Race Relations

Amistad (1997) deserves a special discussion because it represents the state of the white neoliberal agenda on race relations in contemporary America. When Steven Spielberg directed *Schindler's List* (1993), he was accused by some African Americans of ignoring the longest and largest genocide in human history: the African slave trade to the Americas. With *Amistad*, Spielberg appears to rectify that oversight, attempting to do for African American history what *Schindler's List* did for Jewish history. Like *Schindler's List,* this film is an upbeat, Hollywood version of a holocaust, focusing on an exceptional incident, on the heartwarming tale of a few who won their freedom rather than on the millions who suffered and died in bondage. If *Schindler's List* was made for his Jewish family, then he says *Amistad* was made for his two adopted black children.[1]

We are concerned here not with the film's many virtues but with the distorted version of history it presents in the interest of drama and of ideology. Spielberg changes and embellishes the historical facts to make the story pleasing to contemporary sentiments. The historian Simon Schama calls *Amistad* "the most recent, and most impressive, example of filmed history as costume civics, chronicles of latter-day saints and martyrs, right in line with *Glory."*[2]

We argue that *Amistad,* ostensibly the story of the quest of enslaved Africans for freedom, becomes in the Spielberg version yet another sincere fiction of the white self. *Amistad* seems to be on the side of enslaved Africans, but it actually validates white civilization and the American legal institutions that enforced slavery. In *Amistad,* as in *Schindler's List* and *Saving Private Ryan* (1998), Spielberg tells the story of a noble, white Christian male messiah.

White Americans love fictions in which blacks do well, especially if the characters are aided by crusading white men. As we saw in our analysis of the white messianic self,

Amistad: *The rebellion aboard the Amistad involved the killing of the male authority figure, the* captain. *Copyright 1997 Dreamworks.*

these fantasies help to reassure the white conscience of its righteousness and goodness. However, in *Amistad,* the messianic white self acts through the institutions of white society. The reassurance here is that, despite the evil that individual whites may do to people of color, white institutions are fundamentally good. In fact, the movie is a saga about the goodness of the law and reliability of American courts, which supposedly guarantee freedom and justice for all.

We examine this film to illustrate two aspects of the sincere fictions of the white self. The first concerns the intertwining of economic and symbolic power essential to produce a film and the fictions it contains. In Hollywood films, economic power is transformed into the symbolic power of a film to persuade, produce, and reproduce the supposed meaning of things in the world. Through profits, the symbolic power of a film is then transformed back into money. This movie illustrates how the meanings conveyed by a film are determined not only by the filmmakers' intentions but also by the more general project to which films can be said to belong. When a project such as racism is systemic in a society, its influence is ubiquitous in shaping social life.[3]

The second concerns Spielberg's prestige, his symbolic or cultural capital, which draws the public into the movie theaters. His prestige and track record of filmmaking success translates into the creative freedom to engage in projects such as *Amistad.* The money flows to Spielberg because he is certain to entertain or to uplift but hardly to challenge or to offend audiences. Thus the Hollywood system, and the sincere fictions they promulgate, tend to be self-reinforcing. As the film historian Thomas Cripps says, "I think Steven Spielberg's internalized sentimental politics and the sentimental politics of Americans . . . is as one, and therefore there's no risk here."[4] In effect, just as he does in *Saving Private Ryan,* in *Amistad* Spielberg wraps himself in the American flag.

Slavery in Hollywood Films

It is helpful first to place *Amistad* in the history of Hollywood treatments of plantation slavery and the slave trade. The film industry first dealt with slavery in Edwin S. Porter's version of *Uncle Tom's Cabin* (1903). From the beginning of the twentieth century through the 1940s, Hollywood films such as *Birth of a Nation, The Littlest Rebel,* and *Gone with The Wind,* which we analyzed in chapter 2, denied the horror of slavery by sentimentalizing it.

Disney's *Song of the South* (1946), a groundbreaking mixture of live action and animation, is one of the last instances of sentimentalizing slavery in Hollywood film. It concerns a lonely little white boy, the grandson of the owner of the plantation. While his father is separated from the family, he finds solace in the stories of Uncle Remus, a wise and kind old slave who serves as a surrogate parent. The movie fosters the same plantation myths and racialized images as *Birth of a Nation* and *Gone with the Wind.* Its marketing to children and use of animation seem to guarantee its harmlessness, yet the technical innovations of *Song of the South* are placed at the service of a particular version of slavery in which slaves are docile and happy to serve and to love the white masters. The family values that the movie teaches apply only to whites, for Uncle Remus, like Mammy in *Gone with the Wind,* seems to have no family of his own. James Snead writes, "the salvation of the white family . . . has come at the cost of the black family unit."[5] The NAACP condemned the film for its racist representations,[6] and, today, Disney does not sell video or laser disc versions of the film in the United States.[7] However, a Disney World attraction still features Brer Rabbit and Brer Fox, the animated characters in the movie, as well as "Zip-a-dee Doo-dah," its Oscar-winning song.

As America moved into the civil rights era in the 1950s, Hollywood moved on to a higher form of liberal sentimentality in its treatment of slavery. Perhaps because slavery seemed too touchy a subject at the time, the only direct treatment of the subject in Hollywood film in that decade was *Band of Angels* (1957), in which Sidney Poitier portrays a rebellious slave. *The Defiant Ones* (1958), released the next year, might be considered an indirect treatment of slavery, since Poitier portrays an escapee from a 1950s southern chain gang who is heading north. But the film displaces the slavery allegory by chaining him to a white prisoner. Both films feature dignified, complex black heroes rather than docile clowns, yet both assuage the white fear of the potential violence of liberated blacks by having the black hero reconcile with a white man at the end. In *Band of Angels,* Poitier repents at the last moment and forgives his former master; in *The Defiant Ones,* he sacrifices his chance at freedom, abandoning the train heading north to stick with his wounded white buddy. (We consider *The Defiant Ones* in detail in chapter 10.)

In the 1970s, in the wake of the Civil Rights movement, two "blaxploitation" films about slavery were aimed primarily at black audiences: *Mandingo* (1975) and its sequel *Drum* (1976). These movies drove a stake through the heart of the plantation genre. "All of *Mandingo's* scenes are clearly shot from a point of view sympathetic to the African American perspective, depicting whites as cruel, degenerate slave masters and not, as in dominant cinema's past, as aristocratic ladies and gentlemen distanced from the brutality of slave ownership or the labor system of the plantation."[8] Unfortunately, Hollywood seemed to have abandoned the sentimental view of slavery only to exploit interracial sex and violence. "Finally, black audiences could experience the catharsis of seeing a slave rise up against the white power structure. But even these films exploited confrontation between the races and seemed simply to trade one stereotype for another. In the place of the childlike fool, we had the noble savage who threatened to sexually conquer the white master's women." This was scarcely an advance from *Birth of a Nation.*[9]

The epic 1977 television series *Roots,* based on Alex Haley's fictionalized account of his family's history, from his African ancestors through the present, enthralled millions of American viewers, both white and black. After *Roots,* "antebellum America seemed to be the purview of prime time, in part because TV, especially cable channels, have been more willing to tackle controversial issues, and in part because they can stage period dramas more cheaply."[10]

Since the 1980s, as Ed Guerrero notes, "While the slavery motif and the plantation genre have ended . . . , fragments of the motif still resonate as sedimented themes, metaphors, and icons in the content of many contemporary films." He points to such films as *Blade Runner* (1982), *The Toy* (1982), *The Brother from Another Planet* (1984), and *The Color Purple* (1985).[11]

In the late 1990s, Hollywood returned to more direct, serious treatments of slavery in films such as *Jefferson in Paris* (1994) and *Beloved* (1998). *Jefferson* attempts to come to terms with some of the ambiguities of American history as Thomas Jefferson confronts the issue of slavery and his love for his slave Sally Hemmings. Unfortunately, the movie invents history by showing the teenage Sally seducing the middle-aged slavemaster Jefferson. This white view of slavery is countered by the African American perspective of *Beloved,* based on the novel by Toni Morrison. Unlike the "blaxploitation" films of the 1970s, *Beloved* aims to educate and to move the audience rather than to shock and to titillate. Although it has some powerful and haunting imagery, audiences found it too long, slow, and confusing.

The Making of *Amistad*

Neither *Jefferson* (1994) nor *Beloved* (1998) was a hit. Indeed, Hollywood was afraid that films about slavery were too painful for both white and black audiences and represented box-office poison. In the early 1990s, African American producer Debbie Allen proposed a film about the *Amistad* case of 1839–1841, in which African slaves took over the ship *Amistad* from their Spanish masters, were captured by an American naval vessel, imprisoned, placed on trial in New Haven, Connecticut, and finally freed by the U.S. Supreme Court. But Allen found Hollywood reluctant to make such a film. Even black directors such as Spike Lee and John Singleton passed on the project, afraid they could not get funding. "I'd love to make stories about our history, and I would if I thought people would see them, but that hasn't been the case," said African American director Keenan Ivory Wayans. "Look at *Glory*—it barely made its money back, and as a black director I can't afford that."[12]

Allen finally turned to Steven Spielberg, the most successful and powerful director in Hollywood, because he was the only one with sufficient clout to make the film. Spielberg had already worked with black actors when he directed *The Color Purple* (1985), and his success with *Schindler's List* (1993) had established his credentials as a filmmaker unafraid to tackle controversial material. In addition, Spielberg had just formed a film studio, Dreamworks, with partners David Geffen and Jeffrey Katzenberg. *Amistad* would be his first directing job under the aegis of the new company.

The Fundamental Goodness of White Institutions

Amistad is praiseworthy in many respects. The graphic images of the middle passage have never before been represented in such horrifying detail.[13] Spielberg has brought to life the only time before the Civil War that American courts sided with rebellious blacks, and in Cinqué he presents an admirable African hero. *Amistad* wants to make both black and white audiences feel good about their common history. It appeals to the black audience by presenting a strong, historically real African hero, casting Africans in African roles, and allowing them to speak in the African language Mende. In addition, it sometimes shows events through the Africans' perspective. (In this regard, it follows the lead of *Dances with Wolves* [1990] in portraying Native Americans on the screen.) It appeals to the white audience by presenting an instance in which white institutions operated in a morally correct fashion and gave Africans their freedom, at a time when millions suffered slavery in the United States. Finally, it performs an important didactic function by bringing this historical incident to the attention of millions of Americans. It was released with a companion educational package intended for classroom use.[14]

Amistad: *The graphic images of the middle passage have never before been represented in such horrifying detail. Copyright 1997 Dreamworks.*

Despite its good intentions, *Amistad* is nevertheless a saga affirming the fundamental goodness of white American civilization. According to the anthropologist Thomas Patterson, "Civilization . . . was state-based, class-stratified, and ruled by law; its literate fraction either belonged to the ruling class or held important positions in the state apparatus."[15] The laws existed to guarantee the privileges of the elite. In the film, there are two sets of heroes: two privileged white Americans, Roger Baldwin and John Quincy Adams, both lawyers; and an African "barbarian" who learns the law and thus becomes civilized.

The white self is divided. On the one hand, there are the evil white men: greedy Spanish and Portuguese slavers, slick white Southerners (represented only by Senator John C. Calhoun), and craven politicians (represented by President Martin Van Buren and his secretary of state) who cater to the Southern vote. These characters have "op-pressor" or "coward" written in their every gesture. Against them are the heroic whites: Northern abolitionists, stalwart British sea captains, and crusading lawyers who take on the cause of liberating the captive Africans. Says Thomas Cripps: "The Amistad story is so perfect as a vehicle. It has the foreign heavies, it has the virtuous New Englanders, and . . . it leaves the white South out of it."[16] Some of the ideological caricaturing of the early, racist film *Birth of a Nation* (1915) is repeated here, with the polarity reversed from good Southern white racists to good Northern white liberals. Although the images of blacks have improved, the representation of the white self is not that different.

Two Stories in One

Of the many ways the story could be told, Spielberg chose in *Amistad,* as in *Schindler's List,* to tell two stories simultaneously. In *Schindler's List,* one story concerns the fate of the Jews during the Holocaust, as represented by the "Schindlerjuden." The other is the story of Schindler, a Nazi businessman turned white messiah, a savior of the Jews. The two stories in *Amistad* are of the fate of the masses of Africans caught in the slave trade, as embodied in the group led by Cinqué, and the development of a white messianic movement led by John Quincy Adams, who frees the slaves. In both *Schindler's List* and *Amistad,* Spielberg adopts the Hollywood strategy of telling history as the drama faced by strong individuals. Unfortunately, the effect of this dramatic strategy is to individu-alize and ennoble the white messiahs Schindler and John Quincy Adams at the expense of the Jews and the Africans (except for Stern in *Schindler's List* and Cinqué in *Amis-tad*), who are reduced mostly to background figures. At least many of the Jewish char-acters have names and stories, unlike the Africans, who remain mostly an undifferen-tiated mass.

The morally ambivalent figure of Schindler has no exact equivalent in *Amistad,* al-though Schindler's arc of development is mimicked by the young lawyer Roger Baldwin, who transforms from ambulance chaser at the beginning of the film into selfless hu-manitarian at the end.

Amistad unnecessarily distorts many of the facts in the historical incident. These al-terations align the film with American pop cultural traditions, but they also have ideo-logical effects.

For example, one commentator calls the film's Roger Baldwin "historically absurd."[17] Roger Baldwin was 46 in 1839, when the case began, not in his twenties, like the actor who portrays him, and no ambulance chaser but a highly regarded lawyer chosen by the abolitionists for his prestige and his sympathy to their cause. However, the inexperienced underdog, such as the clever young lawyer who surprises everyone by winning a seem-ingly impossible case, is an icon of American popular culture. Mathew McConaughey, who portrays Baldwin, played a similar role—a white lawyer who defends a black man—in the thriller *A Time to Kill* (1996). Roger Baldwin is also the beneficiary in the film of "the Huck Finn effect": an unlikely white hero is redeemed by his friendship with a black man. Just as Huck recognizes Jim's humanity and decides to help free the slave, Baldwin befriends Cinqué and finds in him a source of strength and eloquence. In Baldwin's transformation lies the hope for the redemption of the white self.

The abolitionists were not the comic religious figures represented here but dedicated, brave crusaders. A United Church of Christ official criticized the film's portrayal of evangelical abolitionists as a caricature: "the movie often misrepresents the abolitionists as arrogant or self-serving. . . . What those Christian abolitionists really did was to create what we now recognize as the nation's first human rights movement."[18]

Lewis Tappan, the abolitionist, was not a fanatic willing to make Cinqué into a martyr. Tappan was the leader of the American and Foreign Anti-Slavery Society and tireless head of the committee that masterminded the strategy that led to the release of the Africans.[19] In the movie, however, Tappan's moral flaw and the abolitionists' religious fanaticism turn them into foils to the true white heroes, the lawyers Baldwin and Adams.

Next, no African Americans were involved in the legal defense of the captives, although there was an African American abolitionist, the Reverend J. W. C. Pennington, who helped the *Amistad* Africans after they were freed because he hoped to make them into missionaries to carry the gospel back to Africa.[20] Instead, the film exaggerates the role of African Americans in freeing the *Amistad* captives by inventing a fictional black abolitionist, called Theodore Joadson (played by Morgan Freeman), to please a contemporary audience. As one critic complains, "he is necessary to maintain a racial quota."[21] Joadson is treated with equality and respect by all the whites with whom he interacts. Unfortunately, as a historian notes, "no such person of the bearing and dignity depicted by Mr. Freeman would have been allowed to exist in the America of 1840. . . . The airy complacency that presumes to withdraw such realities does no service to the historical understanding of anyone in our time, black or white, who aims, even at the expense of feeling good, to grasp the tone and feel of race relations in their then-hideous state."[22]

Moreover, in reality, American law before the Civil War did not protect blacks or enforce equality and freedom. Rather, as in the Supreme Court's 1857 Dred Scott decision (16 years after the *Amistad* decision), it protected the property rights of slave owners by asserting that American-born slaves had no rights under the Constitution.

The movie is also silent about the highly narrow base on which Supreme Court Justice Joseph Story, a conservative from Massachusetts, resolved the case. The Africans were freed on the technicality that the ownership papers of the Spaniards Ruiz and Montes were fraudulent.[23] Notes Simon Schama: "the case turned neither on the morality nor on the legality of slavery in America but on the slave *trade* on the high seas."[24] Another historian says, "As moral victory, the *Amistad* case was muted at best."[25]

Again, unlike the film, John Quincy Adams and Cinqué were not bosom buddies. Adams neither received Cinqué in his house nor relied on him for legal insight, and Cinqué was not present in the Supreme Court. Adams did meet Cinqué once, briefly, in jail, "but there was no meeting of the minds in that encounter."[26] The historian Natalie Zemon Davis says that the film fabricates "from a wish to make patterns of alliance and friendship in New England in 1839–40 resemble egalitarian hopes in late twentieth-century America." She finds such wish fulfillment inappropriate for a historical film.[27] As we mentioned, a similar wish fulfillment operates in the depiction of the relationship between Theodore Joadson and the whites in the film.

Finally, there were no busts of the American presidents in the Supreme Court, and Adams's eight-and-a-half hour speech (reduced to five minutes in the movie) was not a patriotic appeal to return to our roots but "an appeal to the independence of the

Amistad: *There were no busts of the American presidents in the U.S. Supreme Court, and Adams' speech was not a patriotic appeal to return to our roots. Copyright 1997 Dreamworks.*

Supreme Court, and invoked John Marshall and his colleagues, men apparently with too little name recognition for Hollywood."[28]

The Founding Fathers

A contentment of American civilization is its belief in its supposed universality. In his speech in the film, Adams translates Cinqué's African ancestor worship into an appeal to our founding fathers, who are construed as our righteous ancestors. A civilization that can incorporate beliefs as foreign to its Christian ideology as ancestor worship is no doubt a universal civilization. Thus, the movie appears to respect diversity even as it denies it. Simon Schama calls this scene a "feel-good fantasy."[29]

This is a highly patriarchal movie about the American judiciary. There are no female speaking parts, except for the infantile queen of Spain, who is ridiculed as a prepubescent girl who plays with dolls. Thus, the movie's dramatic tension is simply about which white patriarchal system will prevail. In the end, it is the founding fathers of American democracy. Adams says in his speech to the Supreme Court:

> Thomas Jefferson, Benjamin Franklin, James Madison, Alexander Hamilton, George Washington, John Adams, we have long resisted asking you for guidance. . . . Perhaps we feared that an appeal to you might be taken for weakness. But we have come to understand, finally, that this is not so. We understand now . . . that who we are is who we were.

As Simon Schama notes, "When Jefferson duly appears (in bust form), we are evidently not meant to think of the unrepentant Virginia slaveholder."[30] The movie's unintended irony lies in the fact, never mentioned, that, with the exception of Benjamin Franklin, these founding fathers owned slaves, supported slavery, or believed blacks were inferior to whites.

John Adams, American president and father of John Quincy Adams, although not a proponent of slavery, nevertheless firmly believed in white supremacy. Adams said of the British in 1765, before the Revolutionary War: "We won't be their Negroes." Adams insisted that Providence had never intended the American colonists "for Negroes . . . and therefore never intended us for slaves. . . I say we are as handsome as old English folks, and so should be as free."[31]

Patricide versus Love of the Father

The film opens with a bloody act of rebellion against the established authority of the ship. Technically, this is not a mutiny because it did not involve the crew. The rebellion aboard the *Amistad* involved the killing of the male authority figure, the captain. In the beginning the director shows Cinqué and his followers engaging in a sort of patricide. Cinqué's sword not only stabs the prostrate Captain but pierces through his body and penetrates the deck so that blood drips into the compartment below. This extreme rage and shocking, bloody violence must be given a context to be legitimized. What the film must accomplish from that point on is to "civilize" these wild, murderous men: to undo the patricide and the challenge to authority.

Thus, on the one hand, the movie "civilizes" the violence of the opening scene through lengthy courtroom scenes; on the other, it glorifies the American principles that justify that rebellion. In the process, it exalts the founding fathers, who established freedom and equality as the cornerstones of American civilization. Yet it ignores that slavery was also one of the cornerstones of that civilization. It begins with a "patricidal" act of rage and ends with the reestablishment of the patriarchal superego of the great white fathers. "*Amistad* consists of fathers, fathers, fathers, all the way down."[32]

The movie also glorifies the patriarchs of the Supreme Court by having Justice Story, who wrote the opinion in the *Amistad* case, played by retired Supreme Court Justice Harry Blackmun, author of the majority opinion in *Roe* v. *Wade,* thus attempting to create a link between the Court of 1840 and the Court today, implying, as in its view of the founding fathers, an unsullied American history.

John Quincy Adams himself embodies the great father. He is an overdetermined figure, not only an ex-president but also the son of one of the founding fathers. To increase sympathy, he is shown at first as an underdog. In his first scene, he looks like a doddering old man apparently asleep in the U.S. House of Representatives. But we soon see he still has his wits about him. The movie places a lot of dramatic weight on Adams and pumps up the suspense over whether he will defend the Africans.[33] Finally, he redeems himself by winning the case before the Supreme Court, the last great battle of this old chieftain. Adams represents the triumph of the best of the white patriarchal self. "Every time he appears the soundtrack is invaded by a musical motif redolent of patriotism, duty, life, liberty, and pursuit of happiness (and composed by Mr. Fourth of July himself, John Williams)."[34] He is the white messiah of *Amistad.*[35]

Rage and Reason

Whereas the film portrays the Africans, led by Cinqué, as driven by raw anger provoked by the violence against them, it appears that reason and calculation are the defining traits of the whites. President Martin Van Buren is motivated by political calculation in an election year, a desire to win Southern votes and to avoid civil war. The Portuguese and Spanish shipowners, and the U.S. naval officers who recover the ship, are motivated by greed. The Southerners, as represented by John C. Calhoun, are motivated by the desire to perpetuate the status quo of slavery and plantation society. Calhoun says: "We are not as wealthy as our Northern neighbors. To take away our life's blood now . . . they become the masters and we the slaves. But not without a fight." For Calhoun the question is "not whether this ragtag bunch of Africans raised sword against their enemy, but rather, must we?"

According to Thomas Patterson, the invention of civilization involved the creation of categories of the civilized, the barbarian, and the savage. The ruling class of the self-designated "civilized" societies felt it was their right to dominate and enslave lesser breeds they classifed as "savage" or "barbarian." "Savages lacked law, government, and permanent places of residence; barbarians had governments and fixed places of residence but were uncultured and illiterate."[36]

In the 1840s, the struggle over the fate of the Africans from the *Amistad* revolved around definitions of civilization versus barbarism and savagery. For example, one of the American defenders of the Africans wrote that "such blood-hound persecutions of poor defenceless strangers cast upon the shores, should call down the manly and scorching rebukes of universal civilized man."[37] Meanwhile, John C. Calhoun denounced the Africans as "a band of barbarous slaves, with hands imbrued in blood."[38] The evangelical Christian abolitionists wanted to educate the Africans and teach them the Bible so that they could return to Africa as missionaries to spread Christianity and the glories of Western civilization. Even John Quincy Adams, in his speech before the Supreme Court defending the *Amistad* Africans, called them "savage, heathen barbarians."[39]

In the 1950s, in a historical novel based on the *Amistad* incident, *Black Mutiny,* the author describes the encounter between Cinqué and Adams as "a meeting of primitive man and the finest product of civilization."[40]

Cinqué Civilized

Ironically, in 1997, over 150 years after the incident, in the film version of the events the struggle is still over definitions of "civilization." One critic says that Spielberg, by "presenting the bloody uprising before he shows us the brutalizing events that led up to it, and having the Africans speak in their native tongue without subtitles . . . [is] deliberately flirting with the stereotype of the Savage, putting us in the position of a white 19th-century American first encountering the Other and not knowing what to make of him."[41] Another critic complains that the vicious murder in the opening scene is "flagrantly racist . . . , Spielberg's depiction of the bestial Other."[42] Shortly after this opening scene, Cinqué argues with one of his followers over who should be captain. Yet a third critic complains, "In extreme closeup, they howl at each other in an untranslated outburst, head to head. The effect is to make them as unsympathetic as possible."[43] Admittedly, such scenes are balanced later by allowing us "to see white society through the Africans' eyes."[44] Nevertheless, there is a distinct progression in the character in Spielberg's film: Cinqué begins as a murderous, semi-naked savage but ends as clothed and "civilized." But is this truly progress or simply one false image replaced by another?

The civilizing of Cinqué involves his education in legal procedure. As the Africans dance before a bonfire in the prison courtyard, celebrating their second and apparently final legal victory, Baldwin tells Cinqué that they are not yet free, that the case must be tried yet a third time because the president has appealed to the Supreme Court. Enraged, Cinqué removes his shirt and pants and flings them aside as he yells at Baldwin, "What kind of place is this where laws almost work? How can you live that way?" He is silhouetted naked against the raging bonfire, which now suggests the intensity of his anger. In casting off his shirt and pants, Cinqué is rejecting Western values and civilization, temporarily reverting to savagery.

Although the film at this point seems to support Cinqué's view—his African tribe keep their word but American law seems devious—nevertheless his crisis of faith in Western civilization and law must be overcome. The measure of his intellectual capacity is his ability by the end to think in Western terms and to contribute to the legal arguments of John Quincy Adams. When Cinqué begins to advise Adams, and when he appears in the Supreme Court, dressed like a well-bred American man of the era, "in a lace-cuffed shirt and flowered waistcoat and . . . manners to match," we witness his amazing transformation from African barbarian to "civilized" American.[45] Yet these scenes are pure inventions; they never happened.

The end of the film restores both Cinqué's faith and our faith in Western institutions. On the one hand, we have the great white messianic father, John Quincy Adams; on the other, the stability and dignity of American jurisprudence and the memory of the nation's founding fathers, who created American civilization. Never mind that these founders were mostly slave owners or that slavery was legalized by the American Constitution. The film "snuffs out any hint that slavery ever was integral to the founding of this nation."[46]

Spielberg presents us with a revised, profoundly unambivalent view of American history. He "civilizes" and tames the historical person of Cinqué. The movie turns him into an American patriot as Adams compares him to Patrick Henry.

The reverberations of the name Cinqué are far more disturbing to the white self than this movie will allow. For example, in California in 1974, a black ex-convict renamed himself Cinqué and formed the Symbionese Liberation Army, which robbed banks and kidnapped the white heiress Patty Hearst. This Cinqué envisioned himself a revolutionary, an enemy of capitalism and of white civilization. The Symbionese Liberation Army was a small band of fanatics who imagined themselves the spearhead of a revolution. Most of them were wiped out by a police assault. Nevertheless, they were led by a black man who cast himself as Cinqué, a slave in a bloody revolt for his freedom. Spielberg's character denies the truly disruptive and subversive implications of the original Cinqué, as if the African's close friendship with Roger Baldwin and John Quincy Adams were necessary to erase the disturbing memory of the killings of the opening scene.

One French critic complained that all the Africans in *Amistad* are "noble and athletic"—in other words, noble savages. He accused *Amistad* of a "Disneyesque manicheism that is close to *Dances with Wolves* but light years away from the ambiguity of Melville and of 'Benito Cereno.'"[47] Melville's 1855 story is also based on an historical event: in 1799, rebellious slaves took over a Spanish ship, killing most of the crew but keeping the captain alive. A passing American naval vessel rescued the Spaniards, and the slaves were imprisoned and put on trial in Peru. The story thus has abundant parallels to the *Amistad* incident—except for its ending, in which the Africans are returned to slavery and the leader of the slave rebellion is executed and his head displayed on a pole in the main plaza for several days as a warning to other potentially rebellious blacks. "Benito Cereno" is far more representative of the actual role of nineteenth-century white American institutions in enforcing slavery than is *Amistad*.

Conclusion: The Redemption of White Civilization in *Amistad*

This movie is about rage: subversive, destructive, bloody, murderous rage. As presented in the opening scene, the rage is deliberately decontextualized through an extreme close-up of the surface of the black skin of the character who will later be introduced as Cinqué. What is most memorable in *Amistad* is not the extended courtroom drama, with its complicated political and legal maneuvering, but the opening scene of the rebellion and the later brutality of the long flashback to the middle passage. Watching such scenes is painful, which is part of the social therapeutic strategy of what Mark Golub calls "Hollywood redemption history": "watching and acknowledging the suffering of others becomes the price-tag for absolution of responsibility for the very suffering that is so vividly depicted. . . . these films project the ritualized forgiveness that white audiences long to hear."[48] The audience's shock at this graphic violence must be transformed into admiration and acceptance of the system at the end. The discourse of liberalism must transcend the brutality of slavery.

Just as in Spielberg's *Schindler's List,* in which the hero is a good capitalist, so in this film the heroes are the good lawyers, who believe in and practice in the system. Here, the fear of the anger of rebellion is exorcised through the (white) legal institutions of the state. The movie exalts the goodness of the law and the reliability of white American civilization. In *Amistad,* as in *Glory,* "the redemption of the white characters (as well as American Founding Fathers and political institutions) stands in, through an act of identification, for the redemption of the audience"—that is, of course, for a white American audience, because minority audiences may see the films differently.[49]

At the end of Spielberg's *Saving Private Ryan,* Ryan, the white hero, asks his wife for reassurance that he is a good man and she reassures him that he is. *Amistad* provides a similar reassurance for white Americans.

Sincere fictions rest on misrecognition, that is, on the psychological defenses of denial and displacement. To rescue the white self from the indignity of slavery and elevate it, Spielberg distorted history to claim a patriarchal ancestry of high principles and unblemished virtue. The morally reprehensible but at the time legal act of slaveholding is denied, displaced onto caricatured villains: the Spanish, Portuguese, and American Southerners. The centrality of slavery and white supremacy as dynamic elements in the American economy and civilization from its beginnings is denied, shrouded by the sanctity of its institutions.

Amistad contains powerful, unforgettable images. The sequence of the middle passage presents in horrifying detail some of the humiliation, pain, and suffering that whites inflicted on Africans through slavery. Spielberg's standing as a filmmaker allowed him to violate the taboo that had surrounded filmic representations of the horror of the middle passage. However, the same cultural capital that allowed Spielberg to transgress unspoken rules on the treatment of slavery on film, by a sleight of hand, also allowed him to isolate that violence and pain from the institutions that made it legal in the United States. The Supreme Court that freed the Africans in the *Amistad* also enforced the property rights of owners over slaves. In fact, in freeing the *Amistad* Africans, the Court was enforcing the laws that legalized slavery, and it continued to do so until the Civil War.

Spielberg did not romanticize slavery but showed the violence and pain on which it rested and the rage it aroused among the enslaved. And filmgoers should be indebted to him for that. Nevertheless, he chose to romanticize the institutions that made it legal and possible for slavery to exist. *Amistad*, writes one critic, "glorifies the redemptive power of American justice with a reverence verging on religious zeal."[50]

Notes

1. Hornaday, Ann. 1997. "Revising Movie History." *The Baltimore Sun*, November 30, 1997: 1E, 4E, 5E.

2. Schama, Simon. 1998. "Clio at the Multiplex," *The New Yorker*, 73 (January 19, 1998): 38–43 (p. 38).

3. Feagin, Joe R. 2000. *Racist America: Roots, Current Realities, and Future Reparations*. New York: Routledge.

4. Hornaday, "Revising Movie History," p. 5E.

5. Snead, James. 1994. *White Screens/Black Images: Hollywood from the Dark Side*. New York: Routledge, p. 98.

6. Giroux, Henry A. 1999. *The Mouse That Roared*. Lanham, Md.: Rowman and Littlefield, p. 120, n.36.

7. We acquired our copy of the film in Great Britain.

8. Guerrero, Ed. 1993. *Framing Blackness: The African American Image in Film*. Philadelphia, Pa.: Temple University Press, p. 33.

9. Hornaday, "Revising Movie History," p. 4E.

10. Ibid., p. 5E.

11. Guerrero, *Framing Blackness*, p. 40.

12. Samuels, Allison. 1997. "Unchained Melody: Four Years after *Schindler*, Steven Spielberg Directs Another Freedom Song, *Amistad*." *Newsweek*, 129 (April 7, 1997): 70.

13. Ansen, David. 1997. Review of *Amistad*. *Newsweek*, 130 (December 8, 1997): 64.

14. Some historians were bothered by the fact that *Amistad*, with its fictionalizing and distortions, would be used to teach history. See, for example, Foner, Eric. 1997. "Hollywood Invades the Classroom," *The New York Times*, 147 (December 20, 1997): A13; and Paquette, Robert L. 1998. "From History to Hollywood: The Voyage of 'La Amistad.'" *New Criterion*, 16 (March 1998): 74: "Spielberg and his Dreamworks crew, even before *Amistad*'s December premiere, pronounced their film to be a kind of superior history." Some critics also objected to the use of the film as history. For example, Rosen, Gary. 1998. "*Amistad* and the Abuse of History." *Commentary*, 105 (February 1998): 46–51: "Steven Spielberg's film will long contribute to making it harder and harder for us to tell the truth, either about our history or about ourselves" (p. 51).

15. Patterson, Thomas Carl. 1997. *Inventing Western Civilization*. New York: Monthly Review Press, p. 38.

16. Hornaday, "Revising Movie History," p. 5E.

17. Wilentz, Sean. 1997. Review of *Amistad*. *The New Republic*, 217 (December 22, 1997): 25.

18. Official, United Church of Christ. 1998. "*Amistad* Distorts Abolitionists." *The Christian Century*, 115 (January 7, 1998): 8.

19. Wyatt-Brown, Bertram. 1997. *Lewis Tappan and the Evangelical War against Slavery*. Baton Rouge: Louisiana State University Press, pp. 205–25.

20. Rosen, Gary. 1998. Letter to the Editor. *Commentary* 105 (June 1998): 6. See also Wyatt-Brown, Bertram. 1998. Review of *Amistad*. *The Journal of American History* 85 (December 1998): 1174–76: "Joadson's exaggerated role distorts the abolitionist story. . . . He further misrepresents the circumstances by having Joadson treated as a social equal in every scene in which he appears. Sadly, the intensity of northern prejudice was too great for that representation. Only white abolitionists showed much sense of racial justice" (p. 1175).

21. Rosen, "*Amistad* and the Abuse of History," p. 48.

22. See McKitrick, Eric. 1998. "John Quincy Adams: For the Defense." *The New York Review of Books*, April 23, 1998, pp. 53–8 (p. 54).

23. Jones, Howard. 1987. *Mutiny on the Amistad: The Saga of a Slave Revolt and Its Impact on American Abolition, Law, and Diplomacy*. New York: Oxford University Press, p. 190.

24. Schama, "Clio at the Multiplex," p. 38.

25. Dalzell, F. 1998. "Dreamworking *Amistad*: Representing Slavery, Revolt and Freedom in America, 1838 and 1997." *New England Quarterly* 71 (March 1998): 127–33 (p. 321).

26. Ibid., p. 132.

27. Davis, Natalie Zemon. 2000. *Slaves on Screen: Film and Historical Vision*. Cambridge, Mass.: Harvard University Press, p. 128.

28. Schama, "Clio at the Multiplex," p. 38.

29. Ibid.

30. Ibid.

31. Breen, T. H. 1997. "Ideology and Nationalism on the Eve of the American Revolution: Revisions Once More in Need of Revising." *The Journal of American History,* 84 (June): 13.

32. Rogin, Michael. 1998. "Spielberg's List." *New Left Review* 230 (July–August 1998): 155.

33. Alleva, Richard. 1998. Review of *Amistad*. *Commonweal* 125 (February 13, 1998): 17–19 (p. 18). Also see Kodat, Catherine Gunter. 2000. "Saving Private Property: Steven Spielberg's American Dream Works." *Representations* 71:77–105 (p. 83).

34. Ibid., p. 18.

35. Nichols, Bill. 2000. "The 10 Stations of Spielberg's Passion: *Saving Private Ryan, Amistad, Schindler's List.*" *Jump Cut* 43:9–11. Nichols argues that in each of these three films Spielberg creates a white Christian male savior of "those less fortunate or farsighted than themselves" (p. 9).

36. Patterson, "Inventing Western Civilization," p. 100.

37. Wyatt-Brown, *Lewis Tappan*, p. 209.

38. Ibid, p. 211.

39. Adams, John Quincy. 1874–77. *Memoirs of John Quincy Adams, Comprising Portions of His Diary from 1795 to 1848*, ed. Charles Francis Adams, 12 vols. Philadelphia: J. B. Lippincott, vol. 10, p. 358. From the argument of John Quincy Adams before the Supreme Court in the case of *United States, Appellants*, v. *Cinqué, and other Africans*. Delivered on the 24th of February and the 1st of March, 1841.

40. Owens, William A. 1953. *Black Mutiny: The Revolt on the Schooner Amistad*. New York: Penguin, p. 253.

41. Ansen, "Review of Amistad," p. 64.

42. Nichols, "The 10 Stations of Spielberg's Passion," p. 11.

43. Simon, John. 1997. Review of *Amistad*. *National Review* 49 (December 31, 1997): 56–7 (p. 56).

44. Ibid.

45. Klawans, Stuart. 1998. Review of *Amistad. The Nation*, January 5, 1998: 34–6.

46. Kodat, "Saving Private Property," p. 85.

47. Bourget, Jean-Loup. 1998. "*Amistad*: Le Roi Lion, le Vieil Homme et l'Infante." *Positif*, March 1998: 25–7 (p. 27). Translation by Andrew Gordon.

48. Golub, Mark. 1998. "History Died for Our Sins: Guilt and Responsibility in Hollywood Redemption Histories." *Journal of American Culture* 21 (Fall 1998): 23–45 (p. 29).

49. Ibid., p. 39.

50. Johnson, Brian D. 1997. Review of *Amistad. Maclean's*, 110 (December 15, 1997): 62.

CHAPTER 5

Mutiny on the Bounty: Civilization and Its Discontents

Films Analyzed:
Mutiny on the Bounty (1935)
Mutiny on the Bounty (1962)
The Bounty (1984)

In this chapter we examine three film versions of *Mutiny on the Bounty* from different decades across the twentieth century; all feature romance between white males and Asian women. The period in which a film is made accounts for obvious difference in cinematographic technique and casting. But different decades also reshape the dramatic tensions underlying the plot and the teaching it delivers.

Mutiny on the Bounty, in all three versions, concerns the white, imperialist male encounter with "the primitive," the seduction of the crew by Tahitian culture, and their subsequent mutiny against the captain of the ship. Marianna Torgovnick has argued that "the primitive" is a screen on which we project whatever we wish: "For Euro-Americans, then, to study the primitive brings us always back to ourselves, which we reveal in the act of defining the Other."[1] The primitive thus becomes the repository of "otherness," of whatever the white male fears or desires, including the childlike, the feminine, the sexual, and the violent.

The fear of "going native," of being taken over sexually and culturally by what is perceived as the savage other, is a common trait of the white men portrayed in the movies. The assumption is that whites possess a monopoly on "civilization" but that white civilization is fragile and precarious, a veneer that relies on forces of enormous repression, as Freud pointed out in *Civilization and Its Discontents*. White civilization is always in danger of crumbling in the face of the attraction of the seductive, feared other, and therefore is in constant need of defense.

In the American films about the famous mutiny on the *Bounty*, the discipline and punishment is provided by the institution of the eighteenth-century British Navy. These films thus display a deep uneasiness about the white self because they portray a rebellion against authority and the superego: against white civilization itself. Following Freud's *Civilization and Its Discontents* and *Totem and Taboo*, one could argue that interracial romance serves as a form of defiance of fatherly authority, playing out an implicit oedipal drama. The incest taboo is displaced by the taboo against mating with the exotic racial other.

Mutiny on the Bounty *(1935): "This is mutiny, Mr. Christian!"*
Copyright 1935 Metro-Goldwyn-Mayer. Courtesy Museum of
Modern Art, Films Stills Archive.

The three film versions of *Mutiny on the Bounty*—1935, starring Clark Gable as the mutinous First Mate Fletcher Christian and Charles Laughton as the tyrannical Captain Bligh; 1962, with Marlon Brando as Christian and Trevor Howard as Bligh; and 1984, with Mel Gibson as Christian and Anthony Hopkins as Bligh—provide a test case of our thesis.[2] Each film is a drama of the superior white male self; people of color are secondary, almost all women, and exist primarily to serve the needs of white males. Writes Michael Sturma, "The Tahitians . . . exist mainly as an undifferentiated mass—'extras'. . . trapped in the anonymity of colonialism."[3] Each film is also inflected by the particular cultural and ideological needs of its decade.

Why is there such continuing fascination among Americans with this particular story, based on an incident in British naval history, that each generation of Hollywood filmmakers is compelled to remake it? Movies are remade for economic reasons, but the filmmakers must believe that "the audience will continue to buy the story in its new incarnation because the underlying fable is still compelling. . . . Remakes deal with unfinished cultural business."[4] We argue that this drama links two powerful themes about which white Americans remain profoundly ambivalent: romance with a racial other and revolution. It provides us, as critics, with a way of talking about race, sex, imperialism, and rebellion—in other words, of talking about "civilization and its discontents" in different decades of the twentieth century.

The Fascination with Mutiny

A mutiny is a revolution in miniature, striking at the heart of the social order. In chapter 4, we discussed mutiny in relation to the historic slave revolts portrayed in the film *Amistad* and in Melville's story "Benito Cereno." As the sociologist Cornelis J. Lammers mentions, "it seems rather obvious to compare mutinies with similar conflicts between rulers and ruled," such as strikes and revolutions.[5] A mutiny resembles a labor strike yet is far more drastic and illegal. A ship at sea for months at a time is a claustrophobic society, a hothouse environment with the potential for an explosive buildup of destructive emotions. A naval vessel is a powerful metaphor for oppressive working conditions in a capitalist economy, in which the workplace is an enclosed environment and managers can function like tyrants. In terms of the fears of twentieth-century American society, mutiny could stand for worker rebellion or Communist takeover.

In psychological terms, mutiny is fascinating because it expresses our ambivalence toward civilization and authority. Freud writes, "In consequence of this primary mutual hostility of human beings, civilized society is perpetually threatened with disintegration."[6] As Lammers notes, not only is mutiny a capital crime, but also "naval men seldom mutiny" because "they consider legitimate the strong taboo on mutiny."[7] It thus requires special, extreme conditions—prolonged hardship and injustice, disaffection from the leader and from the goals of the organization, lack of alternative means of protest, and lack of concern for the consequences—for the taboo to be broken and a mutiny to occur.

Mutiny evokes the primal sin Freud posits in *Totem and Taboo* as the origin of society: "The expelled brothers joined forces, slew and ate the father, and thus put an end to the father horde."[8] If this seems an unlikely analogy, it is worth considering that eighteenth-century sailors identified ship's captains as fathers, calling them "father of the ship."[9] On one level, then, mutiny is a form of oedipal rebellion.

Mutiny is the very stuff of drama and continues to inspire the artistic imagination and to excite the American public in such films as *The Caine Mutiny* (1954), *Crimson Tide* (1995), and the various versions of *Mutiny on the Bounty*. America was founded on revolution and places a premium on individual autonomy, dissent, and rebellion. Thus, American audiences have a political, cultural, and psychological attraction to the theme. At the same time, American society is profoundly ambivalent about revolution and mutiny since the end of the Revolutionary War because it poses such a threat to social order, as in the Civil War.

Mutiny on the Bounty combines the fascination with mutiny with the fascination with miscegenation; both involve the breaking of powerful social taboos. According to the historian Greg Dening, in the British empire "the greatest threat to civilization . . . were those who 'went native'. . . . Hidden in all the anger at the mutiny on the *Bounty*, we have to see the scandal as well; so many men 'went native'; so many men did not possess natives so much as they were possessed by natives."[10]

To twentieth-century white America, interracial romance or marriage still poses the threat of the breakdown of boundaries, the confusion of strict racial categories, and the eventual dissolution of white identity. In each version of the tale, first mate Fletcher Christian's romance with a Tahitian maiden causes him to "go native" and to lead a revolt against Captain Bligh. Each version of the *Bounty* story expresses the dilemma of the divided white self: the temptation to break the taboos against making love to the forbidden racial other and against overthrowing authority. The two taboos seem unconsciously linked as an oedipal configuration in the narrative: make love to the native woman and next you will want to overthrow the captain.

Each of the three film versions of the mutiny is also a myth for its times, expressing the attitudes of the particular decade toward capitalism, patriarchy, race, rebellion, and civilization and its discontents. The 1935 *Bounty* gives us a New Deal version of events, an upbeat tale of a crisis in capitalism overcome through reform rather than revolution. The 1962 *Bounty* is a Cold War, Kennedy-era version, profoundly ambivalent about rebellion; it ends with the death of Christian. Finally, the 1984 version is a Reagan-era, counterrevolutionary film that attempts to exonerate Bligh as a family man and capitalist entrepreneur and turns Christian into a self-serving rebel.

All three *Bounty* films constitute what we call sincere fictions of the white self. They have little to do with history but much to do with fantasy. There is "no use displaying the inaccuracies of these versions. It was their purpose to be inaccurate. They could not say what they wanted to say without invention."[11] The filmmakers settle for surface historical authenticity in the costumes and sets while playing fast and loose with the historical facts to create myths suitable for their own times.

The three film versions of the mutiny on the *Bounty* reflect not what happened but what the filmmakers sincerely need to believe happened, forcing us, the viewing public, to misrecognize historical reality. The actual mutiny was messy and ambivalent: Bligh was no devil and Christian no saint. The historical events seem to expose the fragility of institutions, the ease with which authority can be overthrown, and the shaky ground upon which civilization stands. We are reluctant to recognize Freud's pessimistic hypothesis: "man's natural aggressive instinct, the hostility of each against all and of all against each, opposes this program of civilization."[12]

The Historical Facts versus the Movie Versions

The mutiny on the *Bounty* has been exhaustively researched for over two centuries. The facts are well documented, although debate still continues among historians as to the characters of William Bligh and Fletcher Christian, the nature of their relationship, and the causes of the mutiny.

Briefly, these are the facts and the major ways in which the three movies disregard or deviate from them. The *Bounty*, a British naval vessel, sailed from England for Tahiti in December 1787. Her crew, unlike those on most ships of the British Navy at the time, did not include sailors forced into service. In fact, the men of the *Bounty* were all volunteers, eager for a chance to see the recently discovered Polynesian islands. "The first thing to remember about the *Bounty*'s company is that, except for the gardener and his assistant, they were all chosen by Bligh personally. . . . He favored those he had sailed with and had proved themselves—and friends of those who had proved themselves."[13] Nevertheless, the 1935 movie begins with Christian leading a press gang to round up sailors in a tavern, falsely implying that the crew did not sign on voluntarily.

This was Fletcher Christian's third voyage under his patron William Bligh. Bligh favored Christian and promoted him several times, including an early promotion to acting lieutenant aboard the *Bounty*. On their second voyage together, "Christian was often in Bligh's cabin in the evenings and . . . had a key to Bligh's liquor chest."[14] Yet in the 1935 film, Bligh requests Christian from the Navy but Christian already dislikes him because of their two previous voyages. In the 1962 version, Bligh and Christian are strangers, with Christian a last-minute replacement officer, and the two despise each other on sight. Only the 1984 film shows the initial friendship between the captain and his petty officer.

The *Bounty* was on a profit-making expedition to pick up breadfruit trees in the South Seas and transport them to the West Indies, where they could be cultivated as cheap fodder for black slaves. The 1935 version applauds Britain's imperial ambitions; the other two films ignore the issue. All three films avoid dealing with the question of white subjugation of people of color, displacing it onto white exploitation of whites. That is, Bligh is portrayed as a slave driver toward British sailors.

The *Bounty* sailed ten months before reaching Tahiti in October 1788. In the British Navy of the late eighteenth century, sailors frequently perished from poor hygiene, poor diet, or accidents. Surprisingly, only one man died aboard the *Bounty* during the ten-month voyage, and the cause of death was listed as scurvy. Yet because of the 1935 portrayal by Charles Laughton and the 1962 version by Trevor Howard, Captain Bligh has become the archetype of the cruel tyrant who drives his crew to their deaths. The historical Bligh was an erratic leader, a foul-mouthed bully given to temper tantrums and to publicly humiliating his officers with verbal abuse. Because he doubled as purser and wanted to make a profit, he was stingy with the food. Nevertheless, by the standards of the time he was a physically lenient officer who flogged the crew far less than Captain Cook. None of the crew died from Bligh's mistreatment.[15] But in the first two films they die one after another from reckless seamanship, thirst, or brutal punishment. These movies need a sadistic Bligh to justify the mutiny.

The *Bounty* stayed five months in Tahiti. All three films imply that, aside from Bligh's cruelty, it was Christian's love of a Polynesian woman that led him to take over the ship and return to Tahiti. But according to the historian Glynn Christian (a descendant of Fletcher Christian), Fletcher Christian consorted with the women but had no single woman as constant companion before the *Bounty* left Tahiti. In fact, Christian avoided returning to Tahiti after the mutiny because he would have to lie to cover up what had happened and also knew Tahiti was the first place the British Navy would look for him. He first tried colonizing another island but quit when the inhabitants proved hostile. Only then did he return to Tahiti, and he did so reluctantly and briefly. So we cannot say that Christian was motivated by love. Like the sadistic Bligh, the loving Christian is an invention by the filmmakers to justify the mutiny.

The mutiny took place in April 1789, three weeks into the homeward voyage, while the ship was bound from Tahiti to Jamaica. In the 1935 and 1962 versions, Bligh's physical cruelty and inhumanity toward the men drive Christian to revolt. In the 1984 version, Bligh is not so cruel but he is unhinged and shows disregard for the lives of the fearful crew. In actuality, the men were in no immediate danger, although they were afraid of the coming passage through the dangerous Endeavor Straits. But the incident that really drove Christian over the brink was a matter of some stolen coconuts. Bligh humiliated Christian by calling him a thief in front of the men. That night, Christian fashioned a raft to desert overboard but impulsively decided to mutiny instead. He was acting not to defend the crew but to gain revenge for Bligh's slights to his honor.[16] His impulsiveness condemned most of the crew to early deaths. The three films embellish or ignore these facts.

We want to consider each of the films in turn as a sincere fiction about capitalism, white patriarchy, race, rebellion, and civilization and its discontents, an American myth for its time. As we said, the 1935 version gives us an upbeat New Deal melodrama about reform and progress; the 1962 version, a bleak, tragic, Cold War, Kennedy-era version of events; and the 1984 version, an unsatisfying, Reaganesque, counterrevolutionary, postmodern fable.

The 1935 *Bounty:* The Noble Rebel

In the 1930s in America there was a crisis in capitalism, indeed in all of western civilization because of the worldwide economic depression. The American government feared instability because of the examples of Soviet communism and German fascism. During the Hoover era (1929–1932), the United States came the closest to revolution during the twentieth century. Unions were actively organizing and violent labor unrest was common throughout the decade. The promise of socialism was an attractive alternative to the squalor and misery brought about by the Depression. The presidency of Franklin D. Roosevelt and his New Deal rescued capitalism and revived the spirits of average Americans through a program of reform rather than revolution. It was during FDR's first term that *Mutiny on the Bounty* was made at MGM Studios, and the film conveys a message of New Deal optimism.

Louis B. Mayer, president of MGM, at first rejected the proposal of a movie about the *Bounty*. He did not want a picture "in which mutineers are heroes. Nor did he like the notion of a film in which the women were uncivilized natives seducing good order."[17] The ingenious solution provided by Mayer's vice president, Irving Thalberg, was "to make a film in which the hero was not the mutineers at all, but the British Navy, and a British Navy that was a weapon of freedom in a threatened world."[18] The film begins with a foreword that states that the mutiny was justified because it was "against the abuse of harsh eighteenth century sea law" and, further, that the mutiny brought about "a new discipline, based upon mutual respect between officers and men, by which Britain's sea power is maintained as security for all who pass upon the sea." Historically, this is patent nonsense. The changes in British sea law did not occur until decades later and had nothing to do with the mutiny. And Britain's sea power only guaranteed security for Britain, not for "all who pass upon the sea." This 1935 film is pro-imperialist, pro–status quo, and pro-reform rather than pro-revolution.

To enhance its message of democratic freedom, the film invents the notion that many of the seamen were impressed into service, whereas actually they were eager volunteers. It portrays Bligh as a cruel slave driver and the crew as white slaves and concocts many abuses that may have happened elsewhere in the British Navy but did not happen aboard the *Bounty*.

Aside from the exaggeration of the narrative, the 1935 version ignores the ways in which not only the English sailors but also the Tahitians and the black Jamaican slaves were exploited by this venture. Early in the film, a nobleman says, "This is England's new venture in science, trade, and discovery." The voyage certainly was intended to be that, but it was science, trade, and discovery in the service of British racism and imperialism, maintaining slavery in the Caribbean colonies and opening up new potential colonies in the South Seas. To turn this voyage into a fable about freedom and democracy (for white Englishmen only, we must note) is strange indeed.

During the trial of the mutineers, the young Midshipman Roger Byam makes a passionate speech attacking Bligh as a tyrant and defending Fletcher Christian as a true British patriot, a liberator. Byam, loosely based on an actual midshipman, is the narrator created by the novelists Charles Nordhoff and James Norman Hall, who wrote the best-selling novel on which the movie was based. But neither the real midshipman nor the imaginary Byam of the novel ever made this ringing Hollywood defense of British freedom.

The film ends with an excited British captain saying to the reinstated Byam, "We're off for the Mediterranean, lad. We'll sweep the seas for England." And over a shot of the Union Jack waving in the breeze, we hear the stirring strains of "Rule, Brittania." "Thalberg's message was that the act of mutiny, wrong in itself, had good effects. The reason was that institutions of power are ultimately responsive to men of good will."[19]

The film tries to have it both ways about revolution by splitting the hero in two: Christian, who mutinies, and his close friend, the younger man Byam, who refuses to mutiny. Christian and Byam represent the best of the white male self. Both are officers and gentlemen, kind to the crew and kind to the Polynesians. Christian takes the young man under his tutelage and protects him from Bligh. They become fast friends.

In fact, the romance between the men and the native women is less developed than the romance between Christian and Byam.[20] Christian apologizes for punching Byam during the mutiny. Byam says, "That didn't hurt. What hurts is that you and I can never again be friends." They soon reconcile. In one scene, they lie blissfully barechested, side by side on the ground, and Christian reaches up, plucks a banana from an overhanging tree, and hands it to Byam. Perhaps such homoerotic suggestiveness could pass unremarked in a 1930s Hollywood movie, but today it seems self-evident.

The romance between Christian and Byam may be a displacement for the other, more disturbing homoerotic undercurrent in the plot: the sadomasochistic relationship between Christian and Bligh, who are obsessed with each other. Several historians have suggested that the falling out between Christian and Bligh may have been a lover's quarrel.[21] (The 1984 film implies that Bligh was sexually jealous of Christian.)

The 1935 film provides a happy ending for both friends, the twin heroes. Christian finds a hidden island paradise with his Tahitian lover, his crew, and their women. Byam stands trial and defends Christian's reputation. With the help of powerful friends, Byam is reinstated as a British officer, but he does not return to his Tahitian wife, who is conveniently forgotten.

The plot subdues various threatening elements: the revolt is punished by the hanging of several mutineers and the system is reformed. The homoerotic threat is also overcome: Christian remains free of his persecutor Bligh, separated from Byam, and married with a child. Finally, the threat of racial intermarriage is contained by being restricted to Pitcairn, a remote, isolated island off the sea lanes. "The price of interracial love is physical, if not social, isolation."[22]

As the defender of the men, Christian (played by Clark Gable, the epitome of 1930s American movie manhood) is a selfless humanitarian and democrat. He is also spirited and confrontational, critical of Bligh's abuses from the start of the voyage, and eager to mutiny. When Christian leads the mutineers to safety on Pitcairn Island, he says, "They can't press gang you there, they can't starve you, and they can't flog you." As the song "Rule, Britannia" goes, "Britons never, never shall be slaves." So the film transforms Christian from leader of a press gang in the opening scene to liberator of the men in the closing.

This movie about English history is really an all-American myth, like most popular Hollywood films. First, it can be viewed as an allegory about the American Revolution: the American Clark Gable (who does not attempt an English accent) leads a rebellion against the British actor Charles Laughton, who stands in for the mad tyrant King George. And second, in the 1930s New Deal capitalist fable the movie is enacting, Christian and Byam represent the new, enlightened managerial class who will rescue capitalism from Bligh, the old-style, sweatshop boss who treats his employees like white slaves.

In terms of the sincere fictions of the white self in the movie, Bligh is the evil racist who makes Christian and Byam, who go native, look good. Bligh treats the natives as godless heathen, childlike primitives. Christian and Byam instead view the Tahitians as noble savages and fall in love with them. Byam says, "Aren't they amazing? I never knew there were such people in the world. They're simple and kind. Yet somehow they're royal."

The truth about the eighteenth-century Polynesians lies in neither view. The ease of the society came in large part from the mild climate and the abundance of food. For the crew of the *Bounty*, Tahiti was an idyllic pastoral interlude, heaven compared with the hell aboard ship. But the Polynesian culture was neither simple nor all that kind: it was a complex civilization, as class-conscious and hierarchical as England, with severe punishments for breaking taboos.[23] If the Polynesians appeared royal to Byam, perhaps that was because, as an officer, the aristocracy was the only native class with which he mixed.

As Freud writes in *Civilization and Its Discontents*:

> . . . voyages of discovery led to contact with primitive peoples and races. In consequence of insufficient observation and a mistaken view of their manners and customs, they appeared to Europeans to be leading a simple, happy life with few wants, a life such as was unattainable by their visitors with their superior civilization. Later experience has corrected some of those judgments. In many cases the observers had wrongly attributed to the absence of complicated cultural demands what was in fact due to the bounty of nature and the ease with which the major human needs were satisfied.[24]

Thus the idealized view of Tahiti in the movie.

The clichés in the 1935 *Bounty* of the romance between the noble English officer and the noble native princess are repeated in the Disney animated film *Pocahontas* (1995). In both films, the British sailors are good guys who like the natives, especially the nubile women. But the crew is under the orders of a greedy, tyrannical captain. In both, the crew shows their goodness by mutinying against the captain. Both films pretend to be history lessons but rely on fantasy and distortion. Both are imperialistic fairy tales: a brave, handsome, gentlemanly officer of the British Navy (Fletcher Christian or John Smith) falls in love with a beautiful, kind native princess and mutinies against a self-serving, ugly, cruel, greedy captain. There is no suggestion in either film that imperialism is essentially racist and exploitative and taints everyone it touches. Instead, evil (identified as greed and tyranny in *Mutiny on the Bounty*, and as greed, ecological imperialism, and racism in *Pocahontas*) is not intrinsic to the system but resides in a few bad leaders, and it can be overcome by the resistance of men of good will and a simple change of attitude. The similarities between the two movies suggest that, despite the surface messages about feminism, ecology, and racial tolerance in *Pocahontas*, very little has changed in underlying American attitudes toward capitalism and white patriarchy in the past sixty years.

The 1962 *Bounty*: The Doomed Rebel

If the 1930s *Mutiny on the Bounty* is an optimistic fable about American democracy and the triumph of the system, then the 1960s version presents us with a tragic, doomed Fletcher Christian, no patriotism, and no progress. This is a defeatist film that implies that rebellion against a ruthless leader is self-defeating. Brando's Fletcher Christian is a sympathetic figure who tries to do the honorable thing but is alienated, neurotic, and effete, a late 1950s, early 1960s antihero, a white man divided against himself.

Unlike the 1930s version, rather than splitting the hero in two and providing happy endings for both, the 1960s version creates an internally divided Fletcher Christian, on the surface a "supercilious poseur" but at heart a passionate idealist and champion of the people, a sort of Zorro or Scarlet Pimpernel. We go from the straightforward, "manly" assertion of that 1930s exemplar of movie masculinity, Clark Gable, to the more complex, self-tortured masculinity of the 1950s male avatar, Marlon Brando.

In 1935, Bligh was a self-made man who liked having the gentleman Christian under his thumb. In 1962, Bligh is still a self-made man, but he says he resents having "a career fop pawned off on me as a first mate." Christian makes his first appearance exiting dockside from a royal carriage. He is dressed in an outlandish party suit and brings aboard two countesses, one of them French. "He is accompanied by two attractive young woman, perhaps so that his sexuality will not be in doubt."[25] Christian speaks French but the stiff Bligh does not. Bligh was not a gentleman, and Christian was.[26]

Brando plays Christian not as a gentleman but, improbably, as an effete nobleman with an arch, upper-crust British accent. The peculiarity of the interpretation is that the aristocratic Christian makes an unlikely champion of working-class sailors against Bligh's self-made captain. He has to be goaded into mutiny by the scheming sailor Mills, who becomes a major figure in the story.

The class conflict may perhaps derive from the fact that it is a Kennedy-era film: Kennedy was the scion of a rich family and followed the code of "noblesse oblige." Many other American presidents, such as FDR, have come from the upper class, but they prided themselves on their common touch. Only Kennedy had the royal association, with the mythology about "Camelot."

Brando's Christian is a particularly isolated figure. Unlike Gable's Christian, his aristocratic posturing separates him from the crew and the officers. He is given a friend in Midshipman Young, but the two are not as close as Christian and Byam in the 1935 version. After the mutiny, he tells the men, "I believe I did what honor dictated, and that belief sustains me. Except for a slight desire to be dead, which I'm sure shall pass," and then he shuts himself up in his cabin, where he broods alone for weeks.

Shortly after they reach Pitcairn Island, Christian dies because of another heroic but futile gesture. Characteristically, he has reached another decision in isolation. Having finally found a safe hiding place, Christian changes his mind and announces that the noble thing would be to return to England. But Mills and his helpers set fire to the *Bounty* to prevent their return, and Christian is fatally injured trying to save the ship and recover the sextant. These events are a fabrication, contrary to history, but then so is most of the rest of the movie.

This internally divided, tormented, depressed, even suicidal Christian reflects Cold War cynicism and the revisionist notions about heroism seen in other movies of the period, such as *Lawrence of Arabia* (1962) and *The Spy Who Came in from the Cold* (1965), in which the heroes are noble, idealistic white men who end up frustrated, disillusioned, and doomed. America in the 1930s still believed in ideology, but America in the 1950s and early 1960s believed it lived with "the end of ideology" (in the words of Daniel Bell), and therefore it was hopeless to attempt to change the system.[27]

In the 1935 version, there are good authorities and bad, but the system is self-correcting. By 1962, however, authorities can neither be trusted nor restored: one mutiny simply leads to another. Brando wanted to present not a "heroic mutiny against tyranny, but the mystery of violence in human nature. Even when the mutineers had a chance to make an island paradise on Pitcairn, they were self-destructive."[28] A sense of futility pervades the film: the mutiny accomplishes nothing, except to prove that Bligh was no gentleman, which was obvious from the beginning. Thus, even if the system produces such bad leaders as Bligh, there is no point in rebelling against it. Mutineers are either insidious and self-serving, like the untrustworthy Mills, or else naïve, self-defeating idealists like Christian. As the movie ends, Christian dies and the camera pans to the ship as it burns and sinks, an image of defeat.

Far more than the 1935 version, the 1962 *Bounty* is about civilization and its discontents, discontents that seem insoluble. Christian rebels in the name of civilization; he calls Bligh a "remarkable pig." Yet this Christian, who seems so cool and hypercivilized, is more violent than in the 1935 version: he knocks Bligh down and stabs him in the arm with a sword. And when Christian lies in his cabin after the mutiny, sunk in despair, his wife Maimiti looks at the mess in which he is living and says, "You pig, pig all over!" Christian has become a pig like Bligh.

Unlike the 1935 Christian, this hero does not find freedom and a new life on the natural paradise of Pitcairn but only self-torment, for he is plagued with depression and guilt. Bligh had said he would never leave Christian, and he doesn't, for Christian has internalized him in his own avenging superego, which will not let him rest. As Freud writes, "the price we pay for our advance in civilization is a loss of happiness through the heightening of the sense of guilt."[29] It is Christian's sense of guilt that dooms him. Nevertheless, his capacity to make moral distinctions and to feel guilt elevates Christian above the other characters, who seem less civilized by comparison.

The Tahitians are no longer the noble savages of the 1935 version: one set of white stereotypes about non-white others has been replaced by another. In 1935, Chief Hiti Hiti was portrayed by a white actor, but he was wise, kindly, and spoke English. Now the chief is played by an Asian, but despite his impressive ceremonial garb, he is a primitive who speaks no English and seems foolish; like a clichéd tribesman in a Hollywood jungle movie, he laughs when he first sees his image in a mirror.

In all three films, the ship is a harsh, all-male prison of brutal work, poor rations, and harsh punishment, whereas Tahiti is soft, fertile, welcoming, and nurturing, a "feminized" place. We see few native men, and they are not hostile to white men or jealous about their women. In all three films, Tahiti is imagined as a tropical paradise and utopia for white males, but the portrayal becomes more overtly sexual over the decades.

In the 1962 version, the women are more eroticized than in 1935: they show more skin and their dances are much more provocative. And this Hiti Hiti actually orders Christian to sleep with his daughter Maimiti. More than in 1935, the women in the 1962 film are all available and eager. According to the voice-over narrator, the Tahitians consider making love a gesture of goodwill and think light skin a sign of beauty, so they find all white men handsome. The filmmakers presume "that their own sexual fantasies of the Tahitians were the reality."[30] The native is a fantasized and feminized other who exists to fulfill the wishes of the white male self.

This holds true for the principal Tahitian woman, Christian's lover, Maimiti. In 1962, she has more spirit than the deferential Maimiti of the 1935 film, even if Christian has less. She also learns more English. But she still defines herself in relation to male authority: her spirit is of the "stand by your man" variety. The fantasy here is of the good woman rescuing the fallen man. When Christian will not come to her after the *Bounty* returns to the island, Maimiti enters his cabin uninvited, gets angry at his condition, lectures him, cleans his messy quarters, and announces she is going with him. Christian is too depressed to object.

Mutiny on the Bounty *(1935),* Mutiny on the Bounty *(1962), and* The Bounty *(1984). Tahiti becomes more overtly sexual over the decades. Copyright Metro-Goldwyn-Mayer 1935 and 1962. Courtesy Museum of Modern Art Films Stills Archive. Copyright Orion Pictures 1984.*

In the 1935 movie, Clark Gable was never this dispirited. Brando's portrayal suggests the existential ennui of the late 1950s, early 1960s, white American male.

The 1984 *Bounty:* The Hero Goes to Hell

Finally, the 1980s version is a postmodern rewriting of the familiar story that changes Bligh from a sadistic martinet into a complex figure, a family man and friend to Christian, and turns Christian into an egocentric rebel. It becomes a much more personal struggle of two friends who turn into bitter enemies. This is the least satisfying version of the three: a deconstruction of the familiar tale, with no principle at stake, no controlling meta-narrative, and no sympathetic hero, neither the repressive Bligh nor the self-serving Christian.

The 1935 and 1962 films were based on Nordhoff and Hall's novel *Mutiny on the Bounty* (1932). The 1984 version instead draws on a history, Richard Hough's *Captain Bligh and Mr. Christian: The Men and the Mutiny* (1972). It thus would seem to have more claim to historical veracity; yet it, too, fabricates, for example by turning Fryer, the master of the ship, into the chief disciplinarian, thereby softening the portrait of Bligh.[31] It also has Christian warn Bligh that the men might mutiny, which Christian never did; his decision to mutiny was actually impulsive and spontaneous.

The 1984 version seems to favor civilization over nature. Bligh gets the happy ending; he returns to England and is exonerated by a naval court of inquiry. Meanwhile, Christian, having led the mutiny, has unleashed dangerous passions. He narrowly averts a second mutiny against himself by finding the crew an island hiding place, but it is no triumph. When they land and burn the *Bounty,* they do not celebrate but instead say sadly, "We'll never see England again." An afterword tells us that when a British ship finally reached the island 18 years later, only one crew member had survived, and it was not Christian. So Christian and the mutineers pay the price for their rebellion. After taking over the ship, Christian screams at Bligh, "I am in hell!" But what he finds through mutiny is not freedom in paradise but exile in hell.

This *Bounty* is filled with more graphic sex and violence than the earlier versions: Hollywood practices had changed over the decades. Almost everything in the film is pushed to extremes: there are lots of blood, screaming, bare breasts, and savage passions. Writes Michael Sturma, "Like so much of popular culture during the decade, the film is simultaneously voyeuristic and moralizing."[32] The cinematic language has also changed. Many scenes express frenzy and chaos through quick cuts and handheld camera: the crew tossed about by a wild storm at sea or the crew attacked by a savage tribe. There are also many close-ups of the sweaty faces of Bligh and Christian or of the face of a sailor grimacing in agony, his mouth gagged as he is flogged. Rather than a buildup of tension, the film seems to be in tension throughout. Scene after scene is overdone and portentous; the inappropriate, intrusive synthesizer score by Vangelis adds to the ominous effect.

The movie is framed as the trial of Captain Bligh by a British Naval court martial in London. Bligh must defend himself, so the film is a series of lengthy flashbacks triggered by his responses to the inquiry, and events are told in retrospect. It ends with Bligh's acquittal and the crew's burning of the *Bounty* once they reach Pitcairn Island. However, the narrative often deviates from Bligh's point of view, showing us events he could not have witnessed or known about.

The Bligh in this movie is a complex character. First, he is ambitious, frustrated at remaining a lieutenant when he should have been promoted to captain, and eager for the glory of circumnavigating the globe. He says, "I don't have your connections, you see, Fletcher. I want to make a name for myself before I'm too old." Second, he is a family man devoted to his wife and two little daughters, and an affable host who has the *Bounty*'s mates Fryer and Christian dine at his home. Christian is his close friend, has served under him on two previous voyages, and knows Bligh's family (Bligh reminds Christian of this family during the mutiny, but Christian says it is too late). Third, he is a concerned leader: Bligh takes measures to improve morale and he doesn't want to lose a single sailor.

Unfortunately, he is also an erratic, short-tempered commander who swears at his officers in front of the men. On the return voyage, he becomes so abusive that Christian is driven to mutiny. Yet after Bligh is cast adrift in the longboat, he recovers his senses and shows extraordinary leadership and seamanship in bringing the men to safety. In other words, the Bligh portrayed by Anthony Hopkins is a mass of contradictions.

Christian is not as complicated as Bligh, but he is not a very sympathetic rebel. Once again, Christian is played by an exemplar of Hollywood movie masculinity. In this case, it is Mel Gibson, who is on-screen a postmodern, 1980s man: arrogant, passionate, and ferocious, verging on psychopathic, but nevertheless hip, often cynical and self-mocking, as in *The Road Warrior* (1981) or *Lethal Weapon* (1987).

Christian is introduced as a dissolute young gentleman among a ghoulish crowd of bettors in a London club who are wagering on whether one of the club members, who has just collapsed in front of them, will live or die. The incident begins a pattern in the film of sadistic entertainment by both the officers and men of the *Bounty*. The sailor Churchill savagely beats two shipmates, the crew roughly initiate young midshipman Heywood when they cross the Equator, and the Master Fryer enjoys having the men bound and gagged. All the Englishmen seem brutal. But, to his credit, Christian later pleads for clemency for two sailors and saves another who is caught in the rigging during a storm. So he is not entirely unheroic.

Nevertheless, this Christian can be not only callous but also egocentric and hedonistic. He rebels for personal reasons, because he is fed up with Bligh's abuse of him, not because he wants to defend the men, and he first prepares to desert, not to mutiny. Although he may correspond better to the historical Christian than either the Gable or the Brando version, it is at first difficult to understand what motivates such a shallow character—Dening calls him "petulant, posturing"[33]—to such desperate acts or to howl at Bligh during the mutiny, "I am in hell! Hell, sir!"

One can only understand Christian if one recognizes that this version of *Mutiny on the Bounty* is an overtly Freudian psychodrama, making manifest the struggle disguised in the two previous films: an oedipal struggle with homoerotic undertones. Bligh as family man is the patriarch and Christian the rebellious youth. Introduce a racially taboo Tahitian woman into the picture and Bligh and Christian are both driven to a frenzy and behave like howling maniacs. Bligh goes temporarily insane because his protegé, whom he has favored and promoted, becomes sullen and disobedient because of a woman. Christian goes crazy because his mentor has turned against him and there is no escape from him aboard ship.

Another way of interpreting the struggle is to say that Bligh represents all the repressive forces of civilization and Christian the rebel against civilization: in other words, it is a struggle of superego versus id, with no balancing ego in between.

This *Bounty* preaches the perils of going native, which is equated here with the pleasures of the id: sensual indulgence and regression. The naval judge asks, "What made them so easy to corrupt?" Bligh replies, "It was the place itself." But the crew seems to have signed on precisely to be subjected to temptation. The day they sail from England, the men talk of the Tahitian women: "All they wear is tattoos." In each version of *Bounty*, the women show more skin and their dances become more suggestive, until here they are bare breasted and their dances are erotic rituals. Writes Sturma, "The *Bounty* films conform to a pattern in which males assume the active role in advancing the storyline, while women's bodies provide exotic spectacle."[34] The Englishmen also go more deeply native in this movie, inscribing their bodies with tattoos, so that Tahiti is carved into their flesh.

Despite the complete eroticization of the women, Tahiti here is not entirely the realm of the id, and the Tahitians are given some dignity and individuality. In particular, the role of Chief Hiti Hiti, now called Chief Tynah, is expanded, making him less of a type and more of a three-dimensional character. As in the 1935 version, he is wise, is good natured, and speaks English, but as in the 1962 version, he laughs when he first sees his image in a mirror. However, Tynah expresses a greater range of emotions than the previous chiefs. When Christian returns after the mutiny, Tynah says, "You shame me by coming here," and tells him to go. When Christian asks that the chief's daughter be allowed to choose whether to accompany him, he permits her to decide since she is pregnant and the chief had married her to Christian. When she leaves, there is a close-up of the chief crying. It is a touching moment.

We also see interesting aspects of Tahitian culture, which were omitted in the earlier versions and which serve to individualize them. For example, the Tahitians here show more compassion than the whites: the women cut their heads and wail in sympathy when one of the crew is flogged.

Only Bligh holds himself aloof from Tahiti, rejecting the offer of one of the chief's wives. The more Fletcher enjoys himself with the chief's daughter, the more uncomfortable and angry Bligh becomes; the older man appears to be sexually jealous of the younger.

They have several long arguments that did not exist in the earlier versions, eighteenth-century quarrels about civilization versus the state of nature. Bligh accuses Christian of setting a bad example for the men: "You're no better than one of these natives. . . . I think your brain has been overheated, sir, and your body overindulged in sexual excess." Christian replies, "I've done no more than any natural man would do." To which Bligh counters, "You've done no more than any wild animal would do!"

Later, aboard ship, Bligh preaches at Christian in the longest speech in the film, a racist argument. He is trying to win him back by seeming reasonable and kind. But it is too late, the desperate last appeal of a friend (or lover) who has been scorned.

> I've seen many men, many good men, lose their heads over native women in these waters. I've never yet seen it come off well. Of course, I understand the excitement. But think to yourself, man. Think. Could you take a woman like that back home to your friends, back home to your family? No, of course you couldn't.[35]

To which Christian replies icily, "Will that be all, sir?"

As the representative of the superego, Bligh punishes himself, Christian, and the crew. He defends against his jealousy and desire for Christian through paranoia and projection, seeing dirt all around him and forcing Christian to have the men obsessively scrub the deck over and over: "Still filthy! I'll not have your vile ways brought aboard my ship, sir." He fears that Christian's "contamination" in going native has infected him as well—the ship is like his body—and he rages against Christian and the crew. Bligh's pathology evokes an equally violent passion in Christian, which leads to the mutiny.

In terms of its racial representations, this is an ambivalent film. Tahitian culture is romanticized, as in the other films, but it is also portrayed as savage and erotic, unleashing wild passions that are dangerous to supposedly rational white men. Both Bligh and Christian are profoundly affected for the worse by their contact with this foreign culture. In response to Tahiti, they move toward extremes, toward the opposing poles of superego and id. There can be no happy resolution of such a split.

There are many mutually compatible ways of reading the conflict between Bligh and Christian. In the 1984 film, for example, it can be read as a postmodern deconstruction of a familiar tale that completely revises our notion of both characters but provides us with no hero; as a tale of civilization and its discontents, and the sorry effects on European imperialists when they go native; as an oedipal fable; or as a tale of superego versus id.

We want to propose one further, final way of viewing this film. As we said earlier, these versions of *Mutiny on the Bounty* are myths for their times. With that in mind, the 1984 film becomes a story about two privileged white men, more 1980s than 1780s, with Bligh the ambitious yuppie and Christian the narcissistic yuppie. One reviewer considered the film a parable about the sexual revolution.[36]

The framework of the film is a trial; symbolically, what is on trial is white patriarchy. In the wake of gay liberation and women's liberation, the hegemony of white European and American males has been called into question. For the first time in the twentieth century, white patriarchy was on the defensive.[37] If the intent of the 1984 film is to re-legitimize white authority, then Bligh must be exonerated. But the movie cannot really restore Bligh's authority because it portrays him as a man so fatally flawed—a friendly family man who is also a paranoid racist and a closeted homosexual—that he contains within himself all the insoluble contradictions of the white male capitalist. Neither is the movie able to glorify Christian as a white hero, for who would want to follow the rebellion of a narcissistic yuppie? This is a postmodern, self-canceling film that deconstructs itself.

Conclusion

Mutiny on the Bounty may have been remade so many times because it presents a modern (now postmodern) dilemma about civilization and its discontents and the West's shifting relation to "the primitive" other. The films keep returning to the late eighteenth century, which was the heyday of western imperialism and white male hegemony but also the beginning of fractures within the system, as in the American Revolution, Haiti's independence, the French Revolution, and events such as the mutiny on the *Bounty*. The films about the mutiny display a profound ambivalence about the white self because they enact a rebellion against authority and against the superego inspired by contact with "the primitive," a challenge that is appealing yet must also somehow be understood and contained. Only the 1935 film provides a satisfactory solution to the dilemma by reaffirming the continuing legitimacy of white patriarchy and the necessity for reform rather than revolution. To arrive at this solution, it forces us to misrecognize historical facts and presents a simplified conflict of good versus evil, in which the system is good. The 1962 version sidesteps the question of the legitimacy of the system but shows the rebel as a neurotic, misguided idealist whose rebellion is ultimately futile. Finally, the 1984 version, released when white hegemonic masculinity itself was finally being called into question, tries to rehabilitate Captain Bligh but ultimately discredits both the authority and the rebel, leaving us nowhere to stand.

Thus, each version of *The Bounty* presents a different sincere fiction of the white self that respectively addresses the political contingencies of the epoch in which it was produced. As George Lipsitz puts it, any film "responds to tensions exposed by the social moment of its creation, but each also enters a dialogue already in progress, repositioning the audience in regard to dominant myths."[38]

Notes

1. Torgovnick, Marianna. 1990. *Gone Primitive: Savage Intellects, Modern Lives.* Chicago: The University of Chicago Press, p. 11.

2. There is a 1916 silent version of *Mutiny of the Bounty* made in Australia.

3. Sturma, Michael. 1995. "Women, the *Bounty* and the Movies." *The Journal of Popular Film and Television* 23 (Summer 1995): 88–93 (p. 92).

4. Braudy, Leo. 1998. "Afterword: Rethinking Remakes," in *Play It Again, Sam: Retakes on Remakes,* ed. Andrew Horton and Stuart Y. McDougal. Berkeley: University of California Press, pp. 327–34 (pp. 328, 331).

5. Lammers, Cornelis J. 1969. "Strikes and Mutinies: A Comparative Study of Organizational Conflicts between Rulers and Ruled." *Administrative Science Quarterly* 14 (no. 4): 558–72 (p. 558).

6. Freud, Sigmund. 1930. *Civilization and Its Discontents,* trans. James Strachey. New York: Norton, 1962, p. 59.

7. Lammers, "Strikes and Mutinies," p. 565.

8. Freud, Sigmund. 1962. *Totem and Taboo,* trans. A. A. Brill. 1913; reprint, New York: Random House, p. 183.

9. Dening, Greg. 1992. *Mr. Bligh's Bad Language: Passion, Power and Theatre on the Bounty.* Cambridge, England: Cambridge University Press, p. 142.

10. Ibid., p. 257.

11. Ibid., p. 346.

12. Freud, *Civilization,* p. 69.

13. Hough, Richard. 1972. *Captain Bligh and Mr. Christian: The Men and The Mutiny.* London: Hutchinson, p. 75.

14. Ibid., p. 76.

15. Christian, Glynn. 1982. *Fragile Paradise: The Discovery of Fletcher Christian, Bounty Mutineer.* London: Hamish Hamilton, p. 84: "Bligh's was the rule of a bad-tempered schoolmaster, petulant and niggling." Christian quotes a lieutenant who sailed with Bligh and says Bligh treated others with "'insolence and arrogance'" and showed "'the fury of an ungovernable temper'" (p. 186). Richard Hough quotes David Hannay, who says that Bligh was not a gross tyrant but had "a foul mouth . . . and he did not know when to stop. He was a nagger" (Hough, p. 303). Dening refutes the notion that Bligh was a sadist by citing statistics on flogging in the British Navy on Pacific voyages during the late eighteenth century.

16. Barrow, Sir John. 1989. *The Mutiny of the Bounty*. 1831; reprint, Oxford, England: Oxford University Press, p. 97.

17. Dening, *Mr. Bligh's Bad Language*, p. 348.

18. Ibid, p. 349.

19. Dening, *Mr. Bligh's Bad Language*, p. 350.

20. Sturma, "Women, the *Bounty* and the Movies," p. 89.

21. Among those who have proposed that Bligh, ten years older than Christian, took the younger man not only as his protegé but also as his lover, see Darby, Madge. 1965. *What Caused the Mutiny on the Bounty?* London: Allen and Unwin, pp. 149–50.

22. Sturma, "Women, the *Bounty* and the Movies," p. 92.

23. On eighteenth-century Tahitian culture, see Barrow, *The Mutiny of the Bounty*, pp. 3–67; Dening, *Mr. Bligh's Bad Language*, pp. 159–237; and Hough, *Captain Bligh and Mr. Christian*, pp. 106–30.

24. Freud, *Civilization*, p. 34.

25. Sturma, "Women, the *Bounty* and the Movies," p. 92.

26. Dening, *Mr. Bligh's Bad Language*, p. 361.

27. Bell, Daniel. 1965. *The End of Ideology: On the Exhaustion of Political Ideas in the Fifties*, rev. ed. New York: Free Press; Collier-Macmillan.

28. Dening, *Mr. Bligh's Bad Language*, p. 160.

29. Freud, *Civilization*, p. 81.

30. Dening, *Mr. Bligh's Bad Language*, p. 360.

31. Ibid., p. 347.

32. Sturma, "Women, the *Bounty* and the Movies," p. 92.

33. Dening, *Mr. Bligh's Bad Language*, p. 346.

34. Sturma, "Women, the *Bounty* and the Movies," p. 92.

35. *The Bounty* (1984).

36. *Newsweek*. 1984. Review of *The Bounty*. May 14, p. 81.

37. Connell, R. W. 1995. *Masculinities*. Berkeley: University of California Press, p. 226.

38. Lipsitz, George. 1990. *Time Passages: Collective Memory and American Popular Culture*. Minneapolis: University of Minnesota Press, p. 169.

CHAPTER 6

Racism as a Project:
Guess Who's Coming to Dinner

Film Analyzed:
Guess Who's Coming to Dinner (1967)

Guess Who's Coming to Dinner: *First romantic kiss between a black man and a white woman in a Hollywood movie, framed in a rearview mirror. Copyright 1967 Columbia Pictures.*

In this book we have conceived of films as involved in the creation of object relations, those mental templates of our relationships with others. We argue that the white self exists as an object relation, a type of relationship, a fictional construction that once disseminated in the minds of individuals guarantees that both the white person and the racial other are perceived without reference to the true basis of the relationship between the two. In other words, their relationship is misrecognized. Sincere fictions construct a persistent, exalted white self-image as powerful, brave, cordial, kind, firm, and generous, a natural-born leader worthy to be respected and followed by those of other races. These fictions also include debased or fantastic images of racial others that have become templates in the mind for people in the United States and around the world. As the black hero of Ralph Ellison's novel *Invisible Man* says of his relationship with whites, "You wonder whether you aren't simply a phantom in other people's minds."[1]

In this chapter we introduce the idea that films are part of a project, part of something that wants to be brought into being. Jean-Paul Sartre writes of the need to study social relations in terms of a "project." To understand any human creation, he argues, we need to understand both the existing conditions and what they are allowed to build in the future, that is, "the field of possibles" open to them. Sartre believes that Marx was correct that people have an objective situation in life: their work. But for Sartre the work only makes sense as an attempt to bring something into being. "Society is presented to each man as a perspective of the future. . . . Every man is defined negatively by the sum total of possibles which are impossible for him; that is, by a future more or less blocked off."[2]

Using Sartre's terms, racism is a *project*; it has something it wants to bring into being in the future. Racism is the *practice,* and white supremacy—looking up to whites or down on people of another color—is the *condition* that has resulted from it. The project of white racism is to make a non-racist world impossible in the future; it aims above all to perpetuate white privilege and its products.

Therefore, to understand the white self, we need to look not only at the conditions of its past and present existence but also at what it wants to make, and makes possible (or impossible), in the future, both for whites and for people of color. We would add that object relations help define the field of the possible; what we conceive of as possible or impossible is shaped by our relations to the object. Racism occurs both externally, as a project, and internally, in the feelings and desires of the white self. The project is thus enabled by the range of object relations available in a society at a given time.

The Project of *Guess Who's Coming to Dinner*

What then does a film such as *Guess Who's Coming to Dinner* (1967) want to bring into being—aside from entertainment and the profits it produces through the appeal to the widest possible audience that we can assume is true of any Hollywood movie? What conditions and events is it trying to bring into being? Under what conditions of possibility? One can ignore these questions only by conceiving of films as aimless inventions that exhaust their reason for being in the act of production.

Guess Who's Coming to Dinner came out in 1967, amid the impact of the Civil Rights movement, which had been in full swing for a decade. It was directed by Stanley Kramer, who was known for producing or directing outspokenly liberal, anti-fascist, "message" films, such as *Judgment at Nuremburg* (1961) and *Ship of Fools* (1965), and anti-racist films, such as *Home of the Brave* (1949), *Pressure Point* (1962), and *The Defiant Ones* (1958). On the surface, the project of this film is anti-racist. It tackles the ultimate American racial taboo of black-white romance. In this film the romance leads to a marriage accepted by both families, demonstrating that "love conquers all." It preaches reconciliation between the generations as well as reconciliation between the races. Ostensibly, the dramatic tension is between bigotry and racial tolerance. It is a well-meaning, social therapeutic comedy, a problem-solving film, a fable about two nice families, one white and super rich, the other black and middle class, who resolve their differences, overcome mutual prejudices, and unite in marriage.

But is this the actual project of the film? In practice, it turns out to be a rather tame, self-congratulatory liberal melodrama that actually expands the white self by announcing, "Look how tolerant we are!" The movie concerns a crisis in white patriarchy, a situation that questions the validity and the power of one particular aging member of the white elite. But it ends by reaffirming the wisdom, power, and tolerance of the white patriarch as he adapts successfully to changing times. *Guess Who's Coming to Dinner* plays not only on the objective situation—the audience's knowledge of the historical conditions—but also on the subjective racism of the audience.

Because of the 1960s' "generation gap," the film's message of reconciliation between the young and old is as central as its message of racial tolerance; in fact, the two are connected. The passions about miscegenation are displaced onto the far safer topic of generational difference. In 1967, the superheated topic of interracial marriage could not be confronted head-on by a Hollywood film but "the generation gap" could. Stanley Kramer says, "Who says it's a story only about the black man? . . . It's about young and old viewpoints, and in this case the bone of contention happens to be the acceptance of interracial marriage. But this film says that the new generation won't live like the last generation simply because that's the way it's supposed to be. Life has moved on."[3] The crisis in American society in the late 1960s was brought about in large part by children acting on the ideals taught them by their parents and their schools. When the parents were shocked by their children's active protests against the Vietnam War or against racism, the children began to view their elders as hypocritical liberals who did not practice what they preached. *Guess Who's Coming to Dinner* reassures the older members of the audience that parents are not hypocrites, that they want the best for their children, but that they are realists concerned about the pace of change, not about the eventual outcome of racial reconciliation. At the same time it congratulates the younger members of the audience, assuring them that racism will fade away because everyone in the younger generation in the film is color blind.[4]

In 1967, interracial marriage was illegal in many states. In the 1960 census, the last before the film was made, black-white couples constituted only one tenth of 1 percent of married couples in the United States. Marriage between whites and blacks had been absent from Hollywood films "for over forty years, since the implementation of the Production Code. No one would touch this most explosive of social issues."[5] Interracial romance and marriage could occasionally be countenanced in historical films, westerns such as *Broken Arrow* (1950), colonial sagas such as *Mutiny on the Bounty* (1935 and 1962), or musicals set in the past, such as *Showboat* (1936 and 1951). And by the late 1950s, contemporary marriage between whites and Asians was an acceptable subject for films such as *Sayonara* (1957) and *South Pacific* (1958) (both based on novels by James Michener). Yet even in the 1960s, it was still considered taboo to depict a screen marriage between a white and a black. The barrier was first breached in the low-budget feature *One Potato Two Potato* (1964), "the screen's first study of an interracial marriage. (Other features had dealt with interracial romances; there is a difference)."[6]

Then, in 1966 William Rose, who wrote *It's a Mad Mad Mad Mad World* (1963) for director Stanley Kramer, pitched Kramer an idea: a daring comedy about a white South African liberal whose daughter falls in love with a black man. Kramer suggested setting it in contemporary America instead: "I thought to myself, 'What a sorry sight to see a front-line liberal come face to face with his own principles right in his own house.'"[7]

Kramer and Rose decided on a light treatment of this heavy subject. "*Guess Who's Coming to Dinner* was conceived as having a consistently light tone; fundamentally a salon comedy, not above using sight gags and double takes, weak jokes, visual ironies, and snappish, cynical humor."[8]

The casting was also intended to win a wide audience for this potentially controversial movie. Kramer cast it with an ideal, beloved white screen couple—Spencer Tracy and Katharine Hepburn—and a black superstar, the paragon of rising black middle-class respectability, Sidney Poitier. These cultural icons legitimized and made believable the story by bringing it in line with cultural expectations of the time.

As Kramer's biographer Donald Spoto remarks, "Tracy is everywhere the mouth-piece for the struggles, hopes and beliefs of Stanley Kramer."[9] Tracy and Hepburn had not worked in years: he was ill and she was taking care of him. But Tracy had often worked with Kramer and agreed to do the picture on the basis of the story idea. Katharine Hepburn persuaded Tracy to play the father by saying she would play the wife.

Hepburn had solid liberal credentials; she was a progressive, a lifelong feminist. Tracy was more conservative, but he, too, was anti-racist. In 1945 he refused to perform a benefit at the National Theater in Washington, D.C., because wounded white World War II veterans were admitted but not wounded black soldiers. Because of Tracy's stand, the segregated theater relented: for one performance only, blacks were allowed in the audience.[10]

Tracy and Hepburn were a legendary pair, two of the greatest actors of their time, a royal couple of the old Hollywood. Their screen careers had begun over thirty-five years before, with the beginnings of Hollywood sound films. From 1942 to 1957, they were teamed in eight pictures, of which the best remembered are four romantic comedies: *Woman of the Year* (1942), *Adam's Rib* (1949), *Pat and Mike* (1952), and *Desk Set* (1957). Ten years passed until they costarred once again in *Guess Who's Coming to Dinner*. Tracy was 67 and Hepburn 57, and they were ideal to portray the parents in this drawing-room comedy. *Guess Who's Coming to Dinner* was their ninth and last film together: Tracy was very ill during the filming and died ten days after its completion. The fact that it is his swan song and that Tracy and Hepburn were offscreen lovers for twenty-five years (she was divorced; he was a devout Catholic who refused to divorce) gives the film added poignance.

Tracy and Hepburn represented a pairing of opposites. Their onscreen roles mimicked their real-life personalities: he was rugged, gruff, the epitome of the common man; she was a New England aristocrat, graduate of the elite women's college Bryn Mawr. Garson Kanin, who wrote two of their romantic comedies, explained the success of the pair: "Nothing more endears a Queen to her subjects than . . . a marriage to a commoner."[11] As Hepburn put it, "Certainly the ideal American man is Spencer. Sports-loving, a man's man. Strong looking, a big sort of head, boar neck, and so forth. A man. And I think I represent a woman. I needle him, and I irritate him, and I try to get around him, yet if he put a big paw out, he could squash me. I think this is the sort of romantic ideal picture of the male and female in the United States.'"[12] In other words, they were role models, one of the best-loved American couples of their generation. Tracy and Hepburn were the apogees of whiteness and gave the project the Establishment seal of approval. When a royal couple speaks your lines, the lines carry more weight. In addition, audience expectations from previous Tracy and Hepburn films ensured that *Guess Who's Coming to Dinner* would be taken more as entertainment, as romantic comedy, than as political message picture.

Once Tracy and Hepburn were aboard, Sidney Poitier, who had also worked before with Kramer, agreed to play the prospective son-in-law, although he doubted a studio would buy it. At that time, Poitier was the leading black male actor in America. If Tracy and Hepburn symbolized the old white establishment, then Poitier symbolized in Hollywood films of the 1950s and 1960s the rising young American black. Poitier was the key to the commercial success of the project because he was well recognized and acceptable to the white audience. One critic writes, "In 1966, he was the only black actor who could conceivably woo a white girl without alienating a large portion of the American film public."[13]

This is a crucial structuring condition of possibility. As the heroine Janie says in Zora Neale Hurston's novel *Their Eyes Were Watching God* (1937), "'De ones de white man knows is nice colored folks. De ones he don't know is bad niggers.'"[14]

Donald Bogle writes:

> Poitier's ascension to stardom in the mid-1950s was no accident. . . . in this integrationist age Poitier was the model integrationist hero. In all his films he was educated and intelligent. He spoke proper English, dressed conservatively, and had the best of table manners. For the mass white audience, Sidney Poitier was a black man who had met their standards. His characters were tame; never did they act impulsively, nor were they threats to the system. . . . And finally they were non-funky, almost sexless and sterile. In short, they were the perfect dream for white liberals anxious to have a colored man in for lunch or dinner. . . . He may have played the old tom dressed up with modern intelligence and reason, but he dignified the figure.

Black audiences also liked him because "he was the paragon of black middle-class values and virtues."[15]

Kramer says, "It's a tribute to Kate, Spence, and Sidney that Columbia went along."[16] Kramer's dedication, his previous successes as producer and director, along with the talent and reputations of Tracy, Hepburn, and Poitier, and the clever script by William Rose, enabled the film about a touchy subject to be made and to become one of the box-office successes of 1967. Tracy said, "'Aw, you know, everyone knocks message pictures. Let me tell you something. They don't object to message pictures, nor does the audience. They object to message pictures *that don't make money.*'"[17] *Guess Who's Coming to Dinner* "was financially the most successful picture of Spencer Tracy's thirty-seven-year career."[18] It was nominated for ten Academy Awards and won in two categories: Best Actress and Best Original Screenplay.

Reviews of the Film

Guess Who's Coming to Dinner appeared shortly after the repeal of the Hollywood Production Code and broke taboos. For example, it showed the first romantic kiss between a black man and a white woman in a Hollywood movie, albeit coyly framed in the rearview mirror of a taxicab as a disapproving cabdriver looks on.[19] Reviewers were divided between those who found it bold and those who thought it "treacly, sentimental, and contrived." The most common criticism was that it was "old-fashioned." *Guess Who's Coming to Dinner* appeared at a transitional time and is an Establishment film that makes some awkward concessions to the then-growing anti-Establishment mood. Hollywood in 1967 was facing the spreading turmoil of the 1960s and trying to recapture young audiences. The movie business was changing so fast in the late 1960s that whereas *Guess Who's Coming to Dinner* might have seemed bold in 1966, by 1967 "it was already out of date." *Guess Who's Coming to Dinner* was "one of the last big-studio glossy pictures whose story could have been lifted from a slick magazine. Kramer, once the great hope of the avant garde, now was called Establishment; *Bonnie and Clyde* and *The Graduate* were the 'new cinema.'"[20] Donald Bogle calls *Guess Who's Coming to Dinner* "pure 1949 claptrap done up in 1940s high-gloss MGM style. . . . the last of the explicitly integrationist message pictures" before the onslaught of the angry or separatist films about black Americans in the 1970s.[21]

Aside from criticism that it was old-fashioned, some reviewers objected that "the race issue is prettified and preguaranteed a happy resolution here because of the extraordinary character of the black man, and the built-in liberal stance of the parents, especially since Poitier represents the quintessentially respectable and unthreatening black, and Tracy and Hepburn represent the settled, establishmentarian liberals who can win over any case and make the nastiest world safe for love and ideals."[22]

Both Kramer and Poitier defended the film against these charges. Kramer says, "We took special pains to make Poitier a very special character in this story and to make both families, in fact, very special. Respectable, yes. And intelligent. And attractive. We did this so that if the young couple didn't marry because of their parents' disapproval, the *only* reason would be that he was black and she was white. . . . The critics simply missed the point."[23]

Poitier argued that

> In 1967 it was utterly impossible to do an in-depth interracial love story, to treat the issue in dead earnestness, head on. No producer, no director could get the money, nor would theatres in America book it. . . . Hollywood was incapable of anything more drastic in 1967. It couldn't have been made, it couldn't have been distributed. But Kramer created an idea and molded it so lovingly . . . that a totally unheard-of theme opened in theaters around the country without incident."[24]

Poitier is saying that the field of possibles was such that this was the only movie that could have been made at that time. He takes the fact that the film played around the country "without incident" as a tribute to the expertise of Stanley Kramer in giving a controversial subject a light touch. But we might read it instead as a testimony to the movie's blandness. Why should a movie about an explosive topic, released during a time of tumultuous racial protest and change in America (there were riots in the black ghettos of Detroit, Washington, D.C., and other American cities in 1967), have aroused so little protest? Clearly it was not strong medicine but a sugarcoated pill guaranteed to pose no threat to the white establishment and thus to ensure its commercial success. In his review, Arthur Knight accuses the film of a "patness" and "surface slickness that inevitably glosses over the urgency of its theme. . . . The very elements that prevent it from coming to dramatic grips with its potentially explosive material are probably also the ones that would commend it to a wide audience—and Kramer's canny enough as a producer to recognize this."[25]

One could argue that movies such as *Guess Who's Coming to Dinner,* which are designed to offend no one, rather than advancing the cause of anti-racism, do the opposite by easing the public's mind, suggesting that there is no real racial divide that cannot be bridged in the course of a day by a meeting of open-minded whites and blacks of good will. *Guess Who's Coming to Dinner* ignores the painful truth of the old joke: "What do you call a Nobel Prize–winning scientist? Doctor. What do you call a black Nobel Prize winner? Boy." These movies overlook the structural racism of American institutions, a racism built into the Hollywood system, in favor of individualistic quick fixes, and reassure the white audience of the fundamental decency and tolerance of the white self. "A conception of racism as a structural phenomenon privileging white Americans just because they are white is simply beyond the film's representational strategies."[26] According to two other critics, *Guess Who's Coming to Dinner* "constructs an idealized world in which institutionalized racism is absent (rendering antiracist activism unnecessary) and steady progressivism and strong heterosexual and patriarchal white families ensure the possibility for full racial integration."[27]

The Crisis of the White Patriarch

Guess Who's Coming to Dinner does not really revolve around the young interracial couple: they fell in love and made up their minds to marry before the film began. Nor does it revolve around the white mother: she is briefly taken aback by the news of the engagement but quickly rallies behind her daughter. Nor does it revolve around the black parents: they are brought in only toward the end, and John is old enough and independent enough that he will marry with or without their approval. Instead, the film revolves around the crisis of the white patriarch who is forced to give his blessing to a union to which he objects. Matt Drayton, the protagonist, is an aging leader of the white establishment, a powerful San Francisco newspaper publisher who lives in an elegant mansion. He is one of the best role models of the white self. The day constitutes a series of assaults in which his hold on power, his principles, his virility, and even his mental faculties are questioned. He is tested and tried. The movie pokes some fun at him. But in his closing speech, he reasserts his hold on power and reaffirms that he is still in control, still a wise old leader worthy of the admiration and love of white women and of black people. "It is Drayton who defines and delimits the black hero's problem as well as the problem of the hero's parents."[28] "In the end, not only is this father of the bride saved from the charge of hypocrisy, but his embrace of his prospective son-in-law vindicates liberalism as a political philosophy and, with it, integration as the solution to the racism of American society."[29]

Mr. Drayton is portrayed in such a way that the audience cannot help but sympathize with him. His wife and daughter adore him. He is a crusading newspaper publisher in San Francisco, a city well known for its tolerance. Setting the movie in San Francisco is one of the conditions of possibility for the film; the audience recognizes that San Francisco is a special case. In 1967, the time of the film, it was the setting of the rise of the counterculture and the Summer of Love.

Drayton's liberal credentials are established even before he appears on the scene by a photo of FDR prominently displayed on his desk. It is even larger than the portrait of his wife and daughter! One of his daughter's friends tells Dr. John Prentice (the character played by Sidney Poitier), "Matt Drayton really stands for something in this town. . . . It's a great paper. And he made it what it is. And there's never been a single public issue on which Matt Drayton didn't take a stand and spell it out."

As the crusading liberal whose tolerance is tested within his own home, Drayton is the target of much of the film's comedy. For example, in his first appearance, his wife, his daughter, and her black fiancé try to break the news of the engagement to him gradually, so as not to upset him, but they do it so gently that he doesn't even get it. He leaves and starts to loosen his tie, getting ready for golf. His back is to them and to the camera when the light suddenly dawns on him and he turns around in shock. During the scene that follows, his tie is askew, mirroring his befuddlement.

Later, when he goes driving with his wife to get out of the house and momentarily distract them from the crisis, he appears like a forgetful old man. He stops at an ice cream parlor and requests the special flavor he had the last time—except he can't remember its name. The waitress, a young, gum-chewing blonde, rapidly recites the menu. He chooses boysenberry, tries it, then calls her back, stating that it wasn't the flavor he was thinking of, but that, on second thought, he likes it anyway. The pretty young waitress tries to be polite but seems to be having difficulty not rolling her eyes at this doddering codger.

As he reverses his car out of the parking lot of the ice cream parlor, he hits a sports car driven by a young black man, who loudly denounces Drayton to the approving crowd as an old man who ought to have his driver's license taken away. The effect of the ice cream parlor scene is to make Drayton look for a moment like a foolish old man, out of touch with the young, and perhaps losing his grip.

Nevertheless, the scene also shows Drayton's positive side: his acceptance of the new flavor of ice cream, which was not what he wanted but he liked it anyway, anticipates his later acceptance of his daughter's black fiancé.[30] He is not completely closed to change—although preferences in ice cream are not really comparable to attitudes toward race.[31] And he refrains from making any racist retorts, even though the angry young black man publicly insults him.

In other slapstick scenes, Drayton is so rattled by his daughter's engagement that he slaps his shaving brush into his drink rather than into the shaving cup, rips his sock while putting it on, and spills the sock drawer on the floor.

However, the comedy directed against Drayton is largely gentle. The 1967 audience was familiar with Spencer Tracy in the role of the crusty, lovable, but flustered father in such films as *Father of the Bride* (1950) and *Father's Little Dividend* (1951). The associations from those sympathetic roles carry over to this domestic comedy.

The comedy in *Guess Who's Coming to Dinner* is also related to an underlying oedipal rebellion. Drayton the patriarch is being challenged in his own home by a stranger, a young black man who has suddenly appeared out of nowhere to marry his daughter and demands his acceptance or rejection of the marriage the same day he meets him. That is why Drayton is made to seem hypocritical, foolish, and perhaps even senile at times: his authority and his manhood are being questioned.

As Frantz Fanon questions, "Granted that unconscious tendencies toward incest exist, why should these tendencies emerge more particularly with respect to the Negro? In what way . . . does a black son-in-law differ from a white son-in-law?"[32] According to Fanon, it is because, in the white unconscious, "the Negro is taken as a terrifying penis."[33]

Drayton makes a few racist comments, revealing his ignorant acceptance of stereotypes. First, he has an assistant check the credentials of Dr. Prentice. Next, he wonders to his wife, "How do you suppose a colored mailman produced a son with all the qualities he has?" And finally, he asks Prentice, "Are you saying they [black people] don't have a special sense of rhythm?"

Mr. Drayton's objections to the marriage, however, are not permitted to appear as racist. Instead, the crisis in the film stems from a series of dramatic contrivances: it was a whirlwind romance that took place out of state; the Draytons knew nothing about it because their daughter did not bother even to phone them from Hawaii; and now they meet their prospective son-in-law for the first time and are expected to give the couple their blessing on the spot because Dr. Prentice is flying to New York and Geneva that night. The pressure-cooker atmosphere intensifies during the day when Joanna decides to fly on with her fiancé and when she unwisely invites the Prentices to dinner. Mr. Drayton's objections appear then as the sensible reservations of a responsible father who does not want to be pressured into a snap decision about such a momentous life choice, not as the irrational objections of a bigot.

The racism of Drayton and his wife is further tempered by several other devices in the film. The first is their disdain for overt bigotry. Mrs. Drayton, who is even more anti-racist than her husband, says of their daughter Joanna:

> The way she is is just exactly the way we brought her up to be. . . . We told her it was wrong to believe that the white people were somehow essentially superior to the black people—or the brown or the red or the yellow ones, for that matter. People who thought that way were wrong to think that way. Sometimes hateful, usually stupid. But always, always wrong. That's what we said. And when we said it, we did not add, 'But don't fall in love with a colored man.'

Their daughter Joanna, however, is so color blind as to seem naïve. Dr. Prentice says, "It's not that our color difference doesn't matter to her. It's that she doesn't seem to think there is a difference." One wonders if she is a liberal saint or an overprivileged white girl blithely unaware of the racial turmoil of her country.

According to Samuel Kelley, "The film's function is not to explore white racist attitudes toward interracial marriage, but to communicate the Draytons' liberal image toward interracial marriage by showing how harshly they deal with racists."[34] When Hillary, Mrs. Drayton's employee at her art gallery, makes bigoted comments about the engagement ("I simply couldn't believe it. I mean, it's so unlike Joey to do anything so appallingly stupid. . . . Darling, what you must be going through!"), Mrs. Drayton coolly fires her on the spot. The incident makes Mrs. Drayton appear principled and heroic. The audience loves this scene because Hillary is "the kind of repulsive character that most people love to hate." Kramer is "following the familiar approach of using the most obnoxious types to represent racial prejudice."[35] Hillary is a caricature, easy to dismiss, especially because Mrs. Drayton is her boss.

Displacing Racism

Another device to make the Draytons appear anti-racist is to displace the racism onto some of the black characters, such as Tillie, the Draytons' maid. "While they are severe with white racists such as Hillary, they do not seem the least bit perturbed by the maid from whom they tolerate the most vicious kind of racism."[36] Tillie is used as comic relief. Her role is similar to that of Mammy in *Gone with the Wind*: the live-in maid, a bossy, fiercely loyal family retainer who has raised the white daughter, seems to have no family of her own, and so identifies with the white family that she aggressively protects what she sees as their interests. Tillie is hostile to Dr. Prentice from the moment he enters the house and makes no effort to disguise her hostility. "Tillie is drawn as childlike and confused, unable to accept or understand what is happening."[37] She asks Mrs. Drayton, "You and Mr. Matt, you gonna put a stop to this damn nonsense foolishness?" She says she doesn't like to see one of her own kind "gettin' above hisself." Both Mrs. Drayton and Joanna brush off Tillie's objections. Joanna tells her, "You know I've always loved you, and you're just as black as he is."

Tillie is given the most vitriolic racist speech in the film. She denounces Dr. Prentice, saying:

Guess Who's Coming to Dinner: *Tillie tells off Dr. Prentice. Copyright 1967 Columbia Pictures.*

> You may think you're fooling Miss Joey and her folks, but you ain't fooling me for a minute. You think I don't see what you are. You one of those smooth-talking, smart-ass niggers, just out for all you can get, with your black power and all that other troublemaking nonsense. . . . And as long as you're anywhere in this house, I'm right here watching. You read me, boy?

The scene is comic because of Tillie's profanity and excessive indignation. But it is also preposterous to believe that she would treat any guest in her employer's home with such lack of respect. Mrs. Drayton fired Hillary for a much milder offense. While Tillie is not fired, "this implies only that, because of both her race and her class position, her opinion simply does not matter."[38]

Two critics note that this scene, awkwardly filmed at oblique camera angles to suggest a skewed perspective, seems out of keeping with the otherwise highly conventional cinematography of the film. Kramer seems to have deliberately chosen a traditional, old-fashioned style of filming to soothe the audience about this potentially disturbing topic. The critics suggest that "the material here may have gotten out of Kramer's control."[39] The sociologist Stanford Lyman complains that the scene is "one of the most subtly debasing ever to blacks," especially because Dr. Prentice is caught while changing clothes and covers his shirtless chest as if to protect his modesty or to ward off the old woman. He claims that "no white star—Redford, Newman, McQueen—would have been asked to play that kind of comedy"[40] Dr. Prentice's humiliation in this scene—caught half-naked and subjected to a racist diatribe by the maid—contrasts to the more gentle comedy directed at Mr. Drayton.

As James Baldwin says, "In *Birth of a Nation*, the loyal nigger maid informs the nigger congressman that she don't like niggers who set themselves up above their station. When our black wonder doctor [in *Guess Who's Coming to Dinner*] hits San Francisco, some fifty-odd years later, he encounters exactly the same maid, who tells him exactly the same thing."[41] Unfortunately, this same form of screen comedy—using blacks to humiliate and keep down fellow blacks—is alive and well fifty-two years after *Birth of a Nation*.

Kelley claims that the racism in *Guess Who's Coming to Dinner* is also displaced onto "Dr. Prentice's parents. . . . They subscribe to an outmoded segregationist notion."[42] Actually, Mrs. Prentice accepts the marriage as much as Mrs. Drayton does. It is Mr. Prentice who cannot accept the notion of his son's marrying a white woman. "Adhering to the familiar strategy of heightening the protagonist's character through the negative portrayal of the antagonists, Mr. Prentice is unsympathetically drawn. Unlike Drayton he undergoes no character change."[43]

The conflict between Dr. Prentice and his father escalates into the most dramatically charged scene in this otherwise rather tame comedy. It is the only scene in which we witness the explosion of the racial and oedipal tensions that underlie the film. Mr. Prentice treats his son like a teenager.[44] He tells him:

> You don't know what you're doing. . . .you've got to stop and think. Have you thought what people will say about you? Why, in 16 or 17 states you'd be breaking the law. You don't change the way people feel about these things. You know, for a man who never put a wrong foot anywhere, you're way out of line, boy.

For the second time that day, Dr. Prentice has been called "boy," but in both cases it was not by a white racist but by a fellow black. Angry, he retaliates to his father's lack of respect with some rudeness of his own: "That's for me to decide, man. So just shut up and let—"

But Mr. Prentice interrupts, telling his son, "You have no right to say a thing like that to me, not after what I been to you. . . . I'm proud of what you made of yourself. But you know I worked my ass off to buy you all the chances you had." He tries to guilt trip his son into obeying him.

Dr. Prentice delivers a fiery speech, the only scene in the film in which he is allowed to show any passion. He says:

> You and your whole lousy generation believe the way it is for you is the way it's got to be! And not until your whole generation has laid down and died will the dead weight of you be off our backs! You understand? You've got to get off my back!

Remorseful at hurting his father, he reassures him that he loves him, but he adds, "But you think of yourself as colored man. I think of myself as a man."

Samuel L. Kelley finds Mr. Prentice's attitude "a gross distortion of black attitudes. . . . Most black people who have not been formally educated, like the Prentices, tend to look up to their college educated children with respect. . . . Certainly one would not expect the outrage and temper tantrums exhibited by Mr. Prentice."[45] The black intellectual Addison Gayle, however, describes the uneasy oedipal relationship between "Black Fathers and Their Sons."[46] Whatever the sociological or psychological truth of the black father-and-son confrontation here, the sudden explosion of emotion only highlights by contrast the tameness and repression in the rest of the film. If we view *Guess Who's Coming to Dinner* as a film whose project is to maintain the white self in a time of racial struggle and change, this scene is yet another displacement of racism, which is again projected and seen as emanating from the black characters rather than from the amiable Mr. Drayton. The black father-son struggle also displaces the primary oedipal struggle in the film, which is that of Dr. Prentice versus Mr. Drayton. Dr. Prentice will marry despite his father's objections, but he will not disregard Mr. Drayton's objections. He gives more weight to the opinion of his prospective white father-in-law than he does to that of his own father.

The Supertom

As we mentioned, object relations are "templates of others in our minds."[47] If we accept that Mr. Drayton is the true protagonist of *Guess Who's Coming to Dinner* and not Dr. Prentice, and that the project of the film is to ennoble the embattled white liberal self, then Dr. Prentice and all the black characters in the film are sincere fictions, constructed according to templates in the white mind.

To overcome the huge, unacknowledged weight of white privilege, Dr. Prentice must be built up into a black superman. His credentials are formidable:

> He's an important guy. . . . Graduated maximum cum laude [sic] Johns Hopkins 1954; Assistant Professor Yale Medical School 1955; three years Professor London School of Tropical Medicine; three years Assistant Director World Health Organization; two textbooks and a list of monographs and medical society honors as long as your arm.

Reviewers complained that Dr. Prentice was contrived and incredible, "a composite Schweitzer, Salk, and Christ colored black for significance."[48] The "wonder doctor . . . had to become a living freak, a walking encyclopedia of rare medical knowledge, in order to have the question of his marriage to a white girl *discussed*."[49]

We might add that Dr. Prentice's intellectual achievements must be exaggerated as well to defend against incest fantasies of the "Negro as terrifying penis" out to rape white daughters.[50] To defend further against these white fantasies, Dr. Prentice is made into not only a genius but also an amazing paragon of sexual restraint who refuses to sleep with his fiancée until after they wed.

Another indication of the weight of white privilege is the mismatch in the couple's accomplishments. If mate selection is conceived of as an exchange between the couple and their families, then there should be a balance in what each offers the other. Here, however, there is a gross imbalance: he is a world-renowned public health doctor, she seems to have no goals other than marrying him. Her accomplishments are being young, white, pretty, and rich. The mismatch extends to the casting as well: Katharine Houghton (Joanna), a novice actor, is far weaker than the other players. The film implies that "a black man has to have a superhero's credentials in order to marry a white woman with no credentials."[51] Blacks are allowed to bridge the ultimate social barrier of intermarriage and to be accepted as equals in the white world—as long as they are superheroes played by superstars like Sidney Poitier. The film really emphasizes how narrow the field of possibility is for black Americans.

There is a further mismatch: to have accumulated all these honors, the character must be made into an older man, thirty-seven years old to Joanna's twenty-three. This presents another problem for the screenwriter. At thirty-seven, Dr. Prentice can't be never married or divorced—either possibility might render him suspect to a 1967 American audience—so he is made into a widower whose wife and son were killed in a train accident, which increases sympathy for him.

As an object created to satisfy the needs of the white self, Dr. Prentice must fulfill contradictory needs: he must be super-accomplished and supremely confident to enter the white world as an equal, yet simultaneously humble so as not to offend that white world.[52] Dr. Prentice is a reincarnation of a figure who has long existed in the white imagination: the tom, here re-imagined as a "supertom." Writes Donald Bogle, "Always as toms are chased, harassed, hounded, flogged, enslaved, and insulted, they keep the faith, ne'er turn against their white massas, and remain hearty, submissive, stoic, generous, selfless, and oh-so-very kind."[53]

The innovation in this new, white liberal film is to shift the blame from whites by making the primary harassers and insulters of the tom into his fellow blacks (Tillie and Mr. Prentice).

The year 1967 was a time of black rage in the United States, with riots in many urban ghettos. But the black characters in *Guess Who's Coming to Dinner* are deferential to the whites. The only black rage in the film is black against black—Tillie versus Dr. Prentice or Dr. Prentice versus his father—a convenient displacement. By centering on whiteness, *Guess Who's Coming to Dinner* ignores "black activism against white racism."[54] The only references to the racial turmoil of the 1960s are a few sarcastic comments by Tillie. "This marginalization of the film's raison d'être both coyly acknowledges its political agenda and betrays its anxiety about how the audience will react"— that is, how the white American audience will react.[55]

Conclusion: Paying Homage to White Privilege

The last word in the film is given to the white protagonist, Matt Drayton, who has kept everyone in suspense by not publicly announcing his decision. In gender stereotyping, the fathers—Mr. Drayton and Mr. Prentice—represent the voice of reason and are against the marriage, whereas the mothers represent emotion and side with the couple. Mrs. Prentice accuses Drayton and her husband of being old men who have forgotten "what true passion is." This final assault on his manhood triggers a change in Drayton. He gathers everyone in the living room and finally speaks his piece. It is the longest speech in the movie and concludes the story. As Joanna's friend had said earlier, "Matt Drayton really stands for something in this town. . . . There's never been a single public issue on which Matt Drayton didn't take a stand and spell it out." This is exactly what Drayton does in his concluding speech: takes a stand and spells it out for everyone. He

Guess Who's Coming to Dinner: *Matt Drayton makes them all sit and listen to him.*
Copyright 1967 Columbia Pictures.

reasserts his manhood and his command as master of the household. He makes them all sit and listen to him, and when his daughter interrupts, he tells her to shut up.

He also brings Tillie in to listen to his speech, introducing her to the Prentices as "Miss Matilda Biggs, who's been a member of this family for 22 years." To call a domestic servant a member in equal standing of the family is a piece of white liberal piety the film never questions.

The film opens with a sappy theme song about "The Glory of Love": "You've got to give a little, / Take a little, / And let your poor heart break a little. / That's the story of, / That's the glory of love." So we don't forget the message, the theme song is repeated later in a nightclub scene and serves as background music in many other scenes. Americans like love stories and like to believe that "love conquers all," and that is the movie's overt message: true love can triumph over all obstacles, even racial barriers. This is what Drayton says in his concluding speech: "The only thing that matters is what they feel—and how much they feel—for each other. And if it's half of what we [Mr. and Mrs. Drayton] felt—that's everything." Nevertheless, except for one brief kiss, the film never shows physical affection between the couple.[56] In effect, it neuters the black hero.

The speech concluded, they go in to dinner together. The final image in the film is of the new, reconstituted American family, white and black together, all sitting down at the same family table, and further blessed by organized religion in the form of dinner guest Monsignor Ryan. Of course, we note they are still being served by the black maid. (We will encounter the constitution of a multiracial family—but without the intermarriage—also in the final scene of *Lethal Weapon 4*.)

Drayton's speech is one that is often repeated in the history of American film: it is the speech of the white liberal messiah coming to the rescue. The same strategy is used thirty years after *Guess Who's Coming to Dinner* in the climax of Spielberg's film *Amistad* (1997) when John Quincy Adams takes a stand and spells it out in a long speech before the Supreme Court (see chapter 4). The white patriarch frees the slaves; the old lion roars again.

By giving Drayton the last word, *Guess Who's Coming to Dinner* legitimates white privilege. The movie offers impassioned speeches about generational difference and the glory of love but only tame platitudes about race. The ostensible project of the film—to increase racial tolerance—is paradoxically only possible as it pays homage to white privilege, which is the unacknowledged root cause of the problem it seeks to overcome. *Guess Who's Coming to Dinner* thus reverses its intended consequences. It turns into a film about a crisis in the white patriarchy successfully resolved. Racial differences can be tolerated, it implies, so long as white privilege is never brought into question.

Our analysis of this groundbreaking film shows that the plot and images of a film are not only determined by the filmmakers' intention, by their individual projects, but also by the social project that provides the codes that make it meaningful. The meaning of a movie, we propose, is embedded in what Sartre called the field of what is socially possible at a certain time and place. Given the ubiquity of racism in U.S. society, the field of possibles greatly restricts the antiracist imagination.

Notes

1. Ellison, Ralph. 1952. *Invisible Man*. New York: Random House, p. 3.
2. Sartre, Jean-Paul. 1963. *Search for a Method*. New York: Knopf, p. 95.

3. Spoto, Donald. 1978. *Stanley Kramer, Film Maker.* New York: Putnam, p. 277.

4. Wartenberg, Thomas E. 1999. *Unlikely Couples: Movie Romance as Social Criticism.* Boulder, Colo.: Westview Press, p. 24.

5. Spoto, *Stanley Kramer, Film Maker,* p. 274.

6. Bogle, Donald. 1997. *Toms, Coons, Mulattoes, Mammies, and Bucks: An Interpretive History of Blacks in American Films.* New York: Continuum, p. 201.

7. Davidson, Bill. 1987. *Spencer Tracy: Tragic Idol.* London: Sidgwick & Jackson, p. 206.

8. Spoto, *Stanley Kramer, Film Maker,* p. 275.

9. Ibid., p. 280.

10. Kanin, Garson. 1971. *Tracy and Hepburn: An Intimate Memoir.* New York: Viking Press, pp. 127.

11. Ibid, p. 80.

12. Davidson, *Spencer Tracy: Tragic Idol,* p. 86.

13. Carey, Gary. 1975. *Katharine Hepburn: A Biography.* New York: Pocket Books, p. 208.

14. Hurston, Zora Neale. 1990. *Their Eyes Were Watching God.* 1937; reprint, New York: Harper & Row, p. 164.

15. Bogle, *Toms, Coons, Mulattoes, Mammies, and Bucks,* pp. 175–76.

16. Davidson, *Spencer Tracy: Tragic Idol,* p. 207.

17. Ibid.

18. Swindell, Larry. 1969. *Spencer Tracy: A Biography.* New York: World, p. 274.

19. Knight, Arthur. 1967. "The New Look," *Saturday Review,* December 16, p. 47.

20. Swindell, *Spencer Tracy,* pp. 274–75.

21. Bogle, *Toms, Coons, Mulattoes, Mammies, and Bucks,* p. 217.

22. Spoto, *Stanley Kramer, Film Maker,* p. 275.

23. Ibid., pp. 275–77.

24. Ibid., p. 278.

25. Knight, "The New Look," p. 47.

26. Wartenberg, *Unlikely Couples,* p. 122.

27. Projansky, Sarah, and Kent A. Ono. 1999. "Strategic Whiteness as Cinematic Racial Politics," in *Whiteness: The Communication of Social Identity,* eds. Thomas K. Narayama and Judith N. Martin. Thousand Oaks, Calif.: Sage, pp. 149–74 (p. 161).

28. Kelley, Samuel L. 1978. *The Evolution of Character Portrayals in the Films of Sidney Poitier, 1950–1978.* New York: Garland, p. 161.

29. Wartenberg, *Unlikely Couples,* p. 112.

30. Spoto, *Stanley Kramer, Film Maker,* p. 278.

31. Wartenberg, *Unlikely Couples,* p.125.

32. Fanon, Frantz. 1967. *Black Skin, White Masks.* New York: Grove, p. 165.

33. Ibid., p. 177.

34. Kelley, *Evolution of Character Portrayals in the Films of Sidney Poitier,* pp. 166–67.

35. Ibid., p. 167.

36. Ibid., p. 168.

37. Ibid., p. 170.

38. Projansky and Ono, "Strategic Whiteness," p. 172.

39. Keyser, Lester J., and André Ruszkowski. 1980. *The Cinema of Sidney Poitier: The Black Man's Changing Role on the American Screen.* New York: A. S. Barnes, p. 118.

40. Dardner, Paul. 1974. "Hollywood is Crossing the Last Racial Barrier." *New York Times,* October 6, section 4, p. 13.

41. Baldwin, James. 1985. *The Price of the Ticket: Collected Nonfiction 1948–1985.* New York: St. Martin's Press, p. 602.

42. Kelley, *Evolution of Character Portrayals in the Films of Sidney Poitier,* p. 160.

43. Ibid., p. 174.

44. Ibid., p. 175.

45. Ibid., pp.175–76.

46. Gayle, Addison. 1970. *The Black Situation*. New York: Horizon Press, p. 144.

47. Greenberg, Jay R., and Stephen A. Mitchell. 1983. *Object Relations in Psychoanalytic Theory*. Cambridge, Mass.: Harvard University Press, p. 11.

48. Morgenstern, Joseph. 1967. "Spense and Supergirl." *Newsweek*, December 25, p. 70.

49. Baldwin, *The Price of the Ticket*, p. 605.

50. Fanon, *Black Skin, White Masks*, p. 177.

51. Kelley, *Evolution of Character Portrayals in the Films of Sidney Poitier*, p. 178.

52. Ibid., p. 163.

53. Bogle, *Toms, Coons, Mulattoes, Mammies, and Bucks*, pp. 5–6.

54. Projansky and Ono, "Strategic Whiteness," p. 157.

55. Wartenberg, *Unlikely Couples*, p. 114.

56. Ibid., p. 126.

Scarlett and Mammy Revisited: White Women and Black Women in Hollywood Films

Films Analyzed:
Imitation of Life (1959)
Boys on the Side (1994)
Losing Isaiah (1994)
The Long Walk Home (1990)
Passion Fish (1992)

Just as a major prototype for the relationship between white and black men in American society is found in the novel *Huckleberry Finn* and the films based on it, the prototype for the relationship between white and black women can be found in the novel *Gone with the Wind* and its 1939 film adaptation. The intimacy between Scarlett O'Hara, the white mistress, and Mammy, her black slave, is a relationship of inequality and exploitation. This relationship requires study, if for no other reason than because, as Jane Gaines has noted, "absolute patriarchy" is "most obtuse when it disregards the position white women occupy over black men as well as black women."[1]

At first sight, the figures of Scarlett and Mammy are opposites: Scarlett is white, rich, young, thin, and beautiful; Mammy is black, poor, middle aged, and fat and has a big, round face. Scarlett does no domestic labor because Mammy does it all. Mammy has raised Scarlett more than Scarlett's own mother has—"I knows you ever since I put the first pair of diapers on you"— calls Scarlett "honey chile," and combines the nurturing characteristics of a mother with the servility of a slave. She knows the true Scarlett—all her mistress' flaws and lies—but loves her just the same. She may scold Scarlett, but she is always loyal and serves even when Scarlett is bankrupt. Indeed, she has no name, just the title "Mammy." Whether slave before the Civil War or supposedly free domestic servant after the war, Mammy never changes and appears to have no family—or memory of a family—of her own, no black children to raise, no black friends, and no life outside of her service in the O'Hara household. The relation between Mammy and Scarlet is the same before and after emancipation, an interesting fact given that the movie is about the changes brought about by the Civil War. As we argued in chapter 2, Mammy is a reassuring figure, a beacon of stability amid the chaos and constant change of Scarlett's world.

The two figures may be opposites, but they are inseparable and interdependent; each defines the other. Mammy makes possible Scarlett's privileged life as a Southern

Gone with the Wind: *Scarlett and Mammy. Copyright 1939 Metro-Goldwyn-Mayer.*

belle; the nurturing and labor of the black servant is indispensable for Scarlett to be her beautiful white self. In a repeated scene, Mammy tightens Scarlett's corset—in a sense, *creating* Scarlett.

Mammy is also a comic figure who functions like Jiminy Cricket in the Disney film *Pinocchio* as the protagonist's conscience. Mammy is pure superego. She enters the film scolding Scarlett and continually upbraids her for her lapses in etiquette and morality, even if Scarlett usually ignores or rebels against her advice. A social conservative, Mammy enforces the Southern hierarchy. She gains her status from association with rich white planters. She may be a slave but she is the head slave in the O'Hara household and bosses all the other house servants and the O'Hara children. More than a servant, she considers herself a member of the O'Hara family and identifies with them so much that she disdains mere "field hands" and "poor white trash."

If Mammy is all superego, then Prissy, played by Butterfly McQueen, the other black woman in the film, is all id. If Mammy is old, big, competent, tough, and honest, then Prissy is young, small, incompetent, cowardly, and a liar. The two servants are foils for each other; yet both express aspects of their mistress: Scarlett has the bossiness, strength, and competence of Mammy along with the childishness and dishonesty of Prissy. In constructing the white character as blending the main traits of the two black characters, Scarlett is made complete, "normal," a full character, while the two other characters are one-dimensional (equivalent to E. M. Forster's distinction between "round" and "flat" fictional characters).[2]

Scarlett's "normalcy," not her superiority, justifies in the film her power over the slaves. She is a three-dimensional character, whereas they are one-dimensional stereotypes, and the audience is asked to believe that these traits are true to the life situation portrayed. The way of relating we call race rests on the categorization and perception of the other as unidimensional. The notion of race involves attributing intellectual, spiritual, and moral traits derived from singular physical traits or geographic origin. The sincere fictions on which figures such as Mammy and Prissy depend are that blacks exist only to serve the white self, that they are born servants always loyal to their master or mistress, that they have no life or identity apart from their function of supporting white privilege, that they never change, and that they are totally content with their existence as slaves or servants. Emancipation makes no difference in the relationship between a white woman and her black caretaker. The ideology behind this incredible flaw in the plot is the belief that white privilege is not built into the law and social structures but rather derives from the individual and group traits of whites and blacks.

There is a kind of lexicon of traits in the movie. The meaning of the traits is determined by the way in which they determine the relations among the people who bear them. For example, loyalty emerges as the single most important trait in blacks. Some traits are common to a class of people—rich whites are or at least should be kind and generous to their inferiors and display impeccable manners; poor whites are trashy; black field hands have no manners—whereas other traits are personal, such as Ashley's weakness, Scarlett's guile, or Mammy's forcefulness.

The paradoxical relationship of Scarlett and Mammy, rich white mistress and her black maid who functions as mother substitute, superego, and servant, persists in American film melodramas about women since World War II, although modified and, in films of the 1990s, sometimes radically revised. In this chapter, we consider the relationships between white and black women in *Imitation of Life* (1959), *Boys on the Side* (1994), *Losing Isaiah* (1994), *The Long Walk Home* (1990), and *Passion Fish* (1992).

Aware of their predecessor, many of these films self-consciously refer to *Gone with the Wind*. For example, in *Imitation of Life* the protagonist is an actress who is offered what she calls "the best part since Scarlett O'Hara." In *Boys on the Side,* the black woman jokes to her white woman friend, "You are saved, Miss Scarlett." And in *Passion Fish,* the white protagonist played a soap opera heroine, "Scarlett."

Imitation of Life: "The best part since Scarlett O'Hara"

In *Imitation of Life,* the Scarlett figure is Lora Meredith and Mammy is her live-in maid Annie Johnson. Like Scarlett, Lora is a beautiful woman struggling after a descent into poverty and flawed by selfishness, blind ambition, and neglect of those who love her. Like Mammy, Annie is a tough and unquestioningly loyal servant. The two are inseparable. And just as Mammy makes possible Scarlett's privileged life, so Annie's nurturing and labor enable Lora to succeed as her beautiful white self. And Lora is very white and very blonde, played by Hollywood sex goddess Lana Turner.

Imitation of Life is a remake of a 1934 film that reflected the new liberalism of FDR's first term. The 1934 film "prided itself on its portrait of the modern black woman, still a servant but now imbued with dignity."[3] In the 1934 version, two widows with young daughters, the white Miss Bea and the black Aunt Delilah, struggle together through the Depression. Bea makes her fortune marketing Delilah's pancake recipe, and the two share the wealth. But both suffer because of their daughters. Bea's daughter Jesse becomes her rival for a man and Delilah's daughter Peola, a light-skinned black, rejects her mother and passes for white. The film ends with Delilah's funeral, when her remorseful daughter returns.

The 1959 film updates the story to reflect the liberalism not of the FDR era but of the early Civil Rights era. It is set not in the Depression but in the post-World War II economic boom, from 1947 through 1959. The women are still single mothers who bond together out of mutual interest. Lora makes her fortune not through exploiting her maid's pancake recipe but through her own talent as a stage and screen actress. Ei-

the street, weeping. Although we feel sorry for her—she does not deserve the violence—the film also makes it clear she brought misery on herself and her mother by living a lie. And both the 1934 and the 1959 versions end with the daughter hysterically sobbing with guilt at her mother's funeral "finally making the character . . . conform to the remorseful mulatto type."[7] By blaming the victim, this presentation displaces guilt from the white self to the black self and leaves intact the racist core of society. Like the 1934 version, the 1959 film prefers the mother, an old-fashioned, long-suffering, black saint who knows her place, to the uppity daughter.

Toni Morrison deals with a similar theme in her novel *The Bluest Eye* (1970) without blaming the victim. Her protagonist Pecola Breedlove, a poor, abused little black girl living in Lorain, Ohio, in 1940, is ironically named after the tragic mulatto Peola in the 1934 *Imitation of Life*. Like her namesake, Pecola longs to be white; she wishes for blue eyes, believing they will make everyone love her. But Morrison blames Pecola's self-hatred on the society that stigmatizes blackness, not on the poor, confused black girl.

Boys on the Side: "You're free, Miss Scarlett"

It seems a long way from *Imitation of Life* (1959) to *Boys on the Side* (1994). The former is pre-feminist and condemns a woman for choosing a career over love and marriage. The latter is feminist and post–*Thelma and Louise;* its title suggests that men are peripheral to the lives of women. As in *Thelma and Louise,* some women friends kill an abusive man and go on the road, on the run from the law. The eccentric trio of single women friends here consists of Jane, a middle-aged black lesbian; Holly, a young, white, pregnant woman—it is her drug-addicted, abusive boyfriend they accidentally kill; and Robin, a middle-class white woman dying of AIDS. This movie sets out deliberately to cross boundaries of sexual orientation, race, class, and age by setting up an All-American, utopian community of women. It implies that sisterhood will prevail when three very different, kooky women get together and that the love of women for each other is powerful enough to overcome every social barrier.

Nevertheless, despite its deliberate attempt to shatter stereotypes and to break taboos, *Boys on the Side* replicates the Scarlett-Mammy relationship of the earlier films. When Jane jokes with Robin as she gets Robin to open up and to use swear words—"You're free, Miss Scarlett"—the allusion unintentionally highlights their similarity to their cinematic predecessors, the black maid and the white mistress.

Although they are supposedly friends and equals, Robin has money whereas Jane makes only a marginal living as a singer. Jane winds up living in Robin's house and becoming her caretaker because Robin is dying of AIDS. If the film really overcame racial barriers, then the situation could be reversed: Robin would be a white lesbian taking care of Jane, a straight black woman dying of AIDS. Such a situation would be difficult for an American audience to believe, yet we accept it as totally normal for a poor black woman to selflessly love and take care of a rich white woman.

Why does Jane have to be played by a black actor? There are no other blacks in the film. Jane sings in all-white bands and has no black friends or black lovers. The black community was not developed in either *Gone with the Wind* and *Imitation of Life*, and Mammy and Annie served in white households, yet Jane is even more isolated than they were.

For that matter, why does Jane have to be further isolated by being made a lesbian who has only straight women friends? There are no other significant lesbian characters in the film and no scenes of lesbian sex, only of heterosexual activity.

The film does not really deal seriously with either race or lesbianism. Instead, lesbianism becomes a way to displace the issue of race. The unquestioning loyalty and love of the older black woman who nurtures her white mistress is explained here by the fact that Jane is a lesbian attracted to straight white women.

The film deliberately avoids race. There are, in fact, only a few references to the issue, and those are primarily by Jane. First, when she meets her, Jane puts down Robin as "the whitest woman in America." Later, Robin asks why Jane isn't attracted to her physically: "Is it a black-white thing?" Jane replies, "It's more a blonde-Carpenter thing," referring to Robin's bland taste in music. So the racial dimensions of social relationships are dismissed by a joke. The only other reference to Jane's racial difference is Robin's mother's initial shocked reaction, but the mother and Jane soon become friends as they care together for the dying Robin. Finally, when Holly's baby proves to be black (Holly had been uncertain about the father), Jane quips, "Don't look at me." But everyone quickly accepts the baby, even Holly's white husband, a conservative cop.

Is this racial color blindness, the liberal ideal? The film pretends that race doesn't matter. Whoopi Goldberg, who plays Jane, is cast in a Sidney Poitier position: the white audience is supposed to identify with her and not to see her as black. When she testifies for Holly (who is on trial for murdering her boyfriend), Jane is mistreated by the prosecuting attorney not because she is black but because she is a lesbian. Once again, race is displaced by sexual orientation.

The film also pretends that the barriers imposed in America by race are no different from those imposed by sexual orientation, class, or age and that love conquers all, surmounting any obstacle with ease. The only issue the film takes seriously is AIDS. Otherwise, it resolves far too easily the divisions of race and class and sexual orientation that divide women, dismissing them with a few jokes or wishing them away. Even Robin's mother, a conservative retired woman, is easily converted to their cause.

For all its good intentions and daring attempt to break down barriers, *Boys on the Side* is a feel-good comedy without any significant social criticism. One of its major failings is that it desexualizes Whoopi Goldberg and turns her into a mammy-nursemaid. The character is neither as bossy and angry as Mammy nor as servile and self-denying as Annie, and she is quick with her witty quips, but she is clearly an updated version of the stereotyped figure we have already seen in *Gone with the Wind* and *Imitation of Life*.

Losing Isaiah: Scarlett Adopts Mammy's Child

Losing Isaiah was also released in 1994, a volatile year in American race relations, when Rodney King was beaten by policemen in Los Angeles and O. J. Simpson was arrested. It is a sensitive drama that tries to present an unbiased view of the difficult topic of interracial adoption. It concerns the struggle between the black birth mother and the white adoptive mother over custody of a black child. Here the black woman is not a servant to the white woman; instead the two are antagonists until the end of the film, when they finally bond for the benefit of the boy.

The movie appears not to take sides but to give the women equal time through parallel editing. We are first introduced to Khaila Richards, a young black woman, a drug addict who supports her habit through prostitution. She leaves her newborn infant Isaiah on a garbage dump before she enters a crack house, and the next morning she panics when she cannot find him. Then we meet Margaret Lewin, a middle-aged white social worker married to an architect, who encounters Isaiah in the hospital after he has been abandoned, grows to love the infant, takes him home, and later legally adopts him.

Several years pass. Khaila is sent to prison for theft, paroled, overcomes her addiction, and gets a job—ironically, as nanny to a white child. She assumed Isaiah was dead, but when she discovers that he is alive but adopted without her knowledge or consent, she hires a black male lawyer to get the child back. Margaret counters by hiring a black woman lawyer. A courtroom battle ensues, presided over by a white woman judge (this film rather mechanically tries to maintain racial and gender balance).

The parallel development makes both women sympathetic: Margaret, who loves the three-year-old boy, has raised him from infancy and is afraid of losing him; and Khaila, who also loves Isaiah, has reformed and wants him back to make up for her mistakes.

Losing Isaiah: *Margaret Lewin and her adopted child Isaiah. Copyright 1995 Paramount Pictures. Courtesy Museum of Modern Art Films Stills Archive.*

Losing Isaiah was released in 1994, the year Senators Carol Mosely-Braun (D-Illinois) and Howard M. Metzenbaum (D-Ohio) and Representative Luis V. Gutierrez (D-Illinois) introduced bills that would cut off federal funds to child welfare agencies that deny interracial adoption solely on racial grounds. A 1972 policy statement by the National Association of Black Social Workers opposed transracial adoptions on the grounds that black children brought up in white families lost their cultural identity and grew unprepared for a racist society. This resolution equated transracial adoption with "cultural genocide." The debate still rages on as the adoption policies of agencies in several states are being challenged and a movement grows toward transracial adoptions.[8, 9]

In court, Khaila's attorney criticizes the Lewins for raising Isaiah in a household devoid of black culture, saying sarcastically, "Who do you think he identifies with? The orange-faced muppet?"

Margaret responds, "That I can't raise Isaiah up to be an honorable man because my skin is white? What about love?. . . and what about Isaiah? How does he fit into all this? Or is it more important that we be politically correct? What we should be thinking about here is what is going to happen to the spirit of this little boy if he is taken away from us. . . . We are all he knows and if you take him away from us, it will kill him."

The lawyer replies, "So only you can save him? You're the great white hope?"

Margaret says, "No. But I am his mother."

And the lawyer concludes, "Are you?"

A white social worker testifies: "I am sick and tired of the attitude that taking black children out of their environment and placing them in an affluent household is better for the child. What kind of values does that suggest?"

The judge awards custody to Khaila. But Margaret's fears prove correct: Isaiah grows depressed and rejects Khaila, longing for "mommy." Finally, Khaila has to call in Margaret to help her calm the disturbed child at school. The movie ends with the two women reconciling as they play with Isaiah. So there is a compromise solution and the boy will retain both mothers.

Nevertheless, despite its parallel development and apparent attempt at balance, the movie skews our sympathy toward the white woman. The film is about the deep love of a white family for a black child. At the end, the overjoyed Isaiah runs toward Margaret's arms, yelling, "Mommy!" proving who is the real mother. Whereas the white American audience takes it for granted that Mammy or Annie would nurture a white child as if she were her own, it is impressed when the reverse happens and a white person adopts a black child. And Margaret seems even more saintly because she willingly adopts a crack baby who has neurological problems and learning disabilities. In addition, Margaret has all the middle-class virtues: she is a professional with a stable home and family who has already successfully raised a teenage daughter. Khaila is a crack whore, the kind of problem social workers like Margaret deal with. Margaret is given more screen time, and her arguments prove correct: Isaiah does suffer severely when he is taken away from her. Finally, it is Khaila and her black lawyer who play the race card, not the Lewins.

The problem with the movie is that it confuses the issue. This is an extreme case; very few adoptions are of crack babies abandoned in a garbage dump by prostitutes. Khaila did not have to be a drug-addicted prostitute. Suppose she were simply any young woman, of whatever race, who put up her baby for adoption because she was unmarried, without resources, and hoping for a better life for her child? Mothers often have a change of heart after giving up a child for adoption. The movie is falsely presented as a question of "political correctness" concerning race, when it is really about the respective rights of birth mothers versus adoptive mothers.

Unfortunately, this movie, which seems at first so sensitive and unbiased, proves to be another sincere fiction of the white self in which a white woman is the better mother for a black child. It is as if Scarlett or Lora Meredith adopted Mammy's or Annie's baby.

The Long Walk Home: Driving Miss Mammy

The last two movies about white women and black women we consider are more progressive than the previous ones mentioned. Both *The Long Walk Home* and *Passion Fish* present situations where a white woman and her black maid gradually develop a relationship of genuine friendship and apparent equality and in which the white woman sacrifices for the sake of the black woman. Nevertheless, these films continue to assume that it is the function of the poor black woman to nurture her rich white employer, so that in a sense they revise but never really escape the Scarlett-Mammy paradigm.

The Long Walk Home, based on a true story, written by John Cork, a white Montgomery native, is set in the beginnings of the Civil Rights movement and concerns the effects of the Montgomery bus boycott of 1955–1956 on two families, one white and one black. Miriam Thompson is a conventional, upper-middle-class, white Southern matron married to a real-estate developer. Odessa Cotter, a working-class black woman, has been the Thompsons' maid for nine years. When the boycott begins, Odessa walks hours to and from work. Miriam begins to give her rides, at first simply for Miriam's convenience, but later in defiance of her husband. Gradually, Miriam becomes aware of the injustice of the system of segregation and volunteers to drive other boycotting blacks. In the climax, Miriam and her seven-year-old daughter Mary Catherine cross the color line to link hands with Odessa and a line of black women who refuse to be intimidated by a mob of angry white men that includes Miriam's husband and brother-in-law. So both women change and grow from the historic events and from their relationship. If anything, the white woman takes a longer walk than the black woman, growing and risking more by abandoning white privilege. The film is a conversion narrative, like *Schindler's List*, which uses a historic conflict to dramatize the story of a white character who is transformed from oppressor to liberator of a minority group.

The film borrows a device from *To Kill a Mockingbird:* the adult Mary Catherine narrates in voice-over events that happened when she was a child. In *To Kill a Mockingbird,* Scout's narrative turned her father into the hero, the great white savior. Here, however, Mary Catherine gives Odessa and her mother equal time. That, at least, is an improvement. As in *To Kill a Mockingbird,* the device has multiple effects: first, it ensures the dominance of a white perspective; second, it absolves the white audience of complicity by presenting the point of a view of an innocent white observer of horrific racial conflict; and third, it connects present and past but distances us in time from the events, implicitly congratulating the audience that we live in a more enlightened age. Two reviewers complained about this pat history lesson: "What are audiences to learn about today's racial antagonisms from a long-ago tug of war between saints (the black underclass) and demons (the Alabama plutocracy)?"[10] "There's an overriding predictability to *The Long Walk Home:* the moral issues couldn't be more cut and dried. . . . Hollywood is uneasy with racism in the present tense. . . . It's easy to be on the side of the angels, but the movies we need must do more than flatter the audience."[11]

Like *Imitation of Life, The Long Walk Home* criticizes white women for neglecting their children by relinquishing child rearing to the black maid. Susie complains in *Imitation of Life,* "Let's face it, momma, Annie's always been more like a real mother. You never had time for me." But in this film, the white mother is more self-critical and aware of her shortcomings. Miriam Thompson admits to Odessa, "O, you do the mothering. I saw the way you held Mary Catherine when she had the chicken pox and you hadn't even had it. . . . I wonder, would I have done that for your daughter?" We see Mary Catherine more with Odessa than with her mother until the final scene, when Miriam, inspired by Odessa, acts as a moral role model for her daughter.

Like *Losing Isaiah,* the film uses parallel editing, cutting between the white and the black households. Unlike *Isaiah,* however, it is not skewed in favor of the white family. Indeed, the film favors the Cotters, although one reviewer objected that they are "all-too familiarly idealized, noble icons."[12] The Cotters come across as more egalitarian, closer, and affectionate than the Thompsons. Both Mr. and Mrs. Cotter work and have a say in the household, whereas Mrs. Thompson is a housewife wholly dependent on her husband's income and therefore under his thumb, which bothers her. We see Mr. and Mrs. Cotter talking in bed several times but we never see such intimacy between the Thompsons. Finally, the Cotters join hands and say grace before they eat whereas the Thompsons rarely eat together. They are more dispersed and seem each to go his or her own way. By the end of the film, it appears as if the Thompsons' marriage may not last, a casualty of her rebellion. (*The Long Walk Home* is thus more feminist than *Boys on the Side,* which, despite its title, ends with a marriage.)

The film opens with a ritual illustrating the absurdity of 1950s Southern apartheid: Odessa and other black maids in white uniforms enter the front of a bus to pay their fare to the driver and then descend and reenter the bus from the rear. The voice-over of the adult Mary Catherine narrates, introducing Odessa: "There's always something extraordinary about someone who changes and then changes those around her."

Next we see a typical morning in the Thompson household as they chatter and prepare for the day. Odessa is silent as she goes about her chores in their midst and receives a stream of orders from Miriam, but we are constantly reminded of Odessa's presence as she moves back and forth, often in the foreground, dominating the shots. This foreshadows the development of the film: the privileged Thompsons ignore Odessa, preferring her as a silent black robot, but she is going to dominate and to transform their household.

The busy Miriam leaves Odessa in the park to take care of Mary Catherine and another little girl. But Odessa is evicted by an insulting white policeman, who tells her that blacks are not allowed in the park. He humiliates her, shouting and treating her as if she is willfully disobedient or deaf or stupid: "Can't you hear me, nigger? What you doing in this park? . . . Don't give me any of that mealy-mouthed crap! . . . Niggers like you best answer with 'yes, sir.' . . . You don't understand nothing, do you?" He intimidates her into silence and obedience.

When she learns of this incident, Miriam, in the first step showing her independent spirit, orders the white officer to come to her home and apologize to Odessa and Mary Catherine. In this instance, class trumps gender: Miriam is asserting her privilege as the wife of an affluent white businessman. At this point she is more concerned with the slight to her and her daughter's status as rich whites than with the racist insult to Odessa. As she says to her husband and her brother-in-law, "I will not have my judgment impugned by a wet-behind-the-ears policeman. . . . It's not like she was parading her own children [in the park]." And as Odessa's husband points out to Odessa, "She's the one sent you to that park and you ain't had no say in it. Policeman's apologizing to her and not to you." Miriam's change is gradual; it is only late in the film that she sacrifices on behalf of Odessa.

Although the 1955 setting predates the renaissance of the American woman's movement in the late 1960s, this film links the Civil Rights movement with woman's liberation.[13] Miriam makes common cause with Odessa in part because she recognizes that she is a victim of the gender hierarchy as much as Odessa is a victim of the racial hierarchy. Being a good white Southern wife means being submissive. Although she has a college degree, she is not allowed to work, and her husband treats her like an ignorant child about the bus boycott, saying, "I know you don't keep up with things," which is similar to the cop's saying to Odessa, "You don't understand nothing, do you?"

This movie demonstrates the links between racism and sexism, showing how apartheid is enforced through verbal and physical violence by Southern white males. *Imitation of Life* had one scene in which a white man beats up a black woman; this film has three, establishing a repeated pattern: first is the scene with the white cop; second, in a scene with overtones of rape, three white teenage boys verbally and then physically assault Odessa's daughter, ganging up on her on a bus and then chasing her through a park; third, in the climax, a mob of hostile white men in business suits scream "Walk, nigger, walk!" at a crowd of black women, trying to force them out of parking lot, repeating on a larger scale the two earlier scenes.

Although there is one sympathetic white woman, Miriam, there are no sympathetic white men in the film; they are all bullies, intimidating and beating up women. Black or white women who defy white men in the slightest threaten their masculine dominance and must be forced back into submission through contempt, insults, threats, and, finally, physical violence.

The white male self here is a fascist self, deriving from sadistic hostility against the weaker—against minorities and women. Being high in the gender and race hierarchy allows them freely to release hostile feelings. This is similar to the Nazi persecution of the Jews. Klaus Theweleit claims the emotional core of fascism is a passionate celebration of violence originating in the fear and hatred of the feminine.[14]

Whereas the white man in this film requires the white woman to reinforce his masculinity by complete submission to the gender and racial hierarchy, the black man wants the black woman to affirm his masculinity by joining him in defiance of white male hegemony. As her husband Norman tells Miriam, "Here I am trying to hold my head up as a white man in this town and you're coddling a nigger maid." In contrast, Odessa's husband tells Odessa, "I'm tired of hanging my head in the shadow of crackers. I want to ride in the front of the bus."

Juxtaposed to the black political meeting, which takes place at church and involves the entire black community, whole families of men, women, and children, is the white citizens' council meeting, which consists solely of businessmen, a Chamber of Commerce protecting its economic interests. We witness the growing strength of black female solidarity in the film's climactic scene, in which the black women triumph over a mob of hostile white men by linking hands and singing a spiritual. In a reversal of the early scene in which the lone Odessa was intimidated and silenced by the white cop, now the white men are silenced, completely taken by surprise. The black women defy white male hegemony through religious solidarity, referring to a higher power. The white male power structure is exposed as morally bankrupt, exerting power solely through violence.

White male violence also drives Miriam to defy their hegemony and ultimately to cross the color line. First, she is disturbed by the bombing of the Reverend Martin Luther King's home. In the climax, one of her husband's friends smashes her car windows because she has been using the vehicle to drive boycotting blacks and her brother-in-law slaps her face. She is told, "You want to act like a nigger, then you just get your daughter and walk with the rest of the niggers." But she won't leave; instead she joins hands with her daughter and Odessa in the line of resisting black women. Symbolically, she has given up white privilege and been blackened by her experience.

The Long Walk Home is more progressive than *Gone with the Wind, Imitation of Life, Boys on the Side,* and *Losing Isaiah* because it shows a functional black family—indeed, a black family that works better than the white one—and more of the black community. It also demonstrates the links between sexism and racism. And its white heroine gives up her place in the privileged white patriarchal order to join with her maid and align herself with the black cause. Nevertheless, even in this film it continues to be the function of the black maid to nurture the white woman. "Instead of the film's simply telling her character's story, the domestic's plight serves to awaken (and humanize) her white employer."[15]

Passion Fish: Tara Revisited

Passion Fish (1992) is a product of John Sayles, a progressive auteur who writes and directs low-budget, independent films that fall outside of the usual Hollywood formulas.

His films have gained critical respect and some popular recognition: *Passion Fish* received Academy Award nominations for best actress for Mary McDonnell and best screenplay for Sayles.

The change in *Passion Fish* is that the black woman and the white nurture each other. The film combines elements of the white mistress–black maid film, such as *Gone with the Wind, Imitation of Life,* or *The Long Walk Home,* with elements of a buddy film about an odd couple who are initially hostile but eventually bond as they discover they need each other, such as *Boys on the Side* or *Losing Isaiah.*

Mary Alice is a successful white actress who played a character ironically named "Scarlett" on a popular TV soap opera. Recently hit by a taxicab in New York City, she has become a paraplegic living in a wheelchair. So she leaves her acting career to return to her house in Louisiana, on the bayou where she grew up. In other words, she retreats back to the South, back to the old plantation, just as Miss Scarlett always returns to Tara to revitalize herself.

But this is Tara with a difference. Mary Alice chooses to live alone, withdrawn from the world, without family or friends nearby to help, and depends on live-in nursemaids. She drinks too much and is self-pitying and unable to accept her disability, taking out her anger on her caretakers and driving away a succession of them until a black woman named Chantelle comes. Chantelle has recently arrived in Louisiana from Chicago. A recovering drug addict who lost custody of her daughter, Chantelle is determined to make good in her new career. She needs the job and stands up to Mary Alice, not tolerating her abuse and trying to help her recuperate.

This is more a relationship of mutual need and equality than in the other films because both women are wounded and trying to rebuild their lives in a new location; one is struggling to come to terms with her recent disability, the other is fresh out of detox. Initially at odds, they gradually become friends by helping each other to heal. We get a parallel development of the two women as each becomes settled in her new life and finds romance: Mary Alice with Rennie, a Cajun fisherman she had a crush on in high school, and Chantelle with Sugar, a horse trainer. But neither can rely on the man to help renew her life; Rennie is married and Sugar is a womanizer. Instead, each woman must depend on herself and on the other woman. With Chantelle's help, Mary Alice becomes stronger, stops drinking and watching TV, becomes interested in photography, and begins to get out of the house. Chantelle, initially insecure, becomes better at her job. Chantelle's father brings her daughter Danita from Chicago to visit, and Mary Alice also helps Danita, so that eventually Chantelle may regain custody. At the end, Mary Alice is offered a chance to return to the soap opera but decides instead to continue her new life with Chantelle in Louisiana.

There is some deliberate inversion of racial stereotypes. For example, although the story is set in the South, both the white woman and the black woman are displaced Northerners, Mary Alice from New York and Chantelle from Chicago. This prevents the relationship from slipping into that of white Southern matron and hired black help. Mary Alice may be "a bitch on wheels," as Chantelle calls her, but she is not presented as a racist. She is nasty to all her nurses, white and black alike. She was a misfit when she grew up in Louisiana, then moved north and lost her accent. Her difference is underscored in a scene where two old classmates, conventional Southern belles and genteel racists ("You don't see as much colored help these days") come calling. They bore Mary Alice and she quickly asks Chantelle to get rid of them. In contrast, Mary Alice is friends with a black actress from New York who later visits. And whereas in the previous films, the black maid raised her white mistress's daughter, here Mary Alice has no children and instead helps Chantelle's daughter. And although the black maid is traditionally the cook, Chantelle can't cook and asks, "Is there some rule all black people got to know how to cook?" In a role reversal, Mary Alice cooks for Chantelle to thank her for her help.

There is a lot of touchy negotiation between the two women about the terms of their relationship. Chantelle insists on her professionalism and her definition of her duties, saying, "I'm not your waitress." Mary Alice says, "What are you, then?" Chantelle also says, "If I'm going to stay, I need to be able to do my job." Later, Mary Alice asks, "Do you have to wear that uniform? It's so nursy." Chantelle replies, "I am a nurse. Not an assistant." When Mary Alice says, "I don't know what to call you," Chantelle says, "I'm not your friend." Yet by the end of the film Chantelle has given up her uniform and, as they becomes increasingly involved in each other's private lives, they cross over from a strictly professional relationship into friendship.

True, *Passion Fish* repeats one stereotype we also see in *Losing Isaiah:* the black woman is a recovered addict who has lost custody of her child. Donald Bogle complains: why couldn't Chantelle "have had some other problem besides the old drug-addict routine?"[16] Yet to balance this, the film also makes the white woman an alcoholic.

One final break with stereotype is in the dialogue. Mammy was critical of Scarlett, but she would never have dared to insult and to curse her in the terms Chantelle uses as shock therapy on her white mistress when she is trying to get her to quit drinking:

> Who made you queen of the whole damned world? You sit around feeling sorry for yourself, you miserable TV-watching, dried-up old witch! You can't even go for more than one day without a drink and you're not even a drunk yet. You're just fuckin' spoiled.
>
> Most mornings I want to get out of the house so bad I can't even breathe. . . . I am going away from you. I don't want to be around your shit anymore. You understand that? Away from you.

Yet this is a turning point, Chantelle's strongest outburst against her employer, and one could also say that she does it for Mary Alice's own good, to help her to change. After this, things improve for both women, and they overcome their hostility and cement their friendship.

Thus we see some progress from the days of *Gone with the Wind.* This "Scarlett" is a new-style Southern aristocrat with Northern attitudes and black friends. And she tries to help her black servant as much as the woman helps her.

Although neither *The Long Walk Home* and *Passion Fish* reasserts white privilege or takes it for granted, as progressive as the films seem to be, they are nevertheless sincere fictions that cannot abandon the persistent fantasy that, deep down, black women truly love their white mistresses and are determined to rescue them. As Donald Bogle questions, "Why does such a fantasy—black women as nurturing, caretaking marvels at helping poor white women untangle the knots in their lives—linger on, even in the mind of a contemporary independent filmmaker?"[17] Over sixty years have passed, but the persistence of such sincere fictions in American films suggests that the relationship of Scarlett and Mammy remains at the unconscious core of white women's interactions with black women in America. At the end of *Gone with the Wind,* Scarlett is left alone in her mansion. But she is not really alone: she still has Mammy. At the end of *Passion Fish,* Mary Alice still has Chantelle. Maybe we are still living inside Tara.

Notes

1. Gaines, Jane. 1988. "White Privilege and Looking Relations: Race and Gender in Feminist Film Theory," in *Feminist Film Theory: A Reader,* ed. Sue Thornton. New York: New York University Press, pp. 293–306 (p. 295).

2. Forster, E. M. 1927. *Aspects of the Novel.* London: E. Arnold.

3. Bogle, Donald. 1997. *Toms, Coons, Mulattoes, Mammies, and Bucks: An Interpretive History of Blacks in American Films.* New York: Continuum, p. 57.

4. Modleski, Tania. 1991. "Feminism without Women: Culture and Criticism in a Postfeminist Age," in *Feminist Film Theory: A Reader,* ed. Sue Thornton. New York: New York University Press, pp. 321–35 (p. 331).

5. Feldstein, Ruth. 2000. *Motherhood in Black and White: Race and Sex in American Liberalism, 1930–1965.* Ithaca, N.Y.: Cornell University Press, p. 124.

6. Bogle, p. 59.

7. Bogle, p. 60.

8. Nationwide, in 2000, about 15 percent of the 36,000 adoptions of foster care children nationwide were transcultural or transracial adoptions. In 1987 these adoptions represented only 8%. Nissman, Cara. 2002. "Growing Together; Mother's Day Takes on Special Meaning for Transracial Adoption Family," *Boston Herald,* May 12, Arts and Life section, p. O49.

9. In 1994, the National Association of Black Social Workers softened its 1972 resolution by adopting a policy statement saying that transracial adoption should only be considered after "documented evidence of unsuccessful same race placements have been reviewed and supported by appropriate representatives of the African-American community." Bell, Ezillia. 1994. "Kids' Best Interest Should Be Guide." *Chicago Sun Times.* April 16, p. 16.

10. Corliss, Richard. 1990. "Dole List," *Time,* December 17, p. 62.

11. Ansen, David. 1991. "History à la Hollywood," *Newsweek,* January 14, 54.

12. Ibid.

13. Ibid.

14. Theweleit, Klaus. 1987. *Male Fantasies.* trans. Stephen Conway, Erica Carter, and Chris Turner. Minneapolis: University of Minnesota Press.

15. Bogle, p. 331.

16. Ibid., p. 359.

17. Ibid., pp. 358–59.

CHAPTER 8

White Out: Racial Masquerade by Whites in American Film I

Films Analyzed:
Gentleman's Agreement (1947)
Black Like Me (1964)
Silver Streak (1976)
Bird (1988)
Trading Places (1983)
Soul Man (1986)
The Jerk (1979)

> At lilac evening I walked with every muscle aching among the lights of 27th and Welton in the Denver colored section, wishing I were a Negro, feeling that the best the white world had offered was not enough ecstasy for me, not enough life, joy, kicks, darkness, music, not enough night. . . . wishing I could exchange worlds with the happy, true-hearted, ecstatic Negroes of America.
>
> —Jack Kerouac, *On the Road* (1957)

> The hipster had absorbed the existentialist synapses of the Negro, and for practical purposes could be considered a white Negro.
>
> —Norman Mailer, "The White Negro" (1957)

Idealizing the Image

What does it mean, socially and psychologically, for a white person to masquerade as someone of a different color or ethnicity? We have argued that the white American self is irretrievably split between adherence to the democratic principles of liberty, equality, and justice for all and the brutal reality of racism. Psychologically, a variety of defense mechanisms—such as projection, denial, splitting, repressing, and displacing—are put in the service of denying the inconsistency of this split.

In the white racial masquerade, the primary defense seems to be idealizing the image. Becoming the racial or ethnic other, at least in the movies, is a way to bridge the racial divide by merging two incompatible objects (incompatible in the American imagination) to create an impossible, fantasy solution: a racial hero who is simultaneously both gentile and Jew, or both white and black, or both white and Indian. The fantasy provides a feeling of omnipotence. It is a way to overcome white self-loathing and racial guilt, to compensate for felt lacks in the self by appropriating the imagined attributes of an idealized other, and to rise into a position of moral superiority. At one extreme, in movies like *Gentleman's Agreement* and *Black Like Me,* the white racial masquerade conceals a Christ fantasy: a person voluntarily gives up white power and privilege; takes on the form of members with another racial or ethnic group and moves among them; is mocked, humiliated, and physically endangered; and is even rejected by the very people he came to save.

As Karen Horney writes, "The idealized image might be called a fictitious or illusory self, but that would be only a half truth. . . . It is an imaginative creation, interwoven with and determined by very realistic factors. It usually contains traces of the person's genuine ideals. While the grandiose achievements are illusory, the potentialities underlying them are often real."[1]

Thus, cinematic fantasies about white race switching are usually liberal and well intentioned, based on genuine ideals. They may even have a liberating effect in making Americans more tolerant. However, because of their mixed (and largely unconscious) motives, they provide a fantastic, unworkable solution to the American racial divide.

The sincere fiction involved in narratives of white racial masquerade is that passing is a redemptive act that will enrich and improve the white self and cure racism. These movies preach redemption through individual epiphanies. None of the white race-switching movies illuminates the institutional nature of racism; these films merely deal with its effects on individuals. Of course, this is a general failing of Hollywood film, although it is difficult to say whether it is the direct effect of ideology or a side effect of the individualism demanded by popular narrative. The problem, of course, is that in matters of racism, we are not dealing simply with individual feelings but with institutional structures and widespread, social ways of thinking, feeling, and acting. Passing as a person of another race or ethnic group will not cure white racism any more than male cross-dressing will eliminate sexism and patriarchy.

Although these movies acknowledge multiculturalism and racial differences, they do not attempt to show how racial differences are produced and constructed. Because the differences are largely taken for granted, the movies can actually end up naturalizing the historically, socially constructed American racial divide. Many of these race-switching movies simply constitute other "sincere fictions" of the white self, seeming to question white hegemony while ultimately helping to re-inscribe it. They pretend to show the discrimination that American ethnic and racial minorities experience, but they do so through what Margaret M. Russell calls "the dominant gaze," that is, the normative white perspective of typical Hollywood film.[2]

Post–World War II White Self-Loathing

Whites have masqueraded as people of another color since the nineteenth century. There is a long tradition in American popular culture of blackface minstrelsy. However, it is only

daughter appears to him in the afterlife in the guise of an Asian airline attendant, since her father had once remarked on the beauty of such a woman. Once again, the female masquerade serves patriarchal power.

Like black passers, white passers usually live with the fear of being exposed. But unlike in the narratives of the tragic mulatto, that fear cannot create real tension in the plot because the white masquerade is usually temporary—they were simply slumming—and the consequences of their being found out are negligible. Socially, numerous values and conventions reward as well as guarantee the impunity of the white masquerader. After all, he can always return to his former, elevated status of white privilege.

Blackface minstrelsy carried over from the music hall stage into silent movies, as in *Birth of a Nation* (1915), and into sound movies as well, beginning with the first talkie, *The Jazz Singer* (1927). White actors also performed onstage in the nineteenth century as Asians, Asian Americans (the tradition of "yellowface"), or Native Americans and continued to do so in silent films and even into American movies of the 1960s and beyond. For instance, in the 1930s, Charles Middleton was Emperor Ming the Merciless, the incarnation of the "yellow peril" in the *Flash Gordon* serials (1936, 1938, and 1940). In the *Charlie Chan* series from 1935 to 1949, Chan was played by Warner Oland or Sidney Toler. In the 1950s, Marlon Brando portrayed a Japanese in *Teahouse of the August Moon* (1956) and Yul Brynner, in his most celebrated role, was the King of Siam in *The King and I* (1956). And in John Ford's *Cheyenne Autumn* (1964), a revisionist western sympathetic to the plight of Native Americans, the leading Cheyenne braves are nonetheless portrayed by Ricardo Montalban (a Latino) and Sal Mineo (an Italian American), as if all ethnic minorities were interchangeable.

The Subversive Potential of Racial Masquerade Films

However, since World War II, as Gina Marchetti notes, racial masquerade films "implicitly critique the racial hierarchy of mainstream American culture, since they feature the conscious and deliberate impersonation of another race, putting aside a supposed racial superiority so as to become part of a supposedly inferior culture." She suggests that the masquerade films are potentially subversive because they imply that "racial differences are not 'natural' but culturally constructed and subject to historical change."[11] The white race-switching movies cast the artificial boundary lines between the races into doubt and, at the extreme, criticize or even dissolve the notion of whiteness.

Indeed, race-switching movies have a subversive potential because they imply that race is not an absolute or essential quality but a matter of performance. Judith Butler has suggested that, "In imitating gender, drag implicitly reveals the imitative structure of gender itself—as well as its contingency."[12] She considers gender "as a *corporeal style*, an 'act,' as it were, which is both intentional and performative, where *'performative'* suggests a dramatic and contingent construction of meaning."[13] If race, too, can be considered a matter of performance, then representations of racial passing can be compared, as we have suggested, to cross-dressing. There is always an ambivalence in transvestitism, which springs from dissatisfaction with one's gender assignment and envy of the gendered "other," as well as hostility toward the other, manifested in exaggeration and parody. There are similarly mixed motives in movies about white racial passing: a critique or deconstruction of whiteness and white superiority, a desire for racial liberation through appropriating the supposed qualities of the racial other, along with a sometimes farcical mockery of racial attributes. Susan Gubar notes that, "given what Homi Bhabha calls 'the ambivalence of mimicry,'[14] we need to understand white masquerades as a mockery of and menace of the Other, as an assertion of difference, but also as a form of competition, as an admission of resemblance, a gesture of identification or solidarity, even a mode of self-mockery."[15]

Nevertheless, white racial masquerade in the movies might be understood not only as subversion of whiteness but also, ironically, as an assertion of white privilege. "Whiteness" has always been conceived as more fluid and less fixed than other racial categories. As Richard Dyer notes, white people are permitted to tan themselves with no loss of prestige: "Not only does tanning bespeak a wealth and life style largely at white people's disposition, but it also bespeaks white people's right to be various, literally to incorporate within themselves features of other peoples." In contrast, black people are mocked for using skin lighteners.[16] Writes Gayle Wald, "White people (especially white men) traditionally have enjoyed a greater liberty than others to play with racial identities and to do so in safety, without permanent loss or costs."[17] Thus, white privilege includes the privilege to temporarily change one's color, to masquerade as non-white.

Gentleman's Agreement: A Christian Savior of the Jews

The template for the white "passing" movie is provided by *Gentleman's Agreement* (1947), which concerns a gentile journalist named Phil Green who briefly poses as Jewish to write a magazine article exposing American anti-Semitism. *Gentleman's Agreement,* based on a popular novel of 1947 by Jewish-American writer Laura Z. Hobson, was produced by Daryl F. Zanuck and directed by Elia Kazan, who were not Jewish. The film was a hit, winning Academy Awards for Best Picture, Best Supporting Actress, and Best Director. It is the kind of melodrama with a message of liberal uplift that the academy likes to reward. Playing on patriotic sentiments fostered by World War II, the movie denounces anti-Semitism as un-American. The hero says of anti-Semites, "They're more than nasty little snobs. . . . They're persistent little traitors to everything this country stands for and stands on, and you have to fight them."

Nevertheless, anti-Semitism was mainstream Americanism, well institutionalized for religious, political, and economic reasons, until a few years before the movie appeared. As Karen Brodkin explains, "The temporary darkening of Jews and other European immigrants [primarily Catholic Irish and Southern and Eastern Europeans] during the period when they formed the core of the industrial working class clearly illustrates the linkages between degraded and driven jobs and nonwhite racial status."[18] During the golden age of American industrialization, from the 1880s to the 1930s, immigrants were forced into difficult, low-paying factory jobs that were considered beneath most white folks. The "dirty" work symbolically "blackened" the immigrants.

However, when economic circumstances changed after 1945, their ethnoracial assignment as "less than white" also changed. "America's postwar economic prosperity and its enormously expanded need for professional, technical, and managerial labor, as well as on government assistance in providing it" opened the floodgates for Jews and other "Euro-ethnics" to enter the middle class and to be admitted to the exclusive club of whiteness.[19] All surveys since 1945 have shown a steady decrease each decade in anti-Semitism among most Americans (except among African Americans and white supremacists), although not its total disappearance.

Thus *Gentleman's Agreement* was a timely movie. In the late 1940s, in the wake of revelations about the Holocaust, Americans were first becoming aware of the dangers of anti-Semitism. Aside from *Gentleman's Agreement,* other late 1940s American novels such as Arthur Miller's *Focus* and Saul Bellow's *The Victim* (1947) dealt with the issue, as did another 1947 movie, *Crossfire.*

Gentleman's Agreement: *"Some of my best friends are Jewish." Reporter Phil Green and his mother serve breakfast to returning serviceman Dave Goldman. Copyright 1947 Twentieth Century Fox. Courtesy Museum of Modern Art Films Stills Archive.*

There are four minor Jewish characters in the film, all assimilated Jews, who represent a spectrum of attitudes toward anti-Semitism. First is the quietism advocated by a wealthy Jewish industrialist who advises the magazine editor not to commission the exposé: "It will only stir things up. We'll handle it in our own way." To which the gentile editor responds, "Irving, you and your 'let's be quiet' committee have gotten exactly nowhere." Second is the self-hating Jew, represented by Phil's secretary Elaine Wales, who changed her name from Estelle Walofsky to be hired, who says, "You don't want things changed around here, do you? Just let them hire one wrong one in here and it will come out of us. It's no fun being the fall guy for the kikey ones." When she discovers in the end that Phil is not Jewish, she is amazed. Phil says, "You still can't believe that anybody would give up the glory of being Christian for even eight weeks, can you?" Third is the liberal intellectual, the physicist Lieberman, an Einstein-like figure who says he's not a practicing Jew but stays Jewish because of anti-Semites: "It's a matter of pride." The implication is that Lieberman's ethnic identity is so superficial that it would disappear were there no anti-Semites.[20] Fourth is the fighting Jew, Phil's friend the soldier Dave Goldman. When Dave is called "a yid" by a drunk in a nightclub, he grabs the man and has to be pulled off him. But even Dave is thoroughly assimilated. He displays no ethnic characteristics. "He functions, when bigots leave him alone, quite well in American society, displaying impeccable manners, knowing what wine to order with dinner, and being a combat war hero."[21]

The Jewish characters are secondary. Gregory Peck plays a lone, crusading white liberal saint surrounded by a sea of bigots, similar to the role he would play in *To Kill a Mockingbird* of crusading Southern lawyer. By pretending to be Jewish, Phil becomes a martyr who suffers a series of humiliating snubs from genteel (and gentile) snobs and bigots, culminating in his being escorted out of a restricted resort after the clerk refuses to allow him to register despite his reservation. As he tells his only Jewish friend Dave, "I'm having my nose rubbed in it, and I don't like the smell." Dave tells him, "You're not insulated yet, Phil. It's new every time, so the impact must be quite a business on you. . . . You're concentrating a lifetime into a few weeks. . . . It just telescopes it. Makes it hurt more."

To increase the stakes and to add to audience sympathy, the crusade must not only martyr the white savior but also threaten his family, as it does in later movies such as *To Kill a Mockingbird* and *A Time To Kill*. Phil's mother suffers a stroke (though this is probably not caused by his masquerade, it adds to his stress), his young son comes home crying because his schoolmates called him "a dirty Jew and a stinking kike," and, worst blow of all, his fiancée Kathy breaks off their engagement (she has a last-minute change of heart and they reunite in the happy ending).

Unlike other white masquerade movies, *Gentleman's Agreement* shows the effect of the masquerade on the family. Kathy, the female lead, a lovely, cultivated woman who suggested the magazine do the exposé, is forced to confront her own anti-Semitism. She can't stand the strain of fighting bigots. Phil's liberal friend Anne accuses Kathy of being hypocritical: "The Kathys everywhere are afraid. . . . They haven't got the guts to take the step from talking to action." If anti-Semitism can take root in such an attractive character, then the implication is that it can find a home in anyone. Kathy says, "I'm not going to marry into hothead shouting and nerves"—as if, by impersonating a Jew, Phil has turned into the stereotypical "pushy Jew."

Unfortunately, despite all its good intentions, the film suggests that there is no difference between Christian and Jew, which is an evasion. For Hollywood, ethnicity is superficial, which is why it is so easy for Phil to pass as Jewish. In the Hollywood version of "the melting pot," modern America "will ultimately eliminate ethnic affiliations in favor of universalist identifications," a common, bland Americanness.[22]

The film also tells us nothing about what it is to be Jewish, only about what it is like for a Christian to pretend to be Jewish and to experience the pains of genteel anti-Semitism. As the screenwriter Ring Lardner remarked sarcastically, "The film's lesson? You should never be mean to a Jew because he might turn out to be a gentile."[23] The one who suffers for the cause is the Christian crusader Phil, the white savior. Yet the title of Phil's exposé, "I Was Jewish for Eight Weeks," is unintentionally ludicrous, showing the paltriness of his crusade. The few snubs Phil suffers are trifling, especially considering that this movie comes only two years after the Holocaust.

The film also says nothing about the long struggle against anti-Semitism and other forms of prejudice by many American Jews because the sole crusader here is a Christian. And it turns American anti-Semitism into a problem of the attitude of certain prejudiced individuals, not an institutionalized practice used to police the borders of whiteness and to preserve white privilege.

Gentleman's Agreement was a popular movie, well-crafted to appeal to a large American audience by focusing on the gentile hero. Michael Taub writes that the movie lacks "a central feature one might have expected in major films about anti-Semitism: Jews. . . . the victims themselves barely make the supporting cast. . . . The picture itself studiously avoids dealing with any aspect of Judaism, Jewish culture, or Jewishly committed Jews."[24] There are no scenes in synagogues or in Jewish homes or neighborhoods.

Even 36 years later, Spielberg's *Schindler's List* (1993), although it tells us something about Jewish life in Poland during World War II, follows a similar Hollywood strategy: appeal to the mass audience by focusing on the white Christian hero, the white messiah who stands up for Jews or rescues the Jews.

Black Like Me: The Divided White Liberal

Black Like Me: *A white man learns how to pass for black. Copyright 1964 Walter Reade-Sterling, Inc. Courtesy Museum of Modern Art Films Stills Archive.*

Black Like Me (1964), a film released seventeen years after *Gentleman's Agreement,* relies on a similar premise. Once again, a reporter masquerades in order to write an exposé of racism, and as the hero is educated, so is the audience. Based on a true story by journalist John Howard Griffin, it concerns a writer who temporarily darkens his skin and travels through the American South to find out what it is like to be black. It is another timely film, in this case an anti-racist film during the Civil Rights era.

Because it is based on a real account, it is more downbeat than *Gentleman's Agreement* and also more realistic and psychologically profound. Its hero is not simply a liberal saint on an anti-racist crusade but a tormented soul who suffers an identity crisis because of his masquerade, is relieved finally to return to his whiteness, and is not universally applauded by the black community because of his temporary charade.

Nevertheless, *Black Like Me* is an unsuccessful film, a choppy collection of episodes loosely strung together, offering no dramatic buildup, and painful to watch because it is almost unremittingly tense and downbeat. Although James Whitmore gives a powerful performance, with his thin lips and long thin nose he is so obviously a Caucasian in blackface that we wonder how his masquerade could fool anyone for a minute. (The same is true of the blackface performances in other "passing" movies.) The *Newsweek* reviewer wrote, "There is no moment at which Horton (James Whitmore) even faintly resembles a Negro, indeed, he hardly looks human . . . . For a while, one almost expects him to burst into 'Mammy' a la Jolson."[25]

John Horton's ordeal is far more serious than Phil Green's. Horton attempts to immerse himself in the black community and to learn about the condition of the Southern black man. As he travels from town to town throughout the South, he is cut off from friends and family, terribly isolated, like a spy in enemy country.

The film really concerns the crisis of white liberal identity in the 1960s. Horton says to his wife, "You take away a man's identity, his face, his color—what's left? If you do think of me as some strange black man, how will I know who I am?" In many scenes, he stares at his image in the mirror, as if he can no longer recognize himself. By comparison, Phil Green can look at himself in the mirror with satisfaction; he is still the same man, still recognized and loved by his mother and his son. Whereas Horton, in loneliness and despair, confesses to a priest, "It horrifies me. It's as though I'm no longer myself. . . . It's as though I've lost my immortal soul." The priest, however, tells him, "What you have lost is your pride of self." Horton says, "Now I find myself acting like an inferior colored man. Filled with anger. . . . I'm filled with prejudice, Father. It's like poison. I thought I had purged myself, but I have not."

In *Gentleman's Agreement,* the struggle was external, between the liberal hero and his hypocritical fiancée Kathy, who must confront her own prejudice. But in *Black Like Me,* the struggle is internal, between Horton as liberal saint and Horton as bigot. He is an image of the divided white self. Because the struggle is never satisfactorily resolved, the psychodrama is tense but static.

Like Phil Green, Horton undergoes constant humiliation at the hands of white people. He is treated with suspicion, contempt, prurience, or hatred: bossed around by bus drivers, refused service by ticket clerks, questioned about his sexual activities and supposed sexual prowess, denied jobs that are not menial and dirty, and physically threatened by a band of white thugs. There are a few exceptions—one non-racist Southern white man who picks him up while he is hitchhiking and the understanding priest—but otherwise he is constantly exploited, put down, and even physically assaulted by whites. The movie suggests that a white man would not be able to endure the abuse that a black man sustains every day.

Horton even comes to hate white people, saying, "They're cruel and vicious and they seem to have a million ways of making you feel like nothing." At one point, he becomes so enraged that he starts to throttle a white man, shouting, "You think you can say anything to a man just because his skin is black!"

One problem with the premise of the film is that it assumes that, simply because a white man dyes his skin black, he will automatically have a black experience. As Kate Baldwin writes, "his 'whiteness' always persists in framing his blackness."[26] What's missing for the character is the experience of growing up and being part of the black community, the shared African American history and culture, something also missing in the other movies about whites who pass as black.

In the film, Horton has no culture to sustain him. Even though he lives in the black community, he keeps apart, isolating himself in rented rooms. Once he dances in a nightclub with a black woman who shows interest in him. But because he is a married man and also because he is afraid of exposing his masquerade, he rapidly retreats.

One virtue of the movie is its ending, which undercuts Horton. He reveals the charade to a black family with whom he is living, showing them one of his magazine articles. But instead of congratulating him on his progressivism, the family who had taken him in is deeply offended by his deception. Their son, a Civil Rights activist, says, "You got a lot of nerve comin' in here pretendin' you're folks! . . . . You wipe that blackness off, they'll treat you like a man."

Nevertheless, just as *Gentleman's Agreement* tells us about anti-Semitism but not about Jews, so *Black Like Me* tells us about white racism but not about the black community. Both films center on white heroes and white agony. There is also the arrogant, colonialist assumption that blacks cannot tell their own story but need whites to interpret it for a white audience. "The implication is that it is wiser to let a 'white man' tell the story of the Negroes."[27]

Bird, Silver Steak, and *Trading Places:* Black-Sponsored Masquerade

The white masquerade is rendered acceptable and even comic in some other movies because it is black-sponsored. A lighthearted treatment of white passing occurs in an episode of Clint Eastwood's filmic biography of jazz musician Charlie Parker, *Bird* (1988). Bird hires Red Rodney, a white trumpet player and aficionado of Parker's bebop, to tour with his band. Rodney is at first terrified they will be lynched because this integrated band will travel through the deep South in the 1950s, but Bird arrives at an ingenious solution, advertising "The Charlie Parker band, featuring 'Albino Red ,'" passing off Rodney as a pigment-deprived African-American. Bird even encourages this white boy to get up and sing the blues. The effect is comic.

Robert Stam, however, criticizes *Bird* because it "downplays the role of a supportive minoritarian community composed of such fellow musicians as Thelonius Monk, Miles Davis, Charles Mingus, and Max Roach in favor of the black-white buddy film evoked by the Bird-Rodney relationship."[28]

The white masquerade is also legitimized by being black-sponsored in *Silver Steak* (1976). The film is a rehash of Hitchcock's *North by Northwest* (1959): a middle-class white businessman is falsely accused of murder aboard a coast-to-coast train. The story is mildly amusing but derivative until the supremely talented Richard Pryor enters and kicks it into another gear. The pairing of white comic Gene Wilder and black comic Pryor was so successful that they subsequently co-starred in several more film comedies. When Wilder steals a police car, he finds the thief Pryor in the back seat. Pryor aids his escape, saying, "Open your eyes, now, 'cause I'm gonna make a criminal out of you yet." The street-smart black man who befriends and educates the naïve white man and enables him to survive outside the law is a staple of American literature and film since *Huckleberry Finn.*

For example, when Wilder's picture is splashed across the front page of the papers as a wanted man, the quick-witted Pryor improvises to rescue his white buddy, just like

Charlie Parker did. He has him blacken his face with shoe polish and teaches him to act black. Wilder at first objects strenuously, but Pryor tells him, "Al Jolson made a million bucks looking like that." Wilder's spastic attempt to imitate a black man makes for the film's funniest scene. Nevertheless, it is an instance of what Ed Guerrero calls Hollywood "neominstrelsy."[29] The encouragement of the black sidekick and his joke about Jolson merely disguise the movie's reversion to the minstrel tradition.

Silver Streak: *"Al Jolson made a million bucks looking like that."* Copyright 1976 20th Century Fox.

Silver Streak further reinforces racial stereotypes, because the only black characters are a servile Pullman porter, a shoeshine man, and a thief. Pryor's character is subordinated to and at the service of his white buddy, which was not the case in *Bird*. Pryor has no reason to aid Wilder once Pryor has crossed the state line and escaped the law. In fact, he is putting himself unnecessarily at risk by continuing to aid his white buddy. This repeats the sincere fiction that the white hero deserves the sacrifice of the loyal black man.

A similar premise—street-smart black con man befriends naïve white man and enables him to survive outside the law—is repeated in *Trading Places* (1983). In this *Prince and the Pauper* scenario, Winthorp (Dan Aykroyd), a stuffy, white commodities broker, is thrown out on the streets and replaced in his home and job by Billy Ray Valentine (Eddie Murphy), a black street hustler.

Winthorp runs amok and vows revenge on Valentine, until Valentine reveals that both of them have been guinea pigs in a malicious game rigged by Winthorp's super-rich white employers, the elderly Duke brothers, who are betting on the relative effects of heredity versus environment. Winthorp and Valentine, white and black, then join forces in a scheme to get revenge on the Dukes.

Their stratagem involves disguising their identities, so Winthorp puts on blackface and dreadlocks and briefly passes as Jamaican. As in *Silver Streak,* the black criminal enables his uptight white buddy to succeed by loosening him up and making him into an outlaw. Once again, the masquerade is acceptable and funny because it is done out of desperation and because it is initiated by the black buddy.

As in *Silver Streak,* blacks are assumed to be con artists, natural performers who can teach whites how to perform. Nevertheless, Valentine performs out of necessity and all the time. In the course of the film, he succeeds by leaving the black world and learning how to perform successfully in the white world. As Susan Gubar points out, "racial impersonation and masquerading are a destiny imposed on colonized black people who *must* wear the white mask."[30] Winthorp's racial masquerade, however, is only temporary, until he can win back his white privileges.

As in *Silver Streak,* there is no reason for the black man to go out of his way to aid the white. In fact, Valentine has abundant reasons to dislike Winthorp: first, Winthrop had Valentine arrested for a theft he did not commit. Later, Winthorp attacks Valentine and attempts to disgrace him by planting drugs in his desk.

Despite all this, Valentine befriends him, they collaborate to get even and to get rich, bankrupt the Duke brothers, and retire to a Caribbean island. The film epitomizes Wall Street insider trading of the 1980s, but the corruption (and the racism) is conveniently displaced onto the old establishment, two elderly white villains. As Alan Nadel claims, *Trading Places* is a cynical Reagan-era movie in which "greed is good" and all the characters are hustlers engaging in illegal activities to get rich.[31] The combination of black street smarts and white insider trading triumphs. If the film celebrates blackness, it is only because, like *Silver Streak,* it believes that blacks are superior hustlers and can teach those skills to their white buddies, who will profit from being thus "blackened."

Soul Man: Criminal Masquerade

When the white masquerade is not sponsored by a black man, it must eventually be legitimized by gaining black acceptance and approval—otherwise, the film has no happy ending, as in *Black Like Me. Soul Man* (1986) is a case in point: this movie treats a criminal masquerade by a Harvard law student as a lark. "Unlike . . . *Black Like Me, Soul Man* uses blackface to portray the issue of crossing the color line as a farcical, frat-boy romp."[32] The dubious ethics of this movie are similar to those of *Trading Places* (1983) and *Risky Business* (1983), another Reagan-era movie in which a high school boy becomes a pimp and profits from his crime by admission into Princeton.[33] One of the assumptions of white privilege is that rich young white men can break the rules with impunity and be rewarded for their initiative.

The plot and the humor of *Soul Man* only make sense in a society where white privilege is the unquestioned norm. The story concerns Mark Watson, a young white man admitted to Harvard Law School but unable to attend because his rich father arbitrarily refuses to fund his education any further. He finds no scholarships for which he qualifies, but there is a scholarship for a black student for which there are evidently no eligible candidates. As the president of the Beverly Hills/Hollywood chapter of NAACP pointed out, the film presumes that "in the whole of the metropolitan area of Los Angeles, with literally hundreds of thousands of African Americans, not one of them is academically qualified for a black scholarship to law school."[34]

Mark takes some pills that darken his skin, dons an Afro wig, and wins the minority scholarship.

Soul Man: *Getting a college scholarship: one of the advantages of passing as black. Copyright 1986 New World Pictures. Courtesy Museum of Modern Art Films Stills Archive.*

The film plays on 1980s white American resentment of the effects of affirmative action.[35] White privilege was no longer automatically guaranteed, and many whites decried this changed set of circumstances as unfair, so-called reverse discrimination, as in the Bakke case against the University of California. Such sentiments would pave the way for the repeal of affirmative action in California and other states in the 1990s.

Although that is the unspoken subtext of the film, the hero is presented not as racist but as naïve. At the start of his masquerade, he says, "These are the '80s. It's the Cosby decade. America loves black people"—thereby confusing a television show with real life. Initially, Mark is an obnoxious character, arrogant and impudent with white privilege. In the course of the narrative, he must learn better. Despite his arrogance, he is also presented as ingenious and resourceful, a sympathetic character.

While posing as black, Mark makes it with Whitney, the daughter of his rich white landlord. Whitney is an opportunist who only sleeps with men of color; she is writing her senior thesis on civil rights. She brings him home for dinner with her wealthy family. In a burlesque scene, each family member projects onto Mark the stereotype he or she wants to see: to the mother, he is a black rapist who is passionate for her; to the young son, he is a rock musician; and to the father, he is a watermelon-eating pimp. Margaret M. Russell complains, "Since Mark is clearly not black and not in a subordinate role to anyone, I was left with the sense that Mark's dilettantish exposure to racism in this scene was somehow equated with blacks' everyday experiences with racists."[36]

One could compare this fantasy scene to one in Woody Allen's *Annie Hall* (1977), from which it borrows: Alvy Singer (Woody Allen), the Jewish hero, is taken by his gentile girlfriend Annie Hall (Diane Keaton) to her family home for dinner. In the eyes of her grandmother, whom Alvy calls "a classic Jew hater," he suddenly turns into a Hasid garbed in black, with a long beard. Unlike *Soul Man*, the *Annie Hall* scene has a satiric bite because we are aware that both Woody Allen and the character he plays are Jewish, not simply masquerading as Jewish.

Stupid bigots such as Whitney's father and the super of Mark's apartment building are included as comic foils, racist buffoons to make Mark look by comparison like a model of tolerance. Such a message, Russell mentions, "discourages viewers from recognizing that often bigotry wears a mask not burlesque-style and latent, but subtle and insidious."[37]

As in *Gentleman's Agreement* and *Black Like Me,* the hero must be educated by being subjected to racial harassment. Two white classmates make racist jokes in Mark's presence. He is arrested for "driving while black" and then beaten in the jail cell by white prisoners. And he is evicted from his apartment. But all these indignities are presented as comic inconveniences, not as the serious matters they are in *Gentleman's Agreement* and *Black Like Me.*

Mark interacts with two major black characters. One is a law professor played by James Earl Jones, who, except for skin color, is the imperious, hard-as-nails law professor played by John Houseman in *The Paper Chase* (1973)—another film from which this movie steals. The presence of Jones, a gifted actor, as the sole law professor in the film obscures the fact that blacks are not really part of the Harvard establishment. As Patricia Williams, an African American law professor, writes, "My abiding recollection of being a student at Harvard Law School is the sense of being invisible. . . . The school created a dense atmosphere that muted my voice to inaudibility."[38]

The opportunistic Mark takes the class because he assumes a black professor will show him favoritism. But the professor quickly makes his position clear: "You will get no special treatment from me, Mr. Watson. . . . And if that means you have to work twice as hard as those little white shits . . ."

Nevertheless, at the end of the film, after Mark's masquerade has been exposed, the professor absolves him. "You must have learned a great deal more than you bargained for through this experience, Mr. Watson. . . . You've learned what it feels like to be black."

But the newly humble Mark says, "No, sir. I don't really know what it feels like, sir. I could always get out. It's not the same, sir."

The professor responds, "You've learned a great deal more than I thought. . . . I won't press charges. You can stay."

Here the dialogue given to the black radical in *Black Like Me*—"You wipe that blackness off, they'll treat you like a man"—is instead delivered by the white hero. And the black professor clears the hero of all blame for his criminal masquerade and even praises him.

The other major black character is Sarah Walker, a pretty young law student who provides the romantic interest. Sarah, a smart, hardworking, principled woman, is made to look particularly good by contrast to the shallow, rich white woman Whitney. Sarah is further rendered sympathetic as a single mother raising a young son; she works in the university cafeteria to support her child and pay her tuition.

Mark becomes conscience stricken when he discovers that his masquerade deprived Sarah of the minority scholarship. He makes reparations: in order to stay at Harvard, he promises to pay Sarah back with interest, to volunteer legal aid to the black community, and to establish a scholarship in Sarah's name.

In the end, Mark is working in the cafeteria, like Sarah before him. He has sold his car, paid her back, and taken a loan from his father. Sarah nevertheless tells Mark she is not interested in an interracial relationship and gets up to leave. Conveniently, Mark is given a chance to play hero: he slugs two white guys who make a racist joke. Just as abruptly, Sarah changes her mind about him. Through this contrivance, the film attempts to reverse American history: when white men have injured black women, they have not usually attempted to undo the harm. Historically, this has not been the basis for interracial love affairs.

The film labors hard to contrive a happy ending by converting Mark from a shallow con man into a redeemed sinner. Mark must be absolved by the black community: he not only receives a pat on the back from the professor but also wins the love of Sarah and her little boy. The solution to racism, the film implies, is to educate the white man so he becomes more aware of what it means to be black. But the film never questions white privilege or the justice of the white establishment. White Harvard Law School graduates only appear to be shallow, racist opportunists; actually, they are good guys.

Mark perpetrates a criminal masquerade that makes a mockery of the black experience and is rewarded with a Harvard law degree and the love of a black woman. "*Soul Man*'s comic effectiveness depends upon the viewer's willingness to accept racial stereotypes as comedy and racial identity as a gag."[39] The black community was offended by this neominstrelsy, and the film was not a commercial success.[40]

The Jerk: Adopted into the Tribe

The white masquerade is also black-sponsored in *The Jerk* (1979), a comedy in which the simpleminded white hero has been adopted by a poor Southern black family and is not even aware at first that he is white. The film plays on the comic incongruity of a white man being raised by a black family. The comedian Steve Martin plays Navin Johnson, who begins the film as a homeless man in an alley. He tells the audience, "I'm not a bum. I'm a jerk. . . . It was never easy for me. I was born a poor black child."

In a flashback to his childhood, we see the black family all happily dancing on the front porch, except that the lone white Navin is hopelessly out of step. Like Martin Mull's droll, made-for-television "mockumentary," *The History of White People in America* (1985), the film makes fun of whites' lack of rhythm and blandness. The comic implication is that whites' impaired rhythm and preference for tasteless food and elevator music is genetic. For example, at Navin's birthday party, the family gives him his favorite foods: Twinkies, tuna fish on white bread, and a Tab.

Navin cries because he doesn't fit in. Then his parents reveal the big secret: "You're not our natural-born child."

Navin says, "You mean, I'm gonna stay this color?"

That night, he hears elevator music on a radio station from a distant city and discovers that he can move to white rhythms. He announces to the family, "I've never heard music like this before! It speaks to me." So he heads out into the white world. His father gives him some ironic parting advice: "Don't never ever trust Whitey."

The film follows the foolish, good-hearted Navin through his misadventures, a series of loosely connected comic episodes tied together by Navin's voice-over narration and letters home, which the family reads aloud. He falls in love, accidentally makes his fortune through an invention, then loses both the woman and all his money and winds up on the streets. But he is rescued in the end by his family. His adoptive father had invested the money Navin sent home and grown rich.

The final scene echoes the opening: the jerk Navin, who was helpless against the white world, has returned to his loving family, where he always belonged, and once again all are dancing on the front porch, this time in an improved Southern shack. Navin's white wife has also rejoined him.

Like Forrest Gump, Navin is a guileless simpleton and therefore assumed to be incapable of racism. Yet the film nevertheless plays on the stereotype of poor black people who are always happy and dancing and on the sincere fiction that whites will always be taken care of by nurturing blacks.

Mark Winokur argues that *The Jerk* harks back to the minstrel tradition and is not mocking whiteness but blackness, not the white who tries to pass but the black: "The Martin role goes back to Zip Coon, the black man trying to imitate the white dandy without understanding the social configurations in which he is trying to place himself. Martin is a version of a black trying to pass for white, a man who looks white yet who does not fit into white culture. He even makes the traditional choice of *Pinky* and *Imitation of Life* to return to his people as a prodigal son. As the audience knows he is white, he is safe to laugh at as were the original white minstrels."[41] *The Jerk* is another instance of neominstrelsy and Navin is yet another "white negro."

Notes

1. Horney, Karen. 1945. *Our Inner Conflicts: A Constructive Theory of Neurosis.* New York: W. W. Norton, p. 108.

2. Russell, Margaret M. 1997. "Race and the Dominant Gaze: Narratives of Law and Order," in *Critical White Studies: Looking Behind the Mirror,* eds. Richard Delgado and Jean Stefancic. Philadelphia, Pa.: Temple University Press, pp. 267–72 (p. 268).

3. Lott, Eric. 1993. *Love and Theft: Blackface Minstrelsy and the American Working Class.* New York: Oxford University Press, p. 55.

4. Baldwin, James. 1961. *Nobody Knows My Name; More Notes of a Native Son.* New York: Dial Press, p. 231.

5. Ibid., p. 228.

6. Lott, *Love and Theft*, p. 53.

7. Fiedler, Leslie A. 1964. *Waiting for the End.* New York: Stein & Day, p. 134.

8. Baldwin, Kate. 1998. "Black Like Who? Cross-Testing the 'Real' Lines of John Howard Griffin's *Black Like Me,*" *Cultural Critique* 40: 1033–43 (p. 1034).

9. Gubar, Susan. 1997. *Race Changes: White Skin, Black Face in American Culture.* New York: Oxford University Press, p. 13.

10. Marchetti, Gina. 1993. *Romance and the "Yellow Peril": Race, Sex, and Discursive Strategies in Hollywood Fiction.* Berkeley: University of California Press, p. 187.

11. Ibid., p. 176.

12. Butler, Judith. 1990. *Gender Trouble: Feminism and the Subversion of Identity.* New York: Routledge, p. 137.

13. Ibid., p. 139.

14. Bhabha, Homi K. 1994. *The Location of Culture.* New York: Routledge, p. 86.

15. Gubar, *Race Changes*, p. 44.

16. Dyer, Richard. 1997. *White.* New York: Routledge, p. 49.

17. Wald, Gayle. 2000. *Crossing the Line: Racial Passing in Twentieth-Century U.S. Literature and Culture.* Durham, N.C.: Duke University Press, p. 162.

18. Brodkin, Karen. 1998. *How Jews Became White Folks and What That Says about Race in America.* New Brunswick, N.J.: Rutgers University Press, p.76.

19. Ibid., p. 37.

20. Friedman, Lester D. 1991. *Unspeakable Images: Ethnicity and the American Cinema.* Urbana: University of Illinois Press, p. 25.

21. Ibid.

22. Friedman, *Unspeakable Images*, pp. 24–25.

23. Taub, Michael. 1998. "Tastefully Pareve: Hollywood Confronts Anti-Semitism." *Jewish Spectator,* Summer 1998, pp. 41–44 (p. 43).

24. Ibid., p. 42.

25. *Newsweek*. 1964. "Cliché Odyssey." May 25, 110.

26. Baldwin, Kate, "Black Like Who?" p. 114.

27. Ibid., p. 120.

28. Stam, Robert. 1991. "Bakhtin, Polyphony, and Ethnic/Racial Representation," in *Unspeakable Images: Ethnicity and the American Cinema*, ed. Lester D. Friedman. Urbana: University of Illinois Press, pp. 251–76 (p. 253).

29. Guerrero, Ed. 1993. *Framing Blackness: the African American Image in Film*. Philadelphia, Pa.: Temple University Press, p. 122.

30. Gubar, *Race Changes*, p. 38.

31. Nadel, Alan. 1997. *Flatlining on the Field of Dreams: Cultural Narratives in the Films of President Reagan's America*. New Brunswick, N.J.: Rutgers University Press, pp. 29–47.

32. Russell, "Race and the Dominant Gaze," p. 271.

33. Gordon, Andrew, and Hernán Vera. 1994. "The *Risky Business* of Being *Home Alone*," in *Literature and Psychology: Proceedings of the Tenth International Conference on Literature and Psychology, Amsterdam*. ed. Frederico Pereira. Lisbon: Instituto Superior de Psicologia Aplicada, pp. 241–52.

34. Guerrero, *Framing Blackness*, pp. 124–25.

35. Russell, "Race and the Dominant Gaze," p. 269.

36. Ibid, p. 271.

37. Ibid.

38. Williams, Patricia J. 1991. *The Alchemy of Race and Rights*. Cambridge, Mass.: Harvard University Press, p. 55.

39. Russell, p. 270.

40. Guerrero, *Framing Blackness*, p. 124.

41. Winokur, Mark. 1991. "Black is White/White is Black: 'Passing' as Strategy of Racial Compatibility in Contemporary Hollywood Comedy," in *Unspeakable Images: Ethnicity and the American Cinema*, ed. Lester D. Friedman. Urbana: University of Illinois Press, pp. 190–211, (p. 203).

CHAPTER 9

White Out: Racial Masquerade by Whites in American Film II

Films Analyzed:
Little Big Man (1970)
Dances with Wolves (1990)
Bulworth (1998)
Finian's Rainbow (1968)
The Watermelon Man (1970)
Zelig (1984)

Little Big Man: Deconstructing Whiteness

White Americans have a profound yearning to be accepted and loved by blacks, despite or perhaps because of their historical mistreatment of African Americans. They long for the loyal, unquestioning friendship of the slave Jim or the forgiving embrace of the black mammy. Something similar occurs with the white romance with Native Americans, exemplified by James Fenimore Cooper's Mohican Chief Chingachgook, the Lone Ranger's faithful companion Tonto, and the lovely Indian princess. To some extent, whites also romanticize and romance Asian Americans and Mexican Americans, but it is the two groups who historically have been worst treated at the hands of whites—the black victims of slavery and the Native American victims of genocide—who are the special objects of white romantic fantasies. Apparently, the greater the burden of guilt, the greater the need to assuage or deny it: "Going native articulates and attempts to resolve widespread ambivalence about modernity as well as anxieties about the terrible violence marking the nation's origins."[1]

Even as they oppressed or exterminated Indians, ever since the Boston Tea Party, white Americans have also been playing Indian as a way to overcome their racial guilt and also to claim an American identity and to assert manhood. For, in the white unconscious, the Indian is somehow male and the black is female. Writes Philip J. Deloria, "Americans had a long history of imagining and claiming an Indianness that was about being indigenous, free, white, and male. Their understandings of African American identity, however, circled around contrasting notions—importation, enslavement, and a sometimes-feminized blackness."[2]

Little Big Man: *Jack and Chief Old Lodge Skins, his adoptive father. Copyright 1970 National General Pictures. Courtesy Museum of Modern Art Films Stills Archive.*

Adoption into the family of people of another color, as we have seen, is one strategy to legitimize white masquerade. The device originates in nineteenth-century American popular literature in James Fenimore Cooper's fictions about Natty Bumppo, a white man adopted by the Mohican tribe, who combines the supposed best of both white and Native American culture. Aside from the many cinematic adaptations of Cooper's *The Last of the Mohicans,* two such narratives of white men who are adopted into the tribe and pass for Indian are *Little Big Man* (1970) and *Dances with Wolves* (1990). "Hollywood and post–World War II Euro-Americans appear to rediscover our genocidal treatment of Native Americans every twenty years."[3]

Little Big Man is based on the 1964 novel by Thomas Berger, part of a wave of satiric, black humor fictions of the 1960s that mix fact and fantasy to revise American history, including *The Sot-Weed Factor* (1960) by John Barth, about colonial Maryland, and *Catch-22* (1961) by Joseph Heller and *Slaughterhouse-Five* (1969) by Kurt Vonnegut Jr., both about World War II. These novels all feature bumbling anti-heroes and debunk heroic myths of American history.

The film *Little Big Man,* directed by Arthur Penn, is very much a product of the late 1960s, a radical critique of whiteness unprecedented in Hollywood film up to that point. Its deconstruction of American whiteness is connected with its indirect critique of American imperialism and colonialism. The ostensible subject of the film is the extermination of the Indians, but its real subject is the Vietnam War, then ongoing, that seemed an extension of white American genocidal expansion parallel to what happened in the nineteenth-century settling of the West. "The moral emptiness of white American society is a primary theme of the film, developed narratively and visually through the motif of the massacre."[4]

The 1960s youth counterculture reacted not only against America's conduct in the war in Vietnam but also against their own white, middle-class identity by identifying strongly with oppressed minorities whom they romanticized, such as the Viet Cong, African Americans, and Native Americans. The hippies even adopted Indian garb and envisioned themselves as a communal, tribal culture. The critique of white savagery and the romanticization of Native Americans in *Little Big Man* was so popular with the youth market that the movie had the second highest box-office gross in America in 1970.

In its scathing satire on whiteness and sympathy for the Cheyenne, *Little Big Man* is light years beyond even a revisionist western such as John Ford's *Cheyenne Autumn* (1964), released only six years earlier. Unlike Ford, director Penn cast a Native American, Chief Dan George, in a central role as the Cheyenne chief. Dan George was nominated for an Academy Award as Best Supporting Actor for his performance.

Race in *Little Big Man* is seen as a cultural construct, a product of upbringing and training. The problem of the protagonist, Jack Crabb, is that he has undergone two completely contradictory sets of training: first as a white man and then as a Cheyenne brave. The 121-year-old Jack, living in a Veterans Administration hospital in contemporary America, is the sole white survivor of the massacre at Little Big Horn. He tells his story in voice-over narration to an interviewer, a naïve white man. Jack is ten years old when his parents are killed by the Pawnee. He and his sister are adopted by the Cheyenne. His sister escapes, but Jack remains and is raised by them. "For a boy, it was a kind of paradise. I wasn't just playing Indian; I was living Indian," Jack says, as he is shown astride his pony, galloping freely across the plains.

As he becomes a man, the confused and divided Jack shuttles continually between Cheyenne and white identities. "Jack's *achievements* are Cheyenne, his *aspirations* are white."[5] Although Jack accepts "the myth of progress and civilization, the myth of white culture that steamrolled the West. . . . he finds the reality inexorably disappointing."[6] The film makes it clear that there is no way for Jack to be a successful white man because success in the white world would contradict all the values he learned as a Native American. Unlike the other whites, he can't be a hypocrite, an Indian hater, or a killer. He tries a gamut of white male careers—as hymn singer, gunslinger, con man, businessman, Army scout, drunk, and hermit—and fails every time.[7] The only time he is happy is when he lives with the Cheyenne, who call themselves "the Human Beings" and are the only humans worthy of the name in the story.

Little Big Man satirizes white masculinity and idealizes Cheyenne masculinity. The epitome of the Cheyenne philosophy is old Chief Old Lodge Skins, Jack's adoptive father. He is the film's ideal man: virile, compassionate, generous, and possessed of a balanced, positive vision of the world. He has the key speeches in the film and remains the only sane, stable, loving figure in Jack's mad world, so Jack returns to him repeatedly. The dignity, grace, and sanity of the Chief are contrasted to the sickness, corruption, and evil of the white men.

When young Jack asks why white men would kill women and children, the old Chief replies, "Because they're strange. They do not seem to know where the center of the earth is. We must have war on these cowards to teach them a lesson." He knows whites are crazy, and he even has his doubts about the blacks: "The black white man . . . not as ugly as the white, but just as crazy." Even after the Battle of Little Big Horn, the Chief is pessimistic about the eventual outcome of the struggle: "You cannot get rid of them. There is an endless supply of white men. But there has always been a limited number of Human Beings. We won today. We won't win tomorrow. . . . It makes me sad. A world without Human Beings has no center to it."

Contrasted to Old Lodge Skins are the white role models who also serve as father figures to Jack: the Reverend Pendrake, a fundamentalist religious bigot and sadist; the snake oil salesman Meriweather, a con artist and a nihilist; Wild Bill Hickok, a gunslinger killer, in a perpetual state of paranoia; and General George Armstrong Custer, a military leader and Indian killer. The attributes of the white male self in this movie thus include religious intolerance, sadism, greed, nihilism, paranoia, egomania, unbridled ambition, racist hatred, and the urge to commit genocide. Reverend Pendrake has the nerve to say, "The Indians know nothing of God and moral right" when he knows nothing of the Indians. The swindler Meriweather directly contradicts the teachings of Old Lodge Skins, telling Jack, "He gave you a vision of moral order in the universe, and there isn't any." Only Hickok has some redeeming characteristics: at least he is kind to Jack and to Louise Pendrake, and he kills only in self-defense.

The epitome of the white self, the whitest of them all, is the blond Custer, who is introduced as a messiah figure surrounded by a halo of sunlight that blinds and dazzles Jack. Gazing at Custer is like staring into the sun. Jack at first idolizes Custer, telling Old Lodge Skins, "Grandfather, all the whites aren't crazy. [General Custer] is as brave as any Human Being."

Custer is presented as a stupid, murderous fool, suffering from delusions of grandeur. Custer, who is almost always wrong, believes he is invincible and omniscient. Jack blindly follows Custer's advice ("Go West. You have nothing to fear from the Indians. You have my personal guarantee.") straight into disaster.

Later Jack comes to hate him after Custer leads the slaughter of his tribe. The massacre by the Washita River, in which Jack watches helplessly as Custer's men gun down Jack's Cheyenne wife and child, is the most shocking scene in the movie. It may well have reminded 1970 viewers of the 1969 My Lai massacre in Vietnam, in which U.S. army soldiers, led by Lt. William L. Calley Jr., slaughtered women and children.[8] The fife and drum music that opens the scene evokes previous Western movies, except that, ironically, here the U.S. Cavalry is not riding to the rescue but to massacre the innocent. The fife and drums are reprised later when Custer leads his men to their doom as they charge into the valley of Little Big Horn, which becomes the Indians' revenge for the previous massacres.

The Battle of Little Big Horn in Montana in 1876, in which Custer and his entire command of 225 men were wiped out by Lakota Sioux and Cheyenne warriors, was one of the most famous events in frontier history, an archetypal, traumatic defeat that resonates in American history like Pearl Harbor.[9] Custer and Little Big Horn have been celebrated repeatedly in American popular culture in many works and represented in numerous movies, from silent films to the present day. Most of these movies glorify Custer as a heroic martyr for the cause of white civilization.[10]

The scathingly satiric view of Custer in *Little Big Man* is a bracing corrective to these previous mythic representations. Custer stands exposed as a vain, pompous ass, an ambitious, crazy fool responsible for leading his men to their doom. His stupidity is expressed through his belief that he is suffering from "poison from the goonads [sic]" and his certainty that he is always right. Custer's grandiose notion of himself as a Western hero is shown in his costume: by Little Big Horn, he has abandoned a military uniform for a dramatic outfit of yellow buckskin with a flowing red neckerchief, like a cowboy in a Wild West show. As his men are cut down around him, he can't believe what is happening: "We're being wiped out! Poor Christian America—wiped out by savages!" He stands alone, an isolated figure, and he retreats into raving madness. In his delusion, he starts to address the president and the Senate. When the wounded Jack tells him to shut up, Custer prepares to execute him, mistaking Jack for his hated rival, President Grant.

But the Cheyenne brave Younger Bear kills Custer and rescues Jack, repaying the life he owes Jack, who once saved him from a Pawnee. Thus Jack, whose white self had always fought with his Cheyenne self, is betrayed by a white man but saved by a Cheyenne.

Custer's madness, which is evil and lethal, contrasts to Jack's madness, which is benign. Jack goes temporarily crazy because he is forced to live in the mad white world. Custer proves the truth of Old Lodge Skin's assertion: "The Human Beings believe everything is alive. . . . But the white men, they believe everything is dead. . . . If things keep trying to live, the white men will rub them out." Custer, who indiscriminately slaughters everything—men, women, children, and horses—represents white death. As Richard Dyer says of the horror film *The Night of the Living Dead* (1969), another critique of whiteness that came out the year before *Little Big Man,* "Whites are dead, bring death, and cannot stand that others live."[11]

In *Little Big Man,* the portrait of Custer represents the New Left's revulsion with the American government in Vietnam and with white civilization circa 1970, which it sees as an imperialist power suffering delusions of grandeur and destroying not only racial others but the white self through genocidal madness.

For all its critique of the myths of whiteness, *Little Big Man* depends on other myths and romanticizes the past.[12] It also romanticizes native Americans[13] and replicates the traditional split in the white view of Native Americans as "noble savages" (the Cheyenne) versus "savage savages" (the Pawnee).[14]

Penn views the nineteenth-century Cheyenne through the lens of the 1960s white counterculture, projecting upon them white countercultural values. For example, an orgy in a teepee where Jack, at his wife's urging, beds her three sisters, suggests that the Cheyenne practiced 1960s-style free love. "In reality Cheyenne women were constrained by strictly maintained rules of chastity."[15]

Finally, like all the other movies about whites passing as racial others, although *Little Big Man* may be sympathetic to the other race, it ultimately views Native Americans from a white perspective, since Jack, the protagonist and voice-over narrator, is a white man. There is a danger in turning the Indian into "a mere substitute for . . . hippie white youth alienated from the modern mainstream of American society."[16]

Dances with Wolves: Sensitive New-Age Guy

Dances with Wolves uses realism, rather than satire, to bring a critical perspective to nineteenth-century white-Indian relations. The film is filled with realistic details so that the plot seems plausible within its historical frame, and the protagonist is an active, heroic figure rather than the largely passive bystander, victim, and antihero of *Little Big Man,* nor are the other characters ridiculed.

Yet beneath the realistic surface, *Dances with Wolves* is no more a history lesson than *Little Big Man;* it is another myth for its times, and a highly romanticized and sentimental myth at that. The film relates the story of Lt. John Dunbar, a brave officer of the Union Army who is wounded in the Civil War and then reassigned at his request to an isolated Western frontier outpost, which he mans alone. Dunbar makes friends with a nearby tribe of Lakota Sioux. In gradual stages, he joins the tribe, in the process relinquishing entirely his identity as a U.S. Army soldier and a white man, becoming instead his best self, totally committed to wife, community, and friends. By the end of the film, the Sioux Chief Ten Bears tells him, "The man the soldiers look for no longer exists. Now there is only a Sioux, Dances with Wolves."

Leslie Fiedler explains that "primitivism is the large generic name for the Higher Masculine Sentimentality, a passionate commitment to inverting Christian-Humanist values, out of a conviction that the Indian's way of life is preferable. . . . From this follows the belief that. . . if one is White, he should do his best, despite all pressures of the historical past, to go Native."[17] If *Little Big Man* does not reflect the Native American in the 1860s and 1870s but the white male desire to go Indian in the American 1960s out of revulsion with the Vietnam War, then neither is *Dances with Wolves* about white-Indian relations during the 1860s but rather about the white male desire to go native in the 1990s, the era of the men's movement. *Dances with Wolves* tries to reconcile incompatible masculine desires to be both a macho warrior and a "sensitive New-Age guy" by uniting both in the old, white American myth of the noble savage, the Native American. "Lt. Dunbar is very appealing to today's audiences precisely because he is a 1990s man, not an 1860s white man. Dunbar is for the Baby Boomer generation the disillusioned soldier seeking personal redemption in a wilderness experience. Could Dances With Wolves be the messiah the New Agers are seeking to lead the white man back to a balanced physical and spiritual embrace with the earth, our mother?"[18] Native Americans are secondary to the narrative. Like in *Glory* and *Little Big Man*, the narrative is controlled by the hero's voice-over and concerns the redemption of a white man.

The movie opens with the wounded Lt. Dunbar about to have his foot amputated in a filthy, bloody Civil War battlefield hospital. Preferring death to dismemberment, he painfully struggles back into his boots and rides a horse across enemy lines and back again, making himself an easy target. The men cheer his mad charge, and it sparks them into battle, ending a standoff between the opposing troops. The white men's battle is portrayed as pointless and absurd, in contrast to the Sioux battles seen later in the film.

Miraculously, Dunbar survives. Through this opening scene, Dunbar has symbolically risked castration and death and been reborn. "Costner's film can be interpreted as a shamanistic allegory of symbolic death and rebirth. From this perspective, Dunbar in fact 'dies' in his suicidal ride."[19]

In voice-over narration, Dunbar tells us, "The strangeness of this life cannot be measured. In trying to produce my own death, I was elevated to the status of a living hero." The opening establishes Dunbar as a man of standing, successful within white culture, although through no intention of his own. This is significant because he will later abandon this successful identity as a white army officer.

Dunbar is on a quest. We next see him arrive on horseback at Fort Hayes in the West. He tells the commanding officer, "I'm here at my own request. I wanted to see the frontier. Before it's gone." Emphasizing the quest, the officer says, "Sir Knight. I am sending you on a knight's errand."

But right after Dunbar leaves, the officer commits suicide by shooting himself. Dunbar is unaware of the suicide of his commanding officer or of the murder of his guide Timmons, who is killed by the Pawnee after he leaves Dunbar at his post. The Army is thus ignorant of Dunbar's presence at the abandoned Fort Sedgewick on the prairie. Through these circumstances, Dunbar is cut off, a lone man at an isolated frontier outpost, which enables him to interact by himself with the Indians.

He doesn't mind the isolation, for he seems to have no friends or family, and he enjoys communing with nature. He longed to see the frontier, and its beauty does not disappoint him. "Dunbar, we sense, is a man dissatisfied with American civilization."[20]

There is little that is attractive in the white civilization presented in the film: the filthy, bloody hospital; the pointless slaughter of war; a lunatic commanding officer who wets his pants and kills himself; and the crude wagon master Timmons, who spits and farts and stuffs his mouth with food and whom Dunbar calls, "Quite possibly the foulest man I have ever met." When Dunbar arrives at Fort Sedgewick, it is deserted and in a shambles. In contrast to all this, the most seductive aspect of the film is its romantic view of the West, which depends on gorgeous, sweeping panoramas of the wide open spaces, the Badlands and the prairie, set to stirring music. Typically, the camera will pull back to an extreme long shot of a tiny wagon crossing the plains or an idyllic Lakota village set against a riverside.

The movie presents a sympathetic, albeit highly romanticized view of the Lakota Sioux. The people of the tribe are played by Indian actors, although not all are Sioux. They speak in Lakota with subtitles, and in a few scenes Dunbar isn't present at all. When he momentarily disappears as observer or narrator, suddenly the Sioux are not framed though white eyes, and it is suggested that the audience is seeing the Indians on their own terms. In the council meetings, for example, the braves speak of whites as dirty and weak.

Nevertheless, the film presents a liberal white perspective on Native Americans, who supposedly live in harmony with nature, as contrasted to the corruption, viciousness, waste, and greed of white society. As in *Little Big Man,* whites represent the "death" principle, signified here by the senseless killing of animals. When Dunbar first arrives at his outpost, he discovers a dead elk polluting the pond, a sign of the pointless destructiveness of white civilization. Toward the end of the film, white soldiers shoot Dunbar's beloved horse Cisco, and, just for sport, kill his pet wolf Two Socks. In another scene, when he is hunting buffalo with the Sioux, they come on a field littered with the skinned bodies of buffalo, killed only for their hides and tongues, whereas the Lakota Sioux use every part of the animal. In voice-over, he says, "Who would do such a thing? . . . a people without value and without soul, with no regard for Sioux rights. . . . My heart sank as I knew it could only be white hunters." This scene corresponds to the one in *Little Big Man* when young Jack asks why white men would kill women and children, and the Chief says, "Because they're strange. They do not seem to know where the center of the earth is." The only difference is that here the white protagonist, not the chief, is the spokesman for the Native American way of life.

The Lakota are idealized as living in harmony with the earth and with one another.[21] Dunbar says, "I've never known a people so eager to laugh, so devoted to family, so dedicated to each other. And the only word that came to mind was harmony." They fight, but they are not imperialist warriors like the whites. After Dunbar's first battle with the Sioux against the Pawnee, he says, "I'd never been in a battle like this one. There was no dark political objective. This was not a fight for territory or riches or to make men free. It had been fought to preserve the food stores that would see us through the winter and to protect the lives of women and children and loved ones only a few feet away."

Dances with Wolves: *Friendship of white man and Indian. Copyright 1990 Majestic Films International.*

After this battle, Dunbar finally rejects his white identity and accepts his Sioux name. "I felt a pride I'd never felt before. I'd never really known who John Dunbar was. Perhaps the name itself had no meaning. But as I heard my Sioux name being called over and over, I knew for the first time who I really was." According to Robert Baird, "This renaming of a white man with a 'natural name' and the shedding of his European name is the quintessential American myth—the self-made man rediscovering both America, and, most importantly, his own true self in the process. "[22]

Dunbar's mentor Kicking Bird tells him he is on the one trail that matters most: "the trail of a true human being." We are reminded that the Cheyenne in *Little Big Man* also called themselves "the Human Beings."

When Dunbar is captured by the white soldiers, who want him to lead them to "the hostiles," he stops speaking English and tells them in Sioux, "My name is Dances with Wolves. I have nothing to say to you. You are not worth talking to." He has now gone completely Indian and renounced white society.

Like *Little Big Man,* the film ennobles the Indian primarily to criticize white civilization. Armando Prats argues that, in *Dances with Wolves,* "as in the centuries of white representation of the Indian, the fully 'human' Other doubled as the white man's censure of his own culture."[23] In that sense, the Sioux in the film are only a white fantasy about the Sioux.

Despite its pretense of realism, the film exaggerates the contrast between the Sioux and the whites by making the Indians noble, wise, and peace-loving but the whites, with the notable exception of Dunbar and his white wife Stands with a Fist, largely stupid, crude, crazy, or vicious.[24] One critic counters this, claiming that "even among the soldiers we find all types—good, bad, insane, and brutal."[25] Nevertheless, toward the end of the film, the evil whites predominate. The illiterate cavalrymen repeatedly beat him senseless, use his journal, especially the page where he declares his love for Stands with a Fist, as toilet paper, and kill his horse and wolf for no reason. The film must make the white soldiers as loathsome as possible to justify Dunbar's killing one of them when the Sioux ride to his rescue. Otherwise he would seem like a traitor to the U.S. Army and to the white race.

Like *Little Big Man,* the film also exaggerates the contrast between the good Indians or "noble savages" (in *Little Big Man,* the Cheyenne; in *Dances with Wolves,* the Sioux) and the bad Indians or "savage savages" (in both films, the villains are the Pawnee, who massacre whites and Cheyenne or Sioux to steal from them, or else suck up to whites by serving as Army scouts). Some Native American critics have objected to this stereotyping of the Pawnee.[26] Yet the film sanitizes the Sioux by omitting a scene in the novel in which they celebrate taking the scalps of the white buffalo hunters.[27]

Because it is a satire, the inaccuracies in *Little Big Man* seem more excusable than those in *Dances with Wolves,* which pretends to historical realism. The novel by Michael Blake focused on the Comanche, but the movie turns them into Sioux.[28] During the Civil War, the Sioux were on the warpath against white settlers, which makes it highly unlikely that Dunbar would try to befriend them or even that they would let him live. In fact, "no officer of the Union Army ever defected to any Indian tribe."[29]

Whereas *Little Big Man* deconstructs the myth of Custer and of the winning of the West, *Dances* constructs (or rather reconstructs) the myth of the noble white man—so noble that he renounces his whiteness to become an Indian. He makes the transition from Dunbar into Dances with Wolves totally, unlike Jack, who is Jack Crabb in the white world and Little Big Man among the Cheyenne and remains confused and unable to integrate his two identities. Dunbar sheds his white identity and ties to white civilization and goes native with improbable ease. In a matter of months, he is accepted by the tribe, learns the language, marries into the Sioux, and fights alongside them.

Ironically, the marriage of Dances with Wolves with Stands with a Fist means that the film does not have to deal with the controversial topic of miscegenation because Stands with a Fist is also white; she was raised by the tribe from childhood after her family was killed by the Pawnee. Kicking Bird's wife tells him that the tribe approves of the match: "It makes sense. They are both white."[30] Thus the best of the white self becomes the best of the Indian self as this white couple preserves the Sioux way of life.

There is much about this film that is admirable and an advance over previous Hollywood treatments of cowboys and Indians. The view of the Native American is more sympathetic. Their roles are played by Native American actors. The white woman living among the Indians does not long to return to white civilization. The white man does not want to kill the Indians but to become one. Jane Tompkins mentions the "earnest idealization" of the film, with its very appealing contemporary message of spirituality and return to nature that offers new models of masculinity through friendship between men and participation in family and community.[31]

Nevertheless, despite its liberal intentions, the film is yet another myth of the white savior. Dunbar is an ideal hero, the best of the white self updated for the 1990s: clean, noble, a natural leader and fearless warrior, defender of women and children, kind, friendly, adaptable, ecologically aware, anti-racist—a sensitive New Age guy.

Ironically, the noblest Indian in the film is a white man. The best of the white self becomes the best of the Indian self as the white couple preserves the Lakota way of life, which is about to become extinct due to genocide. "Dunbar's character ironically demonstrates white superiority even as he goes native."[32]

As in *Gentleman's Agreement* or *Black Like Me,* the main victim of white racism in *Dances with Wolves* is a white man.[33] It is an appealing fantasy but an impossible one that denies American history. When Dunbar becomes the racial other, the film idealizes a transformation that does not exist and is unattainable in real life.

In the final scene, Dunbar and his wife leave the tribe forever. Wind in His Hair, who had initially been hostile to Dunbar, now shouts from the mountainside his everlasting friendship: "Don't you see that I will always be your friend?" This is a white man's fantasy about winning the undying love of an Indian.

An old joke exposes the sincere white fiction about Indians who supposedly love white people: The Lone Ranger and his faithful Indian companion Tonto are trapped in the desert by a band of hostile Apaches. They are completely surrounded and there is no hope of escape. So the Lone Ranger turns to Tonto and says, "Well, old partner, I guess we're done for." To which Tonto replies, "What you mean 'we,' white man?"

Bulworth: Abolishing Whiteness

Another film in which the racial masquerade is legitimized because the white hero is adopted by people of color is *Bulworth* (1998), a biting, often wonderfully funny political satire mocking the corruption of contemporary American politics by big money. It critiques the neglect by both Republican and Democratic politicians of the needs of minorities and of the working class and the poor in favor of serving the rich. Directed by and starring Warren Beatty, a liberal who also made *Reds,* about the American Communist John Reed, *Bulworth* was intended as a political statement by Beatty, who was flirting at the time with running for office.

The film takes the form of a conversion narrative about a white, Democratic senator from California, Jay Billington Bulworth. The film sees whites as inauthentic and white politicians as the phoniest of all. At age 60, Senator Bulworth faces both a political and a personal crisis and undergoes a change of heart. The cure for his hypocrisy, his way to attain authenticity, according to the film, is to act black, specifically to mimic a young, inner city black man. Although Bulworth does not dye his skin, in the course of the narrative he so totally identifies with blacks that he adopts the dress, mannerisms, and speech of a ghetto youth, to the extent of delivering his political speeches in rhyme like a rap singer. He is also adopted by an African-American family whose daughter he romances.

As the film begins, Bulworth is near the end of his campaign for reelection in the 1996 primary. A civil rights crusader in the 1960s, as attested by the photos of Martin Luther King and Bobby Kennedy in his office, now he is running on a neoconservative platform full of coded anti-black statements such as "our welfare system is out of control" and "abolish unnecessary affirmative action programs." He sits alone in his Washington office late at night, weeping as he listens over and over to the hollow statements in his campaign advertisements. He has not eaten or slept in days and is suffering a nervous breakdown, evidently brought on by his political sellout.

In despair, he demands a ten-million-dollar life insurance policy as a bribe from an insurance executive who wants him to bottle up in committee a bill to regulate the insurance industry. Then he asks a mobster to hire a hitman to kill him. He is no longer able to live with what he has become and sees no other way out. The insurance will take care of his daughter.

Bulworth's mental state is highly unstable. Once he returns to the campaign trail in California, he swings from suicidal depression into manic euphoria. Because he knows he will soon die and feels he has nothing left to lose, he decides to speak his mind freely.

This begins when he makes a scheduled appearance at a black church in L.A.'s South Central. To the hostile questions from black constituents, such as why he hasn't kept his promises to help rebuild the community after the 1992 riots, he says, "We told you what you wanted to hear and we pretty much forgot about it." He admits that he did nothing for them because "you haven't really contributed any money to my campaign." When another woman questions him, "Are you saying that the Democratic party doesn't care about the African American community?" He replies, "Isn't it obvious? . . . So what are you gonna do, vote Republican? . . . You can have a Billion Man March, but if you don't put down that malt liquor and chicken wings and get behind somebody other than a running back who stabs his wife, you're never gonna get rid of somebody like me." Bulworth admits that the entire American political system has been corrupted by big money and that he is part of the problem.

Bulworth has so enjoyed speaking the truth that now he begins to swing into full mania. When he was depressed, he lost his appetite, but now he begins to gorge on fried chicken and stuffs his face with canapés at his next stop in a Beverly Hills mansion. There he insults some film producers who are potential big contributors, telling them "how *lousy* most of your films are . . . Must be the money—turns everything to crap." He sees money as the root of all evil in both politics and film.

Bulworth is now followed by an entourage of three young black women from the ghetto, who act as a fan club and a backup group for the impromptu rap songs he begins to perform. He becomes infatuated with the most beautiful and flirtatious of the women, Nina (played by Halle Berry). Nina plays a large part in Bulworth's metamorphosis. His acting black seems inspired not only by his political repentance but also by his desire to win Nina's affection.

His conversion is also prompted by a homeless old black man, who, like the women, follows him everywhere. The old man speaks in parables and at first seems crazy. Repeatedly, he tells him, "You got to be a spirit, Bulworth. Don't be no ghost. And the spirit will not descend without song. You got to sing, Bulworth." But the man is not crazy: he is a prophet who recognizes Bulworth's potential and says that if Bulworth does not act on his political ideals, then he is a ghost, as good as dead. He must express his true spirit by singing. Immediately after first meeting the old man, Bulworth begins speaking in rhyme like a rap singer.

This mysterious figure (appropriately, he is played by the famous African American poet Amiri Baraka) lends the film a spiritual dimension. The film is not only a political satire but also a myth in which Bulworth is the mythic hero who follows the pattern of the monomyth: he leaves the everyday world, is tested and tried, is instructed by a wise old man or wizard (the old homeless man), meets dangerous monsters and kind helpers, descends into the underworld (the L.A. ghetto at night), unites with the goddess (Nina), and returns with the ultimate boon which will restore the culture (campaign finance reform and help for the African American community).

Bulworth regains his desire to live, buoyed by the mania of speaking his mind and acting black, by the advice of the prophet to be "a spirit," and by his pursuit of Nina. (We accept his affair with Nina because his marriage is a sham and his estranged wife is also having an affair.) Bulworth wants to avoid the hitman, so Nina takes him to her family's home to hide out. Ironically, she is leading him into danger, for Nina has been hired to aid the assassination.

He changes from his dirty clothes into the clothes of one of her brothers: outsize shorts and sweatshirt, a knit black cap, and sunglasses. Now not only talking in rhyme but also dressed like a black rapper, he goes into the mean streets of the ghetto at night, searching for Nina.

Bulworth: *The senator defends ghetto kids from white cops.* Copyright 1998 Twentieth Century Fox Corporation.

In the streets he encounters an armed group of little boys who work for a drug dealer. But he wins the boys over by buying them ice cream. When a white LAPD officer begins to bully the children, smashing an ice cream cone into a boy's face, Bulworth intervenes and does the same to the cop. Now Bulworth and the boys face two armed, enraged cops who may arrest or shoot them.

At this point, the younger, smarter, and less violent cop recognizes the senator. Bulworth forces the racist cop to apologize. One of the little boys says with glee, "I waited my whole life for this!"

Bulworth next meets the boys' employer, an African American drug lord who explains that he is giving them "entry-level positions" in the only growth industry in the ghetto. He speaks eloquently of the failure of the government and the schools to relieve the grinding poverty.

Bulworth is now ready to deliver his message to a television interviewer. Still dressed like a black rapper, he rhymes and curses, summing up all that he has learned from his recent experiences and echoing some of the words of Nina and of the drug dealer. He denounces the corporations that own the airwaves, the reporters, and the politicians, and he speaks up for the poor. "Rich people have always stayed on top by dividing white people from colored people. White people got more in common with colored people than they do with rich people."

He launches into the final and most radical part of his presentation: the need to abolish racial divisions by abolishing the races. "We just gotta eliminate them. White people. Black people too. Brown people, yellow people. Get rid of them all. What we need is a voluntary, free-spirited, open-ended program of procreative racial deconstruction. Everybody just gotta keep fuckin' everybody till they're all the same color."

Nina takes him home and reveals her part in the assassination plot. But she has changed her mind after hearing his radical message on TV and instead kisses Bulworth. She is evidently ready to engage in his program of "procreative racial deconstruction," but the exhausted Bulworth falls asleep before that happens.

The next morning, Bulworth has resoundingly won the Democratic senatorial primary, with many write-in votes for president from both Democrats and Republicans. Evidently the public is hungry for a candidate who speaks the truth instead of the same old platitudes. Even the drug dealer is so impressed that he plans to become a legitimate community leader, telling Nina's brother, "We got to take advantage of this crazy motherfucker while he's still crazy."

Despite his victory, Bulworth admits to Nina, "You made me feel insecure. First of all, I'm too old for you. And I'm white." Nina reassures him, "Oh, come on. You know you my nigga!" Bulworth is so happy he kisses her passionately in the middle of the crowd of campaign followers and reporters, publicly declaring his love.

At this point, a sniper shoots Bulworth, who falls to the ground. This scene is eerily reminiscent of the assassination of Bobby Kennedy immediately after he won the 1968 California primary as Democratic candidate for president. The implication of the film is that the rich and powerful will silence any major politician who dares to speak out boldly against the economic or racial status quo.

We are left uncertain whether Bulworth survives. The homeless prophet stands outside a hospital and is given the last word, a direct address to the audience, delivering us the same message he gave Bulworth: "You got to be a spirit. You can't be no ghost."

In its call for campaign finance reform, the film is mainstream, for this is an issue that American politicians both right and left have been advocating for years. By focusing on this issue, John McCain temporarily challenged George W. Bush in the 2000 primary campaign for the Republican presidential nomination. Its strong anticorporate message, however, resembles that of Ralph Nader's failed campaign as the leftist, Green Party candidate for president in 2000.

The film's call for the abolition of whiteness, and, indeed, for the abolition of racial differences by eliminating the races, is its most radical (but also rather utopian and naïve) premise. The problem lies not in having people with different colored skins but, as we have argued, in our psychological constructions, our object relations with racial others, and our sincere fictions about race. The notions of white supremacy and white privilege have to be eliminated, not the differences in skin colors. *Vive la difference!*

Despite its critique of whiteness, *Bulworth* is not free of the sincere fictions of the white self. First, Bulworth is still in the mold of the white messiah coming to the rescue of oppressed people of color, especially in the scene where he gets to play the hero by tackling a racist white cop who is bullying little black boys. As white messiah, he improbably inspires the overnight metamorphosis of a black crack dealer into a community leader.

Second, Bulworth's conversion is too quick and too easy. In the course of a weekend, he becomes an "honorary black man" simply by doing a poor imitation of a black rapper. He is adopted by Nina's family and accepted by Nina as "my nigga," thus reversing what her brother told Bulworth in an earlier scene: "You ain't no nigga," meaning that he did not belong in the black nightclub and he did not belong with Nina.

Third, the notion that if whiteness is inauthentic then blackness is automatically authentic is a romantic projection by white people, not that different from Kerouac's lament (quoted at the beginning of chapter 8).

Fourth and finally, the character of Nina is incredible, part plot contrivance and part white man's fantasy. She is required to play many incompatible roles: vamp, hired killer, loving sister, well-educated and astute leftist political analyst of the African American community, and finally lover to Bulworth. It is difficult to believe that this beautiful, 26-year-old black woman would fall for a 60-year-old white politician who is suffering a nervous breakdown. Although the African American critic Patricia J. Williams praises Bulworth as a "smart, funny, hopeful movie, filled with the possibility of reform," she complains that "Berry's role never quite rises above the most ancient of clichés: Tragic Mulatta as bridge between black and white."[34]

Nevertheless, despite its failings, *Bulworth* is as far to the left as any contemporary Hollywood film dares to go. It is a bold film we admire for its crazy political courage.

Finian's Rainbow: A Bigot Transformed by Magic

When racial masquerade is not excused by a journalistic assignment, by the encouragement of friends of another color, or by adoption into the tribe, it is explained away by fantasy. We look next at a series of movies in which a character is suddenly transformed against his will into a person of another color by magic: *Finian's Rainbow, Watermelon Man,* and *Zelig.*

Finian's Rainbow (1968) is a version of a 1947 musical comedy, an odd and uneasy mixture in which a Southern bigot is transformed by an Irish leprechaun. Late 1940s concerns about Dixiecrats are transposed to the late 1960s era of black power, but the movie nevertheless seemed dated even when it appeared, like *Guess Who's Coming to Dinner* (1967).

In the Kentucky of *Finian's Rainbow,* Woody Mahoney is president of the Rainbow Valley tobacco cooperative, in which blacks and whites work together. This isolated, biracial utopia is threatened by the greed and racism of the surrounding society. The bigoted Senator Rawkins (apparently a satire on the actual Senator Rankin of Mississippi) writes a law making it a felony for whites and blacks to live together, so that he can take their land.

Meanwhile, Irish immigrant Finian dances into the valley seeking his fortune. Finian has taken a pot of gold from his village, and he is trailed by a leprechaun who wants it back.

The fantasy element of the leprechaun Og and the pot of gold provide the plot complications and resolution. Finian's daughter Sharon, angry at Senator Rawkins, wishes him black, and the racially transformed senator flees into the forest, ashamed. Og soon transforms the miserable senator into a happy man. Immediately, the senator begins singing "Oh, dem golden slippers," and soon he joins a black gospel quartet. In the end, he is transformed back, but now he is a happy, anti-racist white man.

There are a number of problems with the movie: in the biracial utopia of Rainbow Valley, although blacks and whites live and work together, there is no black-white ro-

Finian's Rainbow: *Og the leprechaun and the transformed Senator Rawkins. Copyright 1968 Warner Bros. Seven Arts, Inc. Courtesy Museum of Modern Art Film Stills Archive.*

mance or marriage. Woody, the white hero, remains in charge. Black characters are reduced to minstrel roles, except for Woody's assistant, the college-educated chemist Howard. The movie sees racism solely as a Southern problem and also assumes that ordinary people are not racist, only those in power, such as the senator and his flunkies, the lawyer and the sheriff.

Irish Americans, who historically were prejudiced against African Americans because the "whiteness" of the Irish was for a long time in question, here are seen instead as paragons of racial tolerance "To be acknowledged as white . . . it was necessary that no Negro be allowed to work in occupations where Irish were to be found. Still better was to erase the memory that Afro-Americans had ever done those jobs."[35] In *Finian's Rainbow*, however, as the Irish immigrants—Finian, Sharon, and Og—become Americanized, they rescue the biracial utopia of Rainbow Valley. Nevertheless, except for the gospel quartet, Irish music and dance dominate the film.

The movie ridicules stereotypes. In the funniest scene, Howard the chemist accepts a job as the senator's servant. He is instructed by the senator's white assistant on how to "act black," which involves speaking in a thick dialect and moving with a slow shuffle. But Howard uses this very slowness to gain revenge when the senator needs a Bromo for severe heartburn.

Nevertheless, the movie also indulges in stereotypes: the Irishman as drunken, irresponsible dreamer and, worst of all, the senator transformed into carefree, singing darky. The major problem is that the movie is so lighthearted that it trivializes the issue of race, wishing it away through fantasy.

The Watermelon Man: Black Magic

Strictly speaking, *The Watermelon Man* (1970) does not belong in this book because we said that we were limiting ourselves to films by white directors so that we could see the way whites represent themselves, and Melvin Van Peebles, the director of *The Watermelon Man*, is African American. Nevertheless, we make an exception in this case because *The Watermelon Man* concerns a white racial masquerade and provides a useful comparison with *Finian's Rainbow*.

Both films deal with a white racist who learns a lesson and loses his bigotry by being magically transformed into a black man. But *Finian's Rainbow* (1968) is a tame satire on white racism, whereas *The Watermelon Man*, released only two years later, is a far more pointed critique. In the interim, "mounting political pressure combined with the film industry's threatened economic position . . . along with the allure and profitability of a rising black box office, proved irresistible."[36] Hollywood movies began to turn away from the integrationist mode of *Guess Who's Coming to Dinner* and *Finian's Rainbow* to more militant, "black power" films made by young black directors.

Melvin Van Peebles directed independent films until he entered the Hollywood system and launched the "blaxploitation" boom of the early 1970s. *The Watermelon Man*, which comes just before his breakthrough hit, *Sweet Sweetback's Baadasssss Song* (1971), is a transitional film on the way to blaxploitation. It has many of the earmarks of such films: a low budget, the experimental techniques of independent film, a black director, a black star, black music (also by Van Peebles), a black-focused plot, and unsympathetic white characters. But it is a comedy that lacks the macho heroism and violence of the blaxploitation genre.

The Watermelon Man is a heavy-handed satire on white racism, fitfully amusing but uneven and often overdone, opting for slapstick farce. In the end, it abandons comedy for drama. The protagonist, Jeff Gerber, is an average, 1970 middle-class white man with a wife, two children, a house in the suburbs, and a job in the city as a successful insurance salesman for a large white company. Jeff is an arrogant, loudmouthed bigot who derides the inner-city rioters he sees on television as "uppity darkies." Thinking he is funny, he makes racist cracks to every black he meets, who are all service people: a bus driver, a counterman at a restaurant, and an elevator operator. His wife Althea represents the liberal viewpoint and tells Jeff, "I think white people have to show greater interest and understanding."

What makes the film a neat inversion of the standard white masquerade is that Jeff is played by the black actor Godfrey Cambridge (a stand-up comedian known for his caustic racial commentary). Cambridge's whiteface makeup, unfortunately, is as unconvincing as the blackface on the white heroes in *Black Like Me* and *Soul Man*. Later in the film, when he becomes black, he simply removes the white makeup.

Jeff wakes up to discover that he has been transformed overnight by magic into a black man. This is his worst nightmare realized. "Ah, I'm black! I'm a nigger!" he cries. "I want my whiteness back! Turn me white, Rinso White!" He becomes hysterical and tries prayer and long showers. Later he resorts to other ridiculous solutions: skin creams, a white mask that hardens on his face, and milk baths, all in vain. "These creams don't work! No wonder Negroes riot!" Like Senator Rawkins in *Finian's Rainbow*, he at first retreats from the world out of shame.

The hero stares into a mirror, unable to recognize himself, and his identity comes into question. His wife screams when she first sees his transformed self, thinking there is a strange black man in the bathroom. When he insists he is still Jeff, she asks, "How do you know you're you?" No one responds to him the same way anymore: the police try to arrest him as a thief for running in a white neighborhood, his coworkers are shocked, and the doorman refuses him entry into an exclusive white club (a scene reminiscent of *Gentleman's Agreement*).

His neighbors threaten him with anonymous phone calls: "Move out, nigger." Finally, a neighborhood committee arrives to buy him out. They offer $50,000 for the house, but he holds out for twice that amount.

As in *Gentleman's Agreement*, the hero's marriage falls apart because of the change. Jeff's wife accuses him, "You took advantage of them because you're colored." He asks, "What happened to the flaming liberal I was married to?" She says, "I'm still liberal, but to a point." She sends the kids away, stops sleeping with him, and finally moves out to join the kids.

Jeff turns to Erika, a Norwegian coworker who used to dislike him and becomes interested when he becomes black. But after they have sex, he rejects her. "I want you to love me because of what I am, not because I'm a Negro. . . . You're such a great bang, but you're a bigot, Erika." She screams at him, "You black bastard! Get out of here, you nigger!" Sarcastically, he congratulates her on her attitude: "Why, in a few years, you'll be qualified for American citizenship!" As he leaves, she screams out the window, "Rape!"

Later, like the senator in *Finian's Rainbow*, he accepts his new identity and assimilates into the black community. Unlike the senator, however, he is not transformed back into a white man. Jeff quits the white company and opens his own insurance office in the ghetto. In the final scene, he is practicing martial arts with a group of fellow black men, brandishing a broom like a spear, suggesting he has become militant.

The Watermelon Man announces the arrival of a new, black-militant, separatist stance in Hollywood film. The film even makes fun of its immediate predecessors. In one scene, Jeff calls home and announces to his wife, "Hello, Althea. Guess who's coming to dinner!"

Nevertheless, for a film that satirizes stereotypes, like *Finian's Rainbow,* it also indulges in some. In particular, although *The Watermelon Man* punctures Jeff's bigotry, Jeff is also a sexist and the film sides with his objectification of women.

The Watermelon Man also rests on the same flawed premise as *Finian's Rainbow:* the notion that blackness is somehow a punishment that should be visited as a curse on white bigots to teach them a lesson. Donald Bogle calls *The Watermelon Man* "the classic tragic mulatto story of the early separatist 1970s. . . . That old black blood—which always brews trouble—had made his life wretched and intolerable." *The Watermelon Man* "dramatized a great white fantasy-nightmare (and perhaps marginally a great black fantasy about whites)—that of mysteriously losing lily-whiteness and turning coal-black." Bogle finds such a premise remote from the black experience.[37] In that sense, like *Finian's Rainbow, The Watermelon Man* is a masquerade film that participates in the sincere fictions of the white self.

Zelig: The Assimilation of the Jews

Zelig (1984) is the final film we comment on in which the racial masquerade occurs by magic. *Zelig,* a clever use of fantasy to illuminate racial and ethnic difference, is a "mockumentary" or parody of a documentary about the life of a fictional character, Leonard Zelig, who is presented as an American celebrity of the 1920s and 1930s. Woody Allen wrote, directed, and starred as Zelig, another version of the lovable, neurotic Jewish-American *shlemiel* Allen always plays. The film is a satiric spoof about assimilation, for Zelig is a "human chameleon" able to change almost instantly into anyone around him. Zelig is the everyman who shows up everywhere and fits in wherever he goes. In the presence of a black, he turns black, among Indians, he transforms into an Indian, and so on. As the narrator comments, "To the KKK, Zelig, a Jew who was able to transform himself into a Negro or an Indian, was a triple threat." But Zelig is so malleable that he can as easily become a Nazi, as he does late in the film.

Questions about identity, particularly about Jewish identity, figure in many of Allen's films. For example, in a scene in *Take the Money and Run,* he plays a prisoner who volunteers for an experimental drug. The side effect is that for twenty-four hours he turns into a Hasidic rabbi. In *Annie Hall,* he plays a comedian named Alvy who is paranoid about his Jewishness and imagines insults everywhere. When he has lunch at the home of his gentile girlfriend Annie, Alvy sees himself through the eyes of Annie's grandmother, whom he calls a "classic Jew-hater," and imagines himself transformed, again into a Hasidic rabbi.

Zelig is the ultimate passer: lacking any core identity, he desires only to fit in. The son of a Yiddish actor, as a boy he was frequently bullied by anti-Semites. Under hypnosis, while he is being psychoanalyzed, he expresses the wish "to be safe . . . to be like the others. . . . I want to be liked." So he becomes a protean self, an actor, a great impostor, and the ultimate passer. Allen includes cameo appearances and fictional commentary on Zelig by the real-life Jewish intellectuals Susan Sontag, Bruno Bettelheim, Saul

Bellow, and Irving Howe. Howe's commentary is to the point: "His story reflected a lot of the Jewish experience in America: the great urge to push in, to find one's place, and to assimilate into the culture. He wanted to assimilate like crazy."

Historically, the Jews were criticized as "human chameleons." They were seen as insidious by anti-Semites because many Jews look just like other "white" people and assimilate readily in any Western culture.

According to two critics, "Zelig exemplifies as well . . . the sometimes caricatural ethnic switch-abouts typical of Yiddish-derived theatricality, of Fanny Brice performing 'I'm an Indian' or Al Jolson in blackface belting out 'Mammy' or of Mel Brooks's Yiddish-speaking Indian in *Blazing Saddles*."[38] This was one Jewish method of becoming American by imitating American racial minorities to differentiate themselves from them.[39]

The film is of course not only about the Jewish experience in America but also a critique of assimilation and a commentary on the fluidity of American identity and the pressure to conform in a mass society. Zelig is the "ultimate conformist," says Bettelheim. Most immigrants to America desire to pass, to assimilate, to become like everyone else. Zelig is a celebrity in the film because, "by being the quintessential symbol of adaptability, Zelig helps to perpetuate the notion that the American dream is achievable."[40] But if you assimilate too much, the film also warns, you run the risk of dissolution of self, of becoming a freak with no identity of your own.

Zelig is the only movie about racial masquerade that views passing as a sickness, a psychological aberration. Zelig is treated by a psychiatrist, Dr. Eudora Fletcher, who ultimately cures and marries him.

Conclusion: Wearing the Mask

According to Eric Lott, white mimicry of blacks began in nineteenth-century minstrelsy because of "how precariously nineteenth-century white working people lived their whiteness." Blackface minstrelsy therefore operated out of mixed motives of "a nearly insupportable fascination and a self-protective derision with respect to black people."[41] In the course of twentieth-century Hollywood films, blackface minstrelsy has evolved from the vicious mockery of *Birth of a Nation* to the idealization of blackness and the critique of whiteness of *Bulworth*. Ralph Ellison notes that white American identity has always depended on wearing the mask of a racial other. "Americans began their revolt from the English fatherland when they dumped their tea into the Boston harbor, masked as Indians, and the mobility of the society created in this limitless space has encouraged the use of the mask for good and evil ever since."[42]

At its best, the white masquerade offers the possibility of imaginative play and of deconstructing whiteness. Stam and Shohat, for example, see a positive aspect to the experience of Zelig in Woody Allen's movie, for it shows the potential of "creative adaptability, artistic transformation," of "transcending fixed roles and ethnic positions, this possibility of an exhilarating indeterminacy."[43] Ultimately, by revealing the arbitrary nature of the color line and the fluidity of racial identity, masquerade exposes the dependency of white identity on racial others and the fictionality of whiteness. As Ellison writes, "For out of the counterfeiting of the black American's identity there arises a profound doubt in the white man's mind as to the authenticity of his own image of himself."[44] Or, as Daniel Bernardi claims, "There are no white people, only people who pass as white."[45]

Nevertheless, there is a flaw in the notion that white masquerade is a subversive strategy. Blacks are forced by the white majority to act white, to wear, as Frantz Fanon puts it, "white masks": "The black man wants to be like the white man. For the black man, there is only one destiny. And it is white."[46] Blacks like Valentine in *Trading Places* perform out of necessity and all the time. As *Imitation of Life* shows, the cost for a black person of passing for white is constant fear of exposure due to the mockery and hatred of white society, isolation from and rejection by black society, and self-hatred. But for whites to masquerade as people of another color is, by and large, voluntary and temporary, a form of play with usually only comic consequences. According to Michael Rogin, there is a significant difference "between the costume as a way of life and as a part that can be discarded at will."[47] As a black man tells the masquerading white hero of *Black Like Me*: "You wipe that blackness off, they'll treat you like a man."

In the movie *Tootsie* (1982), the male protagonist, an unemployed actor, temporarily disguises himself as a woman to get a job on a television soap opera. At the end, after abandoning the disguise, he declares to his girlfriend that pretending to be a woman made him a better man. The white singer Janis Joplin modeled her stage persona on the black blues singer Bessie Smith and said, "Being black for a while has made me a better white."[48] In both instances, there is a double standard operating. Whereas black passing is viewed as transgressive and dangerous, white passing, like white male cross-dressing, is viewed as educational and self-improving. There has never been a comedy about a woman who passed as male and then claimed that she did so to become a better woman, nor can one imagine a black female singer passing for white and saying, "Being white for a while has made me a better black."

The crucial difference lies in the realm of *privilege*: just as males are the privileged gender, whites are the privileged race. And that privilege includes the option to cross the lines, to masquerade without serious consequences. As Gayle Wald points out, "Racial imperatives—or in the case of 'white' identities, a relative *freedom* from such imperatives— implicitly elevates 'white' passing to the status of an educative and ennobling enterprise, while casting 'black' passing as a form of racial disloyalty and ideological entrapment."[49] So long as white privilege remains in place, individual acts of white passing, in the movies or in real life, will not really serve to educate or to liberate us from the bonds of race. According to Michael Rogin, "The more the freedom to perform any role, the less subversion in the play."[50]

Notes

1. Huhndorf, Shari M. 2001. *Going Native: Indians in the American Cultural Imagination.* Ithaca, N.Y.: Cornell University Press, p. 2.

2. Deloria, Philip Joseph. 1998. *Playing Indian.* New Haven, Conn.: Yale University Press, p. 146.

3. Hopkins, George W. 1998. "Constructing the New Mythic West: *Dances With Wolves,*" *Studies in American Culture* 21(no. 2): 71–83 (p. 72).

4. Kasdan, Margo, and Susan Tavernetti. 1998. "Native Americans in a Revisionist Western: *Little Big Man,*" in *Hollywood's Indian: The Portrayal of the Native American in Film,* eds. Peter C. Rollins and John E. O'Connor. Lexington: University Press of Kentucky, pp. 121–36 (p. 129).

5. Landon, Brooks. 1989. "The Measure of *Little Big Man.*" *Studies in American Fiction* 17 (no. 2): 131–42 (pp. 140–41).

6. Ibid., p. 140.

7. Kilpatrick, Jacquelyn. 1999. *Celluloid Indians: Native Americans and Film*. Lincoln: University of Nebraska Press. "It is interesting that in the Indian world his identity is consistent, but in the white world he tries on personalities and lifestyles like one tries on costumes. If this is really a search for identity, then it is a white identity Crabb is looking for, but each one he tries on ends up unfulfilling because of the hypocrisy, greed, dishonesty, and general craziness of the whites" (p. 85).

8. Kasdan and Tavernetti, "Native Americans in a Revisionist Western," p. 130.

9. Pearson, Roberta E. 1996. "The Revenge of Rain-in-the-Face? or Custer and Indians on the Silent Screen," in *The Birth of Whiteness: Race and the Emergence of U.S. Cinema*, ed. Daniel Bernardi. New Brunswick, N.J.: Rutgers University Press, pp. 273–99 (p. 278).

10. Ibid., p. 279.

11. Dyer, Richard. 1997. *White*. New York: Routledge, p. 211.

12. Braudy, Leo. 1971. "The Difficulties of *Little Big Man*," *Film Quarterly* 25: 30–3 (p. 30).

13. Cowen, Paul S. 1991. "A Social Cognitive Approach to Ethnicity in Films," in *Unspeakable Images: Ethnicity and the American Cinema*, ed. Lester D. Friedman. Urbana: University of Illinois Press, pp. 353–78 (p. 370).

14. Pearson, "The Revenge of Rain-in-the Face?" p. 273.

15. Kasdan and Tavernetti, "Native Americans in a Revisionist Western," p. 132.

16. Berkhofer, Robert F. 1978. *The White Man's Indian: Images of the American Indian from Columbus to the Present*. New York: Knopf, p. 103.

17. Fiedler, Leslie A. 1968. *The Return of the Vanishing American*. New York: Stein & Day, p. 169.

18. Castillo, Edward. 1991. Review of *Dances With Wolves*. *Film Quarterly* 44 (no. 4): 14–23, (p. 22).

19. Ibid.

20. Grenier, Richard. 1991. "Indian Love Call," *Commentary* 91 (March 1991): 46–50, (p. 47).

21. Ostwalt, Conrad. 1996. "*Dances With Wolves*: An American *Heart of Darkness*," *Literature/Film Quarterly* 24 (no. 2): 209–16 (pp. 210–11).

22. Baird, Robert. 1998. "'Going Indian': *Dances With Wolves*," in *Hollywood's Indian: The Portrayal of the Native American in Film*, eds. Peter C. Rollins and John E. O'Connor. Lexington: University Press of Kentucky, pp. 153–69 (p. 161).

23. Prats, Armando Jose. 1998. "The Image of the Other and the Other *Dances With Wolves*: The Refigured Indian and the Textual Supplement." *Journal of Film and Video* 50 (no. 1): 3–19 (p. 6).

24. Grenier, "Indian Love Call," p. 47.

25. Castillo, Review of *Dances with Wolves*, p. 17.

26. Ibid., p.15.

27. Ostwalt, "*Dances with Wolves*," p. 215.

28. Castillo, Review of *Dances with Wolves*, p. 17.

29. Grenier, "Indian Love Call," p. 48.

30. Huhndorf, *Going Native*, pp. 3–4.

31. Tompkins, Jane. 1994. "Saving Our Lives: *Dances with Wolves, Iron John* and the Search of a New Masculinity," in *Eloquent Obsessions: Writing Cultural Criticism*, ed. Marianna Torgovnick. Durham, N.C.: Duke University Press, pp. 96–106 (p. 99).

32. Huhndorf, *Going Native*, p. 3.

33. Prats, "The Image of the Other," p. 8.

34. Williams, Patricia J. 2000. "Bulworth Agonistes," in *Cinema Nation: The Best Writing on Film from* The Nation, *1913–2000*, ed. Carl Bromley. New York: Nation Books, pp. 317–19 (p. 318).

35. Ignatiev, Noel. 1995. *How the Irish Became White*. New York: Routledge, p. 112.

36. Guerrero, Ed. 1993. *Framing Blackness: The African American Image in Film*. Philadelphia: Temple University Press, pp. 85–6.

37. Bogle, Donald. 1997. *Toms, Coons, Mulattoes, Mammies, and Bucks: An Interpretive History of Blacks in American Films*. New York: Continuum, p. 234.

38. Stam, Robert, and Ella Shohat. 1987. "Zelig and Contemporary Theory: Meditation on the Chameleon Text." *Enclitic* 9: 176–93 (p. 186).

39. Rogin, Michael Paul. 1996. *Blackface, White Noise: Jewish Immigrants in the Hollywood Melting Pot.* Berkeley: University of California Press, p. 6.

40. Feldstein, Richard. 1985. "The Dissolution of the Self in *Zelig*." *Literature/Film Quarterly* 13 (no. 3): 155–60 (p. 158).

41. Lott, Eric. 1993. *Love and Theft: Blackface Minstrelsy and the American Working Class.* New York: Oxford University Press, pp. 4 and 6.

42. Ellison, Ralph. 1964. *Shadow and Act.* New York: Random House, p. 68.

43. Stam and Shoat, "Zelig and Contemporary Theory," p. 190.

44. Ellison, *Shadow and Act,* p. 68.

45. Bernardi, Daniel, ed. 2001. *Classic Hollywood, Classic Whiteness.* Minneapolis, Minn.: University of Minnesota Press, p. xxii.

46. Fanon, Frantz. 1967. *Black Skin, White Masks.* New York: Grove, p. 228.

47. Rogin, *Blackface, White Noise,* p. 34.

48. Joplin, Janis quoted in Ledbetter, James. 1993. "Imitations of Life." *Vibe,* November 1993:112.

49. Wald, Gayle. 2000. *Crossing the Line: Racial Passing in Twentieth-Century U.S. Literature and Culture.* Durham, N.C.: Duke University Press, pp. 15–16.

50. Rogin, *Blackface, White Noise,* p. 34.

CHAPTER 10

Black and White Buddies I

"With us it's still Jim and Huck Finn. . . . I'm Huckleberry, you see. . . ."

—The white liberal Mr. Emerson Jr. speaking to the black hero in Ralph Ellison's novel, Invisible Man (1952)[1]

Films Analyzed:
The Defiant Ones (1958)
In the Heat of the Night (1967)
Brian's Song (1970)
Blazing Saddles (1974)
48 Hours (1982)

The White Male Quest for Self-Definition

The Defiant Ones (1958) established the pattern for the Hollywood interracial buddy film, a formula still popular today, easily incorporated into many genres, including mysteries like *In the Heat of the Night* (1967), sports films like *Brian's Song* (1970), police action films like *48 Hours* (1982) and the *Lethal Weapon* series (1987, 1989, 1992, 1994), comedies like *Blazing Saddles* (1974) and *Men in Black* (1997), prison dramas like *The Shawshank Redemption* (1994) and *The Green Mile* (2000), as well as many other movies we do not have space here to discuss, like *The Last Boy Scout* (1991), *White Men Can't Jump* (1992), and *Independence Day* (1996).

The formula was established in *The Defiant Ones:* two men, one bigoted white and one proud black, are thrown together by circumstance and forced to work together for a common goal. At first they are hostile and fight bitterly, but because they must work closely and depend on each other, gradually they undergo male bonding and learn respect and even love. By the time of the "color-blind" buddy pictures, beginning with

Lethal Weapon in 1987, the racism of the white hero—or indeed, almost any mention of race as an issue in the United States—has disappeared.

Although *The Defiant Ones* coincides with the emergence of the Civil Rights movement, which it appears to advance, it paradoxically works as a way to assert the white self and to contain black aspirations. The white buddy acts as "ideological chaperone" to the black.[2] Feminist critics argue that this interracial male bonding excludes women, both white and black, and represents white male liberal fantasies. The films express only "the white masculine's quest for self-definition" because the black male buddy "is offered, in the end, no narrative, theoretical, or social release."[3] Such films "project the black male masculinity imagined by white male liberals in search of perfect partners."[4]

The story of the white man whose best friend is a man of another color is nothing new in American popular culture: it is a sincere fiction deeply embedded from the beginning in the white American imagination. As the literary critic Leslie Fiedler points out, the dream of interracial male comradeship goes back to nineteenth-century American literature and the works of James Fenimore Cooper, Herman Melville, and Mark Twain and continues in twentieth-century popular culture in such partnerships as that of the Lone Ranger and Tonto. As Leslie Fedler mentions, "The myth of an earthly paradise for males only has died hard. . . . it was for the first time expressed without camouflage or disguise in a popular movie: a film called *The Defiant Ones*."[5]

The Defiant Ones: Buddies in the Garden of Eden

The Defiant Ones won Academy Awards in 1958 for Best Picture, Best Director (Stanley Kramer), and Best Original Screenplay. Sidney Poitier became the first African American nominated for an Academy Award for best actor, although he did not win that year. *The Defiant Ones* is a pioneer film, the first of the black-white buddy films of the Civil Rights era. It appeared in the wake of such events as the 1954 Supreme Court decision on school desegregation in *Brown v. Board of Education of Topeka, Kansas,* the 1955–1956 Montgomery bus boycott, and the 1957 use of federal troops to integrate Little Rock's Central High, landmark events that moved the urgent need for racial change to the center of American consciousness. The film makes no mention of these momentous events, but *The Defiant Ones* is a message film that would have been inconceivable even a few years earlier in the decade. It was "one of the earliest 'cross-over' movies, capable of attracting both black and white audiences."[6]

This film was enabled not only by the political and social changes taking place in America but also by changes in the movie industry in the late 1950s: "Television, antitrust actions, and high overhead had weakened the studios, new cameras and film made location shooting easier, censorship standards were loosening, and an age of independent productions was at hand," with the rise of socially conscious producers and directors such as Stanley Kramer.[7]

The Defiant Ones tries to match the integrity of its social message with a spare, realistic style that adapts some of the devices of a low-budget film to a big-budget Hollywood production: black-and-white film stock, location shooting, and only natural, diegetic sound (all sound originates in the story space, so there is music only if a character is singing or listening to the radio).

The story concerns Noah Cullen, a poor Southern black man, and John "Joker" Jackson, a poor Southern white man, prisoners who escape when the truck transporting their chain gang crashes. Cullen and Joker run cross country, bound together at the wrists by an 18-inch length of steel chain. Joker and Cullen clash from the beginning and are near to blows when the truck overturns. They are in the same fix, but Joker considers himself better because he is white and constantly enrages Cullen with racist remarks. Their conflict makes their escape even more difficult because the posse is betting "they will probably kill each other before they go five miles."

To maintain suspense, their scenes are crosscut with the progress of the posse. The pursuit is led by Sheriff Max Muller, not a stereotypical tough, bigoted Southern sheriff but a humane lawman. The sheriff is pressured by the governor to capture the escapees and also must contend with an aggressive state police captain and a deputy who values his dogs more than the lives of the convicts. The sheriff must keep the posse going and keep them under control, and he prevents them at the end from killing the escaped convicts.

Not only the sheriff but all the characters are believable individuals rather than stereotypes. Sidney Poitier was excited by the chance to play Cullen, his best role to date: "the role of Cullin [sic] would represent for me and other black actors a step up in the quality of parts available to us, and at the same time afford the black community in general a rare look at a movie character exemplifying the dignity of our people—something that Hollywood had systematically ignored in its shameless capitulation to racism."[8] Cullen, the only black person in the film, is a complex character who shows intelligence, dignity, pride, rage, and also deep compassion.

The white characters represent a range of human responses: there are kind white men like the sheriff and Big Sam, an ex-prisoner who saves Cullen and Joker from a lynch mob, and bigoted whites, like the insensitive captain and the deputy, or Mac, the sadistic leader of the lynch mob, or the woman on the farm who shelters the prisoners for the night but deliberately misdirects Cullen. Finally, there is Joker, who changes from a selfish racist to a friend who sacrifices for Cullen.

"The characters are complementary personalities. . . . The complementarity is further highlighted when Curtis [Joker] has to blacken his face with mud so as not to be seen in the moonlight—he thus becomes the man to whom he's chained!"[9]

Stanley Kramer made his message clear in an interview: "In *The Defiant Ones*, it was my purpose to stress the idea about all human beings having basically the same nature. To show this, I took two individuals on the lowest possible level in order to tell the glory of the sacrifice for a man, to stress the need they have for each other. This is symbolized by the chain they wear together."[10]

The Sentimental Ending of *The Defiant Ones*

Nevertheless, despite the film's dramatic power and moments of realism, toward the end, in its effort to be didactic, it turns sentimental and false. Joker and Cullen are taken in for the night by a lonely white woman on a farm, who gives them a hammer and chisel to break the chain. As James Baldwin writes, "The logic of actuality would now strongly indicate, given their situation, and what we have seen of their relationship, that they separate. For one thing, each fugitive is safer without the other, and, for another, the woman clearly wishes to be alone with the white boy."[11] Yet Cullen won't leave Joker because Joker is ill, even though Joker has the woman to nurse him.

In the night, the woman seduces Joker. The next morning, she persuades him to escape with her. Then she sends Cullen off with false directions that would have led to his death in the nearby swamp. Again, notes Baldwin, there is no real need for her to do this except to open "our white hero's eyes to the bottomless evil of racial hatred" and make him abandon this treacherous woman to rush to the aid of his black comrade.[12]

Joker, shot in the shoulder as he flees by the woman's young son, finds Cullen in the swamp. Although the chain is broken, they are now linked by friendship. Joker is stumbling, weak with loss of blood, and Cullen urges him on, saying, "Come on! You're dragging the chain."

With the dogs hot on their trail, they race to the train to freedom. Cullen jumps aboard the moving train. In a close-up, he stretches out his hand toward Joker and Joker reaches out to him. But Joker can't make it, and Cullen drops off the train to be with his friend. Donald Bogle says of this ending, "When he saved his honky brother, he was jeered at in ghetto theaters."[13] As James Baldwin explains, "He jumps off the train in order to reassure white people, to make them know that they are not hated."[14]

The black comedian Dick Gregory parodied the ending of *The Defiant Ones*: "You remember that movie where me and my white buddy, we escape from the chain gang? And we run through the fields and across the river, chased by the dogs, me and my white buddy, chained together. And finally we break the chain and we run toward the train and I hop aboard, but my white buddy can't make it, so as the train moves down the track, I reach out my arm to him. Yes, I reach out and I wave my hand, and I yell, 'Bye, baby!'"

In the final scene, Cullen sits on the ground beneath a tree, holding the wounded Joker in his arms, in a scene critics have compared to a pietà.[15] This pietà image is repeated 31 years later, at the end of *Lethal Weapon 2* (1989), in which Murtaugh (Danny Glover) cradles his wounded white partner Riggs (Mel Gibson). We wonder why the white imagination needs to repeat this particular icon of a black man nursing his white friend. It seems to suggest a fantasied mutual sacrifice that unites the races: the white Christ figure needs a black male Virgin Mary to comfort him.

Because the white hero in *The Defiant Ones* has rejected the evil white woman to be with his black buddy, James Baldwin suggests that this demonstrates that "A black man and a white man can come together only in the absence of women."[16] Indeed, the pietà implies that the loyal black man substitutes for the treacherous white woman. As Leslie Fiedler argues, *The Defiant Ones* is "the dream of a Garden of Eden with two Adams—one colored, one white—and no Eve."[17] As we will see, this white male racial fantasy also underlies the black-white buddy films in the decades that follow *The Defiant Ones*.

The Defiant Ones: *This pietà image of black man holding his wounded white partner is repeated thirty-one years later at the end of* Lethal Weapon 2 *(1989) when Murtaugh (Danny Glover) cradles Riggs (Mel Gibson). Copyright 1958 United Artists. Courtesy of Museum of Modern Art Film Stills Archive. Copyright 1989 Warner Bros.*

In the Heat of the Night:
Another Fable of Interracial Amity

In the Heat of the Night (1967) appears nine years after *The Defiant Ones,* nine years further into the American Civil Rights movement. Although it is a "whodunit," it has the same structure as *The Defiant Ones:* the co-heroes, a proud, angry black man and a bigoted, angry white Southern man, are thrown together by circumstances. Although they are initially hostile, they are forced to cooperate to achieve a common goal. Along the way, they fight and undergo male bonding, which gradually leads to their gaining mutual respect and even love. *In the Heat of the Night* works as a mystery, character study, and social problem drama. Whether it is really a step forward from *The Defiant Ones* or simply perpetuates some of the same sincere fictions is the question we will consider.

In this case, Virgil Tibbs (Sidney Poitier), a supersmart black homicide detective from Philadelphia, and Sheriff Gillespie (Rod Steiger), the tough, bigoted chief of police of Sparta, Mississippi, must cooperate to solve the murder of Mr. Colbert, a prominent white Northern industrialist. If they don't, his widow threatens to withdraw their planned factory from the town. Despite abuse from Gillespie and, later, repeated mortal danger from a white lynch mob, Tibbs stays, out of stubbornness and pride, to solve the case. And Gillespie has to put up with Tibbs, despite his deep-rooted prejudice, because the mayor leans on him so the town can have the factory.

In the Heat of the Night represents the best that Hollywood film could do in 1967 in the treatment of race relations. It was made by a group of earnest white activists: director Norman Jewison, cinematographer Haskell Wexler (who had been investigated by the FBI as a subversive), editor Hal Ashby, and actor Lee Grant (who had been blacklisted during the 1950s). They had the best pedagogical intentions. Jewison wanted the film to make a difference at the time: "The commitment to social change was a motivating factor by practically everyone on that film. . . . We wanted to express what we felt about ourselves and our country. . . . We as artists in Hollywood were connected to the people. That connection is gone."[18]

The film was so successful with audiences and critics that it won five Academy Awards, including Best Picture, Best Actor (Rod Steiger), Best Adapted Screenplay, Best Sound, and Best Editing. Poitier went on to portray detective Tibbs in two later films, *They Call Me Mister Tibbs* (1970) and *The Organization* (1970), and *In the Heat of the Night* became the basis for a television series from 1988 to 1994, starring Carroll O'Connor (famous for playing another lovable bigot, Archie Bunker, in the earlier television series *All in the Family*) as Sheriff Gillespie and Howard E. Rollins Jr., as Tibbs. The fable of racial amity, of cooperation, respect, and love between black man and white man that the story provides, has therefore been deeply satisfying to the American public over a period of almost 30 years.

In the Heat of the Night Compared with *Guess Who's Coming to Dinner*

A good point of comparison is with another hugely popular, Academy Award–winning film dealing with black-white relations released the same year, and also starring Sidney Poitier: *Guess Who's Coming to Dinner* (see chapter 6). Both films—*Guess Who's Coming to Dinner*, a domestic comedy, and *In the Heat of the Night*, a mystery—demonstrate how social change can be accommodated within the formulaic constraints of standard Hollywood genres. As George Lipsitz writes, "The racial crises of the 1960s in the U.S. gave rise to 'genre anxiety,' to changes in generic forms effected by adding unconventional racial elements to conventional genre films."[19]

Unfortunately, in the end, *In the Heat of the Night* is as preposterous a fable and almost as much a sincere fiction of the white self as *Guess Who's Coming to Dinner*. It has some of the same problems: once again, Sidney Poitier is cast as a black saint. "Poitier's critics lambasted him as the black man whom white people loved to watch, as 'St. Sidney,' because his roles always had an antiseptic quality to them, rendering him soft-spoken, quiet, patient, asexual, and unthreatening."[20] In the 1960s, Poitier, a great actor, was forced to play improbable black characters, "supertoms" shaped according to the needs of white fantasy. In *Guess Who's Coming to Dinner,* he is a sort of black Albert Schweitzer and a paragon of sexual restraint. In *In the Heat of the Night,* he must be smarter than all the white people, the best homicide detective in Philadelphia, brave enough to face down a lynch mob, and exhibit "a somewhat unexpected knowledge of varieties of plant life as well [the care and feeding of rare orchids]"[21] to be considered the equal of one white sheriff.

In addition, the notion of a black supercop fighting for the dignity of the race is yet another white sincere fiction, meeting the stereotype of black inferiority with an equally unreal counterfiction. As James Baldwin reminds us, "Blacks know something about black cops too, even those called Mister, in Philadelphia. They know that their presence on the force doesn't change the force or the judges or the lawyers or the bondsmen or the jails. . . . They know how much the black cop has to prove, and how limited are his means of proving it: where I grew up, black cops were yet more terrifying than white ones."[22]

In *Guess Who's Coming to Dinner,* only the older whites are prejudiced. The younger generation are all quite tolerant, the cheerful implication being that race prejudice in America is simply an old-fashioned vice that will disappear within a generation. *In the Heat of the Night* proposes another false dichotomy typical of Hollywood film: white racism is a disease confined to the South, and all Northerners are liberal. Up North, Tibbs is a respected, well-paid police officer called "Mr. Tibbs." Evidently Tibbs never had to contend with the barriers of discrimination until he ventured into Mississippi. And Mrs. Colbert, the sole white liberal in the film, is also a Northerner. Such portrayals allow white Northerners to congratulate themselves on their open mindedness in comparison to these benighted Southern rednecks.

Both films also work hard to dispel the threat of black sexuality. *Guess Who's Coming to Dinner* reassures white American parents that, "We won't rape your daughters. Instead, we will refrain from taking them to bed until we have humbly begged you for their hand in marriage. Then we will immediately leave the country so as not to bother you anymore." In *In the Heat of the Night,* Poitier is desexed even further and allowed no romance, neither white nor black. When, in the climax of the film, Tibbs is caught in the most compromising possible situation for a black man in the South—with his hands on a young white woman—he is of course innocent because he only collared her to solve a homicide. And naturally he is quick-witted enough to face down and defeat the white mob, who would castrate and lynch him on the spot, by diverting their attention to the white murder suspect. The scene is thoroughly improbable. *In the Heat of the Night* titillates the audience by raising the specter of the ultimate taboo in the white racial unconscious, only to neutralize it immediately.

The Homosocial Relationship of the Buddies

As in all the black-white buddy movies under consideration, the sexual tension is channeled away from heterosexual relationships and into the sadomasochistic, homosocial relationship between the buddies. The most intimate scene in the film is the one in

In the Heat of the Night, Amistad, *and* The Green Mile: *Handshakes signify the bond between buddies.* Copyright 1967 United Artists, Copyright 1997 Dreamworks, and Copyright 2000 Warner Bros.

which Gillespie invites Tibbs to his home late at night and opens up to him. Gillespie, who has had too much to drink and is lying down on his sofa, reveals to Tibbs his isolation and loneliness: "I got no wife. . . . I'll tell you a secret. Nobody comes here. Never." And he questions Tibbs on whether he has ever been married or if he gets lonely. In other words, Tibbs is Gillespie's first "date" since the sheriff came to town.

The final sincere fiction of the film is the elevation of the sheriff into a white messiah, the friend and protector of a black man, like the small-town Southern sheriff turned FBI agent (Gene Hackman) in *Mississippi Burning* (1988). *In the Heat of the Night* posits that a bigoted white Southern sheriff such as Gillespie, a character based in part on the notorious racist police commissioner Eugene "Bull" Connor of Birmingham,[23] could in the course of a few days overcome the conditioning of a lifetime and come to respect and love a black man. Only in white liberal fantasies could this happen. "Black men know something about white sheriffs. They know, for one thing, that the sheriff is no freer to become friends with them than they are to become friends with the sheriff." [24] James Baldwin further speculates that had the widow demanded the death of Tibbs as the price for building the factory, Gillespie would not have hesitated for a moment. "In *Birth of a Nation,* the Sheriff would have been an officer of the Klan . . . . And Virgil Tibbs would have been the hunted, not the hunter."[25]

For James Baldwin, "the effect of such a film [as *In the Heat of the Night*] is to increase and not lessen white confusion and complacency, and black rage and despair. . . . It is not that the creators of the film were inspired by base motives, but that they could not understand their motives, nor be responsible for the effect of their exceedingly complex motives, in action."[26] In other words, in attempting to expand the potential of Hollywood genre film and make an anti-racist statement that would sound a hopeful note in a time of racial turbulence and change, Norman Jewison and his cocreators unintentionally reinforced numerous old sincere fictions of the white self.

Brian's Song: The Male Pastoral

Brian's Song (1971), an award-winning, made-for-television movie, is based on the true story of the friendship of Chicago Bears teammates Brian Piccolo (James Caan) and Gale Sayers (Billy Dee Williams), who in the late 1960s were the first white and black professional football players to room together. Brian helps Gale recover from a knee injury and then Gale stays by Brian's side as he suffers from lung cancer and dies. The film was highly popular because of its true-life basis, because of the moving performances of Caan and Williams, and especially because of the inspirational message about coping with injury and fatal illness through interracial friendship. It showed something new for television: football players who cry and love each other and male bonding across the color line. Released in 1970, after years of riots in urban black communities across the country and the rise of black nationalist and black power sentiments, the story was reassuring to white audiences. It was remade, again for television, in 2001. Thus, like *In the Heat of the Night,* it represents the remarkable persistence of a sincere fiction of the white self.

Brian's Song is part of a tidal wave, beginning in the 1970s and continuing today, of television and movie images of interracial amity. This flood of wish-fulfilling pop-cultural images creates a "friendship orthodoxy" as a salve to black anger and white guilt. [27] In the new friendship orthodoxy, white racism is not a matter of centuries of slavery and systematic exploitation and oppression, of institutional structures, of restricted access to opportunity, or of entrenched caste differences between white and black, and it no longer requires political or governmental intervention. No, racism is simply a misunderstanding that can be overcome if individuals just have the right *feelings* in their hearts. If we can only be friends and recognize that we are all really the same inside, then racism will vanish with handshakes and hugs. All white people need to do is to smile at their black maids or take a black friend to lunch. This is the dominant ideology in the post–Civil Rights era. Social scientists have called this a new, "color blind" racism.[28]

The friendship orthodoxy was codified in popular culture as early as 1967, in Matt Drayton's (Spencer Tracy's) big speech at the end of *Guess Who's Coming to Dinner:* "The only thing that matters is what they feel—and how much they feel—for each other" (see chapter 6).

Utopian and sentimental, *Brian's Song* is a male pastoral, an interracial romance that focuses almost entirely on the two men. Even their wives play minor roles, and their children are eliminated from the story. The movie emphasizes the idyllic relationship of the men through such devices as sentimental music and a repeated, slow-motion shot of the two running together through the woods as Brian helps Gale recover from his injury.

Like all the black-white buddy movies, it must cope with its uneasiness over two taboos: racial difference and homoeroticism. The film finesses race by suggesting that Brian is never prejudiced and that his initial hostility toward Gale is due to competitiveness and male rivalry and not to race. When Gale shows up to try out for the team, Brian plays a joke on him by lying that the coach is deaf in one ear, so that Gale makes a fool of himself when he first meets the coach. Next, Brian causes Gale to be fined for talking during a meal. The film treats these practical jokes as comic, as Brian's way of initiating Gale into professional football. The sequence also follows the pattern of the traditional Hollywood romance, in which the couple must first be hostile before they realize they really love each other.

Nevertheless, because of the racial difference, there is another possible reading of Brian's practical jokes: a white man is trying to hurt a black rival by humiliating him. We are reminded of the scene in chapter 15 of *Huckleberry Finn* when Huck plays a cruel joke on Jim. Jim, disgusted with Huck, tells him, "En all you was thinking 'bout wuz how you could make a fool uv ole Jim wid a lie. Dat truck is *trash*; en trash is what people is dat puts dirt on de head er dey fren's en makes 'em ashamed."

The only racial insults in the film are tossed off as comic, as the joking of close friends. For example, when Gale is slow to recover from his injury, Brian forces him to exercise, egging him on by joshing: "Can't make it. Nigger. Chicken nigger." Later, when Brian is in the hospital with cancer, again he jokes with Gale: "You gave me a pint of blood—is that true? That explains it—I had this craving for chittlins all day." Yet, Gale never makes any jocular insults about Brian's whiteness.

In a nice reversal of stereotyping, however, Brian, the white buddy, is portrayed as extroverted and garrulous whereas Gale, the black man, is reserved and close-mouthed, "the stone face from Kansas."

The film deals with the homoeroticism of the buddies through jokes. When Brian first becomes ill, he jokes, "I think I'm pregnant." Later, when Brian is in the hospital and talking to Gale on the phone, he quips, "If you were here I'd kiss you." This same kind of uneasy joking about the white man attracted to the black male is repeated, years later, throughout the *Lethal Weapon* movie series.

There are also open declarations of love between the two men. While Brian is facing another operation, Gale is given the "Most Courageous Player" award. Gale, who was previously tongue-tied about public speaking, seems to have taken on some of Brian's eloquence and makes a moving speech, saying the award really belongs to Brian: "He has the heart of a giant. He spells out courage twenty-four hours a day, every day of his life. . . . I love Brian Piccolo. And I'd like you all to love him too. And tonight, when you hit your knees, please ask God to love him."

These two men are married until death. When Brian dies, it is Gale holding his hand, not Brian's wife. Brian's dying words are about their friendship and rivalry: "I'm gonna get you next training camp. I'm gonna get you." To which Gale replies, "I'll be waiting."

Would this film have been as popular if it were the black man who had cancer and the white man declared in public his love for a black man and held his hand as he was dying? We doubt such a movie would have ever been made. It would have offended white audiences, who need reassurance that black people really love them, yet also know only too well the insulting term applied to whites who love blacks. Thus, Brian is the tragic hero here and Gale the black sidekick who affirms Brian's worth.

This idyllic marriage until death of the white man and the man of color goes far back in American culture, to such works as *Moby Dick*. In chapter 4 of Melville's novel, the white narrator Ishmael is forced to share a bed in a seaport inn with Queequeg, a South Sea Islander. "Upon waking next morning about daylight, I found Queequeg's arm thrown over me in the most loving and affectionate manner. You had almost thought I had been his wife. . . . For though I tried to move his arm—unlock his bridegroom clasp—yet, sleeping as he was, he still hugged me tightly, as though naught but death should part us twain."

Unfortunately, buddy movies like *Brian's Song,* unlike *Huckleberry Finn* or *Moby Dick,* do not really investigate the complexities of the American racial divide. Twain and Melville at least recognized that the clasp between the white man and the black could be as much a death grip as an embrace. By creating a male pastoral, movies like *Brian's Song* erase the conflict with a sentimental wish.

The Alliance of Blacks and Jews in *Blazing Saddles*

Blazing Saddles (1974), directed by Mel Brooks, is a cheerful carnival of bad taste, an anarchic western spoof, irreverent about almost everything. Brooks is an equal-opportunity offender, making jokes about whites, blacks, Jews, Chinese, Indians, women, and homosexuals. It was extremely innovative for its day, the first of what the contemporary film producer Brian Grazer calls "shock comedy." Tame comedies about race like *Guess Who's Coming to Dinner* were no longer believable. "The comedies that preceded it were more gentle and earnest. This one was aggressive and in your face, and dealing in a very smart and startling way with the most intense social issues, from racial bigotry to sexuality. . . . This movie was a kind of singular moment where it was somehow all right to have this kind of racial language in a movie."[29]

The script is credited to five writers—Andrew Bergman, Mel Brooks, Richard Pryor, Norman Steinberg, and Alan Uger—in other words, to four Jews and a black. And the two heroes, Bart (Cleavon Little) and Jim (Gene Wilder), are played by a black and a Jew. The movie is thus really about Jews and blacks banding together to spoof the white self by mocking Hollywood westerns and rewriting Western history. Like *Little Big Man,* it is an anti-Western in the wake of the Vietnam War. Ella Shohat says, "This parody of the Western brings in these elided subaltern histories and suppressed ethnic voices."[30]

In a flashback, Bart, the black hero, tells Jim, his white buddy, how he came West as a child: "Back in '56, my folks and I were part of this long wagon train, movin' West. . . . Well, not exactly part of it. We were bringing up the rear." When the Sioux attack, the settlers circle their wagons, but "the white folks wouldn't let us travel in their circle, so we made our own." The sight gag of the lone wagon driven frantically in circles epitomizes the marginalized, imperiled, and absurd situation of the African American.

The family is captured by the Sioux, but the Yiddish-speaking chief, played by Mel Brooks, lets them go, saying, "They darker than us." This alliance of minorities is simultaneously Indian–black and Jewish–black. "Here Brooks merges Native Americans and Jews as well as African Americans, all marginalized groups excluded from the Anglo-American master narrative."[31]

Mocking Whites in *Blazing Saddles*

Whites are mocked mercilessly in *Blazing Saddles* as cruel and violent racists but also as stupid and easy to fool. With the exception of Jim, whites in the movie fall into two categories: dumb and dumber. "That these white bigots are so stupid . . . lets you watch them without taking offense. And almost everyone in the movie who is an authority figure is an idiot."[32] The audience enjoys watching the smart, hip black hero make fools of these bigoted white buffoons. For example, in the opening scene, set in Colorado in 1874, blacks and Chinese are laying track for a railroad line in the heat, the kind of scene that never appeared in classic Hollywood westerns.[33] A Chinese man collapses, and Lyle, the white overseer, says, "Dock the chink a day's pay for napping on the job." Next Lyle orders the workers to sing: "Now come on, boys, where's your spirit? I don't hear no singin'. When you were slaves, you sang like birds. Come on, how 'bout a good ole nigger work song?" The workers, led by Bart, harmonize in an a capella rendition of Cole Porter's "I Get a Kick Out of You." The bewildered Lyle and his white gang try to show the blacks how to sing like blacks by launching into "Swing Low, Sweet Chariot" and "Camptown Races." The black workers stifle their laughter at this display.

This opening establishes Bart as quick-witted and sophisticated and Lyle and the whites as dense racists unaware they are being mocked. The scene also makes fun of the minstrel show and the arrogant assumption that whites know all about black culture. In a deliberate reversal, the blacks instead appropriate white culture (Cole Porter).

Bart, who is later appointed sheriff of the all-white town of Rock Ridge, is the smartest character in the film and triumphs repeatedly over dim-witted whites. He is like the supersmart black detective Mr. Tibbs triumphing over dumb white southerners in *In the Heat of the Night,* except that Bart plays it tongue-in-cheek whereas Tibbs always takes himself dead seriously. For example, Tibbs (improbably) talks his way out of being lynched by an angry white mob. Bart does the same thing, but Brooks plays it for comedy, emphasizing the preposterous nature of the stunt by having Bart hold a gun to his own head and say: "Hold it. The next man makes a move, the nigger gets it!" As Bart congratulates himself later, "Oh, baby, you are so talented, and they are so dumb!" When he defeats the huge, simple-minded brute Mongo (by delivering an exploding candy-gram), he is equated through image and sound with the cartoon hero Bugs Bunny, outsmarting the stupid white man Elmer Fudd.

In the end, Bart proves that the white morons cannot survive without minorities. After the black and Chinese workers help save Rock Ridge, the whites allow them to settle there, albeit reluctantly: "All right, we'll give some land to the niggers and the chinks, but we don't want the Irish!"

Satire and Sentiment in *Blazing Saddles*

Despite the mockery of dumb white racists, the heart of the movie is a sentimental tale of interracial friendship. Everything else may be played for laughs, but the love between Bart and Jim is portrayed as genuine.

In other black-white buddy movies, until the onset of "color-blind" movies in the late 1980s, the pair must overcome initial hostility before they can become partners. For example, in both *The Defiant Ones* and *48 Hours,* the heroes come to blows before they solidify their friendship. But in *Blazing Saddles,* Jim feels no animosity toward Bart, and the two bond over a game of chess when they meet. Jim is Bart's prisoner, but Bart treats him instead as an ally. Their immediate friendship is sentimental.

Both gain from the partnership. Jim, once a gunslinger called the Waco Kid, gets his manhood back: he quits drinking and recovers his fast draw. And Bart is able to succeed as sheriff with Jim as his deputy. Together, they defeat the bad guys and save the town.

The alliance of Bart and Jim is another male pastoral, the utopian dream in American popular culture of overcoming the barriers of race and of racism by creating a mutual admiration society based on homosociality.

Perhaps the film repeatedly spoofs male homosexuality as a way to deny its presence in the central tale of male bonding. For example, the villain is named "Hedley Lamarr," a name the other characters frequently confuse with that of the actress "Hedy Lamarr." In one scene, Taggart helps Hedley bathe and gropes suggestively in the bath water. And in the finale, the cast engages in a massive fistfight with a chorus of gay male dancers. At times, Brooks punctures stereotypes, but at others he falls for them or simply exploits them.

48 Hours: The Overnight Cure for Racism

48 Hours (1982) is yet another film that has the same structure as *The Defiant Ones:* a white man and a black man, initially hostile, are forced to cooperate for a common goal, learn grudging respect, and end up partners and best friends. In both movies, the white man is able to abandon enough white privilege and racist stereotyping to learn to trust and admire a black man, and the initially hostile black man learns to love the white man.

The utopian premise of *48 Hours,* as in so many interracial buddy movies, is that it only takes a day or two of interaction with a black man to convert a lifelong white racist into an anti-racist. The implication is that the roots of racism are shallow and can be overcome simply through greater familiarity between the races.

In *The Defiant Ones,* however, the interracial partners are on the same level, both convicts. But in *48 Hours* there is a racial hierarchy: "a tough white cop with the soul of a beer barrel . . . and a jivey black con with the spirit of a peacock."[34]

And whereas *The Defiant Ones* is a melodrama, *48 Hours* is a blend of action film and comedy. One reviewer likened it to the archetypal rogue-cop action movie *Dirty Harry* (1971), "with an interracial buddy-buddy formula plot thrown in to lure the crossover action audience,"[35] but others took it as more of "a sendup of *Dirty Harry*"[36] or an "outright parody of the rogue-cop genre."[37] It was also compared to a TV series "dreamed up by Leslie Fiedler" because the white and black odd couple "bitch at each other like lovers in a sitcom—say, Jeff Goldblum and Ben Vereen in the short-lived *Tenspeed and Brownshoe* or Robert Culp and Bill Cosby in *I Spy.* Welcome back to the raft, Huck honey, and it's off on another trip down the Mississippi in the form of endless car chases along the streets of San Francisco."[38]

The partnership is at first a forced relationship of convenience. The black convict Reggie Hammond (Eddie Murphy, in the role that made him a movie star) is temporarily released in the custody of the white cop Jack Cates (Nick Nolte). Jack needs Reggie to find Reggie's former partner Ganz, who has escaped from prison and killed several police officers. Reggie helps only because Ganz knows where some money is hidden. Jack initially has contempt for Reggie and makes it clear who holds the power: "We ain't partners, we ain't brothers, and we ain't friends. I'm putting you down and I'm keeping you down until Ganz is locked up or dead. And if Ganz gets away, you're gonna be sorry you ever met me."

We sympathize with Jack, despite his harsh treatment of Reggie, because Jack seems so woebegone: he drinks and smokes too much, drives a beat-up old car, has trouble with his girlfriend, and gets no respect from his colleagues or his boss. Because Jack is in plain clothes, fellow cops keep stopping him and questioning his identity. In addition, we root for Jack because Ganz is presented as absolute evil, a psychopathic cop-killer.[39]

Reggie is first introduced as he sits alone in his prison cell, singing along loudly to a recording of "Roxanne" on Walkman headphones. Ed Guerrero notes that "dominant cinema constructs and positions the black image for 'the look' of the norm, for the visual and narrative pleasure of the white spectator-consumer." Thus Reggie is positioned as a foolish black convict to whom the white audience can feel superior.[40]

Noah Cullen in *The Defiant Ones* is also introduced as he sings behind bars. But Cullen sings out of defiance, to annoy the white prisoners and guards, especially the white prisoner to whom he is chained, whereas Reggie apparently sings for his own pleasure, because he is a singing fool. And Cullen's song, "Bowling Green," is a black folk song, whereas "Roxanne" is by the white singer Sting, who is imitating black reggae. Thus we get the curious phenomenon of Reggie performing a white imitation of black music. This seems to reaffirm the claim that 1980s films about race embodied "the desire that blackness cease to exist, that it be replaced with at most a white version of who and what blacks are."[41]

Reggie is also portrayed as perpetually horny because he's been behind bars. Donald Bogle notes that "the script frequently plays on the idea of the oversexed black man" and that Jack is given a girlfriend but Reggie is not.[42]

The film denies its own stereotyping by portraying Jack as at first openly racist: he calls Reggie "watermelon," "spearchucker," "a charcoal-colored loser," and "nigger." They trade insults and finally come to blows, but all this seems part of their male bonding ("in movies like this it is only by fighting that men become friends"[43]). Eventually, Jack apologizes, claiming, "'Nigger,' 'watermelon'—I didn't mean that. I was just doing my job, keeping you down." To which Reggie replies, "Well, doing your job don't explain everything, Jack." Keeping Reggie down because he is a convict is not the same as keeping him down because he is black. There is a double power differential operating here: Jack holds the upper hand not only as a cop but also as a white man.

To upset the differential, the film gives Jack a black boss, but then defeats this potentially progressive move by giving the boss the worst racist diatribe in the film. The chief calls Reggie a "nigger" and "a little piece of shit." Jack interrupts the chief, saying, "Wait a minute, goddamit! Let me tell you something about this man. He's got more brains than you'll ever know. He's got more guts than any partner I ever had." This scene seems contrived to deflect prejudice from Jack, who by defending Reggie before his boss, and a black boss at that, demonstrates his change of heart and anti-racism. As in *Guess Who's Coming to Dinner,* blacks are portrayed as worse racists than whites.

Jack has been on the police force a long time and must have dealt with many black officers; he even has a black boss. Yet those experiences do not seem to have eliminated his racism. Instead we have "faith in the miracle cure by change of heart."[44] The film also tries to appear anti-racist by making the criminal gang multiracial: a white man, a black, and a Native American. Nevertheless, the white man is still the leader of the gang.

"I'm your worst fuckin' nightmare"

The funniest and most memorable scene in the movie involves a racial reversal. Reggie bets Jack that he can get some information if Jack lends him his badge. If Reggie wins, he gains free time with a prostitute. Using the badge, Reggie terrorizes a country-western bar filled with hostile whites. He says, "You know what I am? I'm your worst fuckin' nightmare: I'm a nigger with a badge. That means I got permission to kick your fuckin' ass whenever I feel like it." As he leaves, he proclaims loudly, "I want the rest of you cowboys to know something: there's a new sheriff in town, and his name is Reggie Hammond."

The effect here is similar to that in *Blazing Saddles,* a comic turning of the tables: "there's a new sheriff in town." Whites sympathize with Bart, the black sheriff in *Blazing Saddles,* not because he is an impostor but because, like Reggie, he is an underdog getting revenge.

Eddie Murphy often plays impostors, as in *48 Hours, Trading Places,* and the *Beverly Hills Cop* series. But the role playing means that "Murphy's characters pretend to positions of power rather than actually inhabit them."[45] If he really had power, the white audience would become uncomfortable. Instead, by admiring Eddie Murphy as he plays his comic specialty—the fast-talking, role-playing black con man—the white audience can congratulate itself on its anti-racism.

In addition, white audiences never perceive either Bart in *Blazing Saddles* or Reggie in *48 Hours* as threatening. They are simply too likeable. "Everything about Murphy, from his body language to the look in his eyes, immediately signals that he's a nice guy [and] takes any edge off the picture which would have been provided by a more potentially dangerous sort. There's never any threat that he might try to escape or harm Nolte in any way."[46] Notes Mark Winokur: "Murphy's portrayal of a black con man . . . is parodic—we know that although he is a black man with a gun he will not kill anyone important."[47] To maintain the comedy, both Bart and Reggie are made into paradoxical figures: violent black "bucks" who nevertheless are harmless "coons."

The problem is that neither Bart nor Reggie ever gets really angry at the racism to which they are subjected; they shrug it off with comedy or fast quips. In *The Defiant Ones,* the black hero at least expresses outrage at the racist remarks of the white convict.[48]

Just as Reggie is introduced singing along with Sting, so the entire movie seems to portray him as "a white version of who and what blacks are."[49] He is "your worst fucking nightmare" reduced to a joke as a way to neutralize white fears of black aggression or black power.

Notes

1. Ellison, Ralph. 1980. *Invisible Man.* 1952; reprint, New York: Vintage, pp. 187–88.

2. Guerrero, Ed. 1993. *Framing Blackness: The African American Image in Film.* Philadelphia, Pa.: Temple University Press, p. 128.

3. Wiegman, Robyn. 1997. "Fiedler and Sons," in *Race and the Subject of Masculinities,* eds. Harry Stecopoulos and Michael Uebel. Durham, N.C.: Duke University Press, pp. 45–68 (p. 66).

4. Carby, Hazel V. 1998. *Race Men.* Cambridge, Mass.: Harvard University Press, p. 191.

5. Fiedler, Leslie A. 1968. *The Return of the Vanishing American.* New York: Stein & Day, p. 130.

6. Keyser, Lester J., and André Ruszkowski. 1980. *The Cinema of Sidney Poitier: The Black Man's Changing Role on the American Screen.* San Diego, Calif.: A. S. Barnes, p. 48.

7. Ibid.

8. Poitier, Sidney. 1980. *This Life.* New York: Knopf, p. 212.

9. Spoto, Donald. 1978. *Stanley Kramer, Film Maker.* New York: Putnam, pp. 203–4.

10. Keyser and Ruszkowski, *The Cinema of Sidney Poitier,* p. 50.

11. Baldwin, James. 1963. *The Fire Next Time.* New York: Dial, p. 597.

12. Ibid., p. 598.

13. Bogle, Donald. 1997. *Toms, Coons, Mulattoes, Mammies, and Bucks: An Interpretive History of Blacks in American Films.* New York: Continuum, p. 182.

14. Baldwin, *The Fire Next Time,* p. 599.

15. Spoto, *Stanley Kramer, Film Maker,* p. 204.

16. Baldwin, *The Fire Next Time,* p. 599.

17. Fiedler, *The Return of the Vanishing American,* p. 129.

18. *Heat of the Night* (1967) DVD commentary, United Artists 2000.

19. Lipsitz, George. 1998. "Genre Anxiety and Racial Representation in 1970s Cinema," in *Refiguring American Film Genres: History and Theory,* ed. Nick Browne. Berkeley: University of California Press, pp. 208–32 (p. 209).

20. Ibid., p. 221.

21. Baldwin, James. 1985. *The Price of the Ticket: Collected Nonfiction 1948–1985.* New York: St. Martin's, p. 590.

22. Ibid., p. 595.

23. *Heat of the Night* (1967) DVD commentary, United Artists 2000.

24. Baldwin, *The Price of the Ticket,* p. 594.

25. Ibid., p. 593.

26. Ibid., pp. 591–92.

27. DeMott, Benjamin. 1995. *The Trouble with Friendship: Why Americans Can't Think Straight about Race.* New York: Atlantic Monthly Press, p. 5.

28. Bonilla-Silva, Eduardo. 2001. *White Supremacy & Racism in the Post–Civil Rights Era.* Boulder, Colo.: Lynne Rienner, pp. 137–62.

29 Grazer, Brian, interviewed by Rick Lyman. 2001. "Inducing Hilarity by Doses of Shock: Brian Grazer Interviewed." *New York Times,* December 14, E26.

30. Shohat, Ella. 1991. "Ethnicities-in-Relation: Toward a Multicultural Reading of American Cinema," in *Unspeakable Images: Ethnicity and the American Cinema,* ed. Lester D. Friedman. Urbana: University of Illinois Press, pp. 215–50 (p. 244).

31. Ibid.

32. Grazer, "Inducing Hilarity by Doses of Shock," p. E26.

33. Shohat, "Ethnicities-in-Relation, p. 244.

34. Shickel, Richard. 1982. Review of *48 Hours. Time,* December 20, p. 87.

35. Sarris, Andrew. 1982. Review of *48 Hours. Village Voice,* December 14, p. 79.

36. Thomas, Kevin. 1982. Review of *48 Hours. Los Angeles Times,* December 19, Calendar, p. 1.

37. Coleman, John. 1983. Review of *48 Hours. New Statesman,* March 25, p. 30.

38. Asahina, Robert. 1982. Review of *48 Hours. New Leader,* December 27, p. 20.

39. *Variety.* 1982. Review of *48 Hours.* November 22, p. 82.

40. Guerrero, *Framing Blackness,* pp. 125–26.

41. Winokur, Mark. 1991. "Black Is White/White Is Black: 'Passing' as Strategy of Racial Compatibility in Contemporary Hollywood Comedy," in *Unspeakable Images: Ethnicity and the American Cinema,* ed. Lester D. Friedman. Urbana: University of Illinois Press pp. 190–211 (p. 192).

42. Bogle, *Toms, Coons, Mulattoes, Mammies, and Bucks,* p. 283.

43. Schickel, Review of *48 Hours,* p. 87.

44. De Mott, *The Trouble with Friendship,* p. 54.

45. Winokur, "Black is White/White is Black,"p. 201.

46. *Variety,* Review of *48 Hours,* p. 82.

47. Winokur, "Black is White/White is Black," p. 199.

48. Bogle, *Toms, Coons, Mulattoes, Mammies, and Bucks,* p. 282.

49. Winokur, "Black Is White/White Is Black," p. 192.

CHAPTER 11

Black and White Buddies II

Films Analyzed:
Lethal Weapon series (1987, 1989, 1992, 1998)
The Shawshank Redemption (1994)
The Green Mile (2000)
Men in Black (1997)

Lethal Weapon Series as Generic Blend

The *Lethal Weapon* series (1987, 1989, 1992, 1998), one of the most popular movie series of the 1980s and 1990s, represents a new stage in the evolution of the black-white buddy movie. It resembles *48 Hours* but is one of the first of the new cycle of "color-blind" movies beginning in the late 1980s and continuing today. The series pairs two fictional Los Angeles Police Department officers, one white and one black, as best buddies willing to die for each other. The *Lethal Weapon* movies resemble war movies, with a constant escalation of violence and destruction in which the cop partners function as a two-man army.

The innovation in the series is a blending of the elements of the spectacular action film with those of the black-white buddy comedy and the domestic sitcom. One critic calls *Lethal Weapon* "*Mad Max* meets the Cosby show."[1] In postmodern terminology, we could call it a *hybrid* or a *pastiche*. How can the series successfully mix such disparate elements without creating a fatal clash? The idealized closeness of the white and black heroes is the glue that holds it together. We get a fantasy about racial harmony achieved through male bonding in the midst of a world being blown apart. Action films already defy plausibility, so it is easy to add the implausibility of racial harmony to the mix.[2] Racial hostility is displaced into spectacular violence, and the comedy enables us to laugh it all off. "It is not despite, but *through* comic moments that the device of interracial male bonding functions in the *Lethal Weapon* series, comedy which plays off generic expectations as well as a range of stereotypes."[3]

From the action spectacle, we get the usual fights, gunplay, chases, and explosions. From the buddy comedy, we get an odd couple with clashing temperaments who are

171

Lethal Weapon 3: *Riggs depends on Murtaugh for his identity. He needs the unqualified love and loyalty of his black partner in order to exist. Copyright 1992 Warner Bros.*

thrown together by circumstances, get into trouble, bicker, and finally bond into an indissoluble pair. Here they are Martin Riggs (Mel Gibson), a single, reckless white cop, and Roger Murtaugh (Danny Glover), an older, married, staid middle-class black cop, initially assigned against their will as partners by the LAPD. Although they are supposedly equals, Riggs is violent and impulsive, takes the lead in any violent situation, and always has a plan that his black partner Murtaugh follows as Riggs drags him further into danger. Riggs is fearless, even suicidal, but Murtaugh often shows fear, which provides comedy. Riggs is the joker and the top banana; Murtaugh is the sidekick, straight man, and frequent butt of Riggs's jokes. From the sitcom, we get Murtaugh as the flustered father who is comically possessive of his adolescent daughter and does not know what is going on in his own household.

Finally, the buddies become so close that the *Lethal Weapon* series resembles romance as much as it does war movie. A lot of the comedy derives from the attraction between the white cop and the black. The jokes seem a way to deny the uncomfortable homoerotic tension.[4] This is the same underlying tension found in all the black-white buddy movies.

The Tame Black Man

The pairing of Riggs and Murtaugh seems at first to reverse stereotypes: the crazy, violent white man versus the stable, middle-class black family man. In the white imagination, the black male is supposed to be violent. Nevertheless, Murtaugh simply represents the inverse of this stereotype: the tame black man. This trope begins with *Huckleberry Finn* and runs through all the interracial buddy films, "that makes the white guy and his black pal both supposedly equal, brothers-in-arms, yet domesticates the latter while keeping the former out there, wild, on the edge."[5] Donald Bogle also points to "the huck-finn fixation" in *Lethal Weapon,* in which "the good black man brings to his white loner friend an element of calm control and budding maturity."[6]

Riggs is presented in the first movie as living on the edge: trigger-happy, reckless, and suicidal with grief since the death of his wife. Murtaugh stabilizes him by bringing him home to share Christmas with his family. The black hero restores the white hero's sanity by befriending him and integrating him into his family. "*Lethal Weapon*'s evocation of a world beyond race enables the white man to regain identity and power across a seemingly egalitarian representation of the black bourgeoisie."[7]

In exchange, Riggs helps rescue Murtaugh's kidnapped daughter and restores Murtaugh's manhood by encouraging him to shoot to kill. Thus the black man helps to tame the wild white man and the white helps make the black more wild: "The black man seems to receive from the white man's hands not only the capacity for effective violence, but something very like virility itself, both gifts the white male imaginary has often feared it might lack in comparison to blacks who might possess them in excess."[8]

The domesticated black man is "a figure who proved not only that blacks could make it in white society, but that whites could love them and welcome them into their homes, electronically at least, as friends."[9] In the 1960s, the safe black man was portrayed in the movies by Sidney Poitier. In the 1980s, he was portrayed on television by Bill Cosby and in the movies by Danny Glover. Whites need to feel that they can distinguish bad blacks from good ones, and figures such as those portrayed by Poitier, Cosby, and Glover embody "all the ethical codes of white middle-class America"[10] and "hardly threaten white audiences at all."[11] Murtaugh is a middle-aged, middle-class family man with a wife and three kids, a large home, and a boat. His family has also been "Cosbyized": they are black but drained of all ethnic attributes.

Hazel Carby argues that Glover, whose career blossomed during the conservative Reagan years, typically plays the black savior who helps the white hero "save himself from his enemies and, most importantly, save himself from his own weaknesses and fears."[12] Another critic puts it more bluntly: "With interracial male bonding, black men are a cross between toms and mammies: all-giving, all-knowing, all-sacrificing nurturers."[13] Just as Mammy in *Gone With the Wind* is a figure of domestic stability, a foil for the wild Scarlett, so Murtaugh helps to balance the wild Riggs.

We would add that aside from the tom and the mammy, Murtaugh also partakes of two other stereotyped black male figures: the buck and the coon. The filmmakers incorporate the old stereotypes into a hybrid, contemporary black hero who offers something for everyone. The buck is a figure of brutal violence who emerges out of the white unconscious. As we mentioned, in *48 Hours,* Eddie Murphy quips, "I'm your worst fuckin' nightmare: a nigger with a badge," but it is only a joke because Murphy is playing a criminal temporarily impersonating a policeman. In *Lethal Weapon,* the black man really does possess a badge, but the nightmare is tamed for a white audience because the black man is so safely middle class and also subservient to a white partner, who validates his violence.

The figure of the coon presents the African American "as amusement object and black buffoon."[14] Murtaugh is frequently placed in humiliating situations. For example, he is doomed to get no peace and no privacy in his own bathroom. In an early scene in *Lethal Weapon,* Murtaugh is taking a bath as the entire family troops in to wish him happy birthday. The situation is repeated in *Lethal Weapon 3* when they march in to wish him "Happy Retirement Day," except this time his white friend Leo Getz also barges in. In *Lethal Weapon 2,* Murtaugh is trapped all day on the toilet seat in his bathroom because it has been rigged to a bomb. His humiliation increases when the bomb squad, the media, and the entire neighborhood arrive.

He is also the frequent butt of Riggs' practical jokes. In *Lethal Weapon 2,* Murtaugh's daughter Riane appears in a television ad for condoms, and, to tease him, Riggs keeps planting condom trees on his desk. In *Lethal Weapon 4,* Riggs milks for all it is worth the newspaper story about Murtaugh's stripping in public and acting like a human chicken. Whereas Riggs loves risk and is always cool in the face of danger, Murtaugh sometimes displays the fear and trembling characteristic of eyeball-rolling black comedians of 1930s movies, such as Manton Moreland. As James Baldwin writes, "The white man's masculinity depends on a denial of the masculinity of the blacks."[15]

Despite Riggs' practical jokes against Murtaugh, he is dependent on him for his identity. He needs the unqualified love and loyalty of his black partner in order to exist. This becomes clear in a scene in *Lethal Weapon 3.* Murtaugh is ready to retire, and Riggs confronts him on Murtaugh's boat (it's back to the raft for Huck and Jim). Riggs accuses him: "You selfish bastard! You're just thinking about yourself, goddamn it! What about me? We're partners. What happens to you happens to me. After all the shit we've been through. Don't you get it? When you retire, you're not just retiring you, you're retiring us, man." Murtaugh responds, "It's not my problem." Riggs says, "You're the only family I got. I got three beautiful kids, I love them, they're yours. Trish [Murtaugh's wife] does my laundry, I live in your icebox, I live in your life. What am I gonna do? What am I supposed to do?" So Murtaugh says, "You know I love you" and decides not to retire.

Hazel Carby reads this scene as "the accusation of the betrayal of white America by an aggressive black America."[16] Although this is certainly true, the scene also demonstrates the dependency of the white male identity on the black male. As James Baldwin writes, "the danger, in the minds of most white Americans, is the loss of their identity. . . . Well, the black man has functioned in the white man's world as a fixed star, as an immovable pillar; as he moves out of his place, heaven and earth are shaken to their foundations."[17]

The Function of Leo Getz

A feminist critic sees the *Lethal Weapon* series as concerning a crisis of white heterosexual masculinity "desperately seeking to reconstruct itself within a web of social differences, where its opposing terms include not only femininity, but black masculinity and male homosexuality."[18] In this regard, it is worth looking at the function of Leo Getz, a comic character who becomes the third stooge in the series. Getz first appears in *Lethal Weapon 2* and the character is developed in *Lethal Weapon 3* and *4.* He is introduced as a crooked accountant who will testify against the mob and has been placed in protective custody. Riggs and Murtaugh babysit him and repeatedly save his life. Getz is a hotheaded, obnoxious little twerp who jabbers loudly and uncontrollably. "Leo's comic role functions to produce a figure who is both feminised and trivialised by his hysterical speech."[19]

Getz is a white man of unspecified ethnicity, played by Joe Pesci, an Italian-American actor who often portrays psychotic mafiosi. In the fourth film, he is revealed to be Jewish, thus adding to the purported multiculturalism of the series. Like Riggs, he seems blind to Murtaugh's racial difference. He is a comic foil, a little guy who hero worships the partners and tries unsuccessfully to imitate them, even becoming a private eye. He has no life of his own but attaches himself to the heroes, who use him when convenient but otherwise treat him as a pest or play practical jokes on him. Getz thus functions within the crisis of white masculinity in the series. Infantile, reckless, and clinging, Getz is a dwarf version of Riggs, a way to disavow through comic caricature Riggs's own less-than-"masculine" tendencies.

If these are three stooges, Riggs is clearly the head stooge. Although he clowns around, the jokes are never at his expense. Murtaugh and Getz, his black partner and his white ethnic buddy, are the buffoons, subordinated to glorify Riggs.

The Los Angeles Police Department as Anti-racist Crusaders

One could argue that the *Lethal Weapon* movies, like all the other black-white buddy movies, have a utopian impulse, fighting racism by depicting idealized situations of interracial male bonding.

But despite their apparent message of tolerance, in effect the *Lethal Weapon* movies deny the reality of the American racial situation by a fictional sleight of hand that redefines racism as a foreign import and redefines police brutality as an antiracist crusade. The movies displace racial violence outward toward safe, foreign targets such as white, South African drug dealers who represent the forces of apartheid in *Lethal Weapon 2* (1989) or Chinese gangsters who force illegal Chinese immigrants into virtual slavery in *Lethal Weapon 4* (1998). The violence of these evil foreigners makes the audience applaud the brutality of the LAPD. The effect of the movies is to convert the LAPD, whose image is that of one of the most corrupt, racist police forces in the country, into a haven of racial amity. The movies twist contemporary history, transforming the LAPD into heroic, anti-racist crusaders, similar to the way in which two white FBI agents are made the heroes of the Civil Rights movement in *Mississippi Burning* (1988).

In reality, the contemporary LAPD ranks in the top ten police departments nationally in the quantity of malpractice complaints. The police beating of Rodney King in 1991 and the trial of O. J. Simpson in 1995 exposed the racism of the LAPD, but there were many similar incidents that did not receive national attention. After the Rodney King trial, the Christopher Commission found that "racially motivated brutality" was "institutionalized" within the LAPD.[20]

For example, we see the displacement of racism from the LAPD to foreign villains in *Lethal Weapon 2,* in which the antagonists are vicious white South Africans smuggling currency and drugs under cover of diplomatic immunity. Symbolically, they are slave traders. Riggs says, "It's the triangle trade all over again: molasses to rum to slaves." Only now, it's "drugs to dollars to Krugerrands."

Because they are racist practitioners of apartheid who kill casually, they are also cartoon Nazis, ready made to hate. When Riggs meets the South African diplomat Arjen Rudd, he says contemptuously, "O fuck, I'll just call you Adolf." Later, he calls him "the master race." Riggs taunts Rudd:

> I'll make a deal with you, Arjen. Arjen, is it, or Aryan? Whatever the fuck your name is. You fold up your tent and get the fuck out of my country, and I won't do anything to you. I'll leave. Because if you stick around here, I'm gonna fuck your ass. I'm gonna send you home with your balls in a sling.

Rudd responds by calling Riggs "kaffir lover," the South African equivalent of "nigger lover."

The audience is supposed to applaud Riggs's xenophobic aggression (even though it is tinged with homosexual violence: "I'm gonna fuck your ass") because he is the hero and because he is LAPD, the embodiment of American law and order. Riggs is allowed to speak with open hostility and contempt, to curse, to use violence and threats of more violence—questionable behavior for a policeman—because he is the righteous white American defending the land of the free and the home of the brave against Nazis. The friendship of his black partner testifies to Riggs's anti-racist credentials.

The South Africans later declare war on the LAPD and kill several policemen. In addition, they kill Riggs's South African girlfriend, and he discovers that they were also responsible for the car crash that killed his wife. As in *Mississippi Burning*, the last straw that sets the hero on a rampage is not the fact that the villains are racist killers but that *they abuse white women*. Riggs's vendetta thus becomes personal, further justifying his violent revenge. The movie thus helps the audience to misrecognize police racist brutality by converting the LAPD into a haven of interracial amity and anti-racist crusaders.

The same effect is created in *Lethal Weapon 4*. In this movie, the foreign menace is not crudely stereotyped South Africans but crudely stereotyped Chinese gangsters. Riggs treats the head of a Chinese American gang with the same xenophobic contempt and violence he showed toward the South African boss. Here, however, the supposedly anti-racist crusader Riggs makes racist jokes, mocking the Chinese accent with stupid cracks to their face about "flied lice."

To make up for its use of Chinese villains, the movie includes a group of saintly Chinese boat people that Murtaugh rescues and Riggs and Murtaugh defend against the villainous Chinese thugs. The movie counters one stereotype—the "yellow peril"—with another: the helpless Asian refugee.

Just as the South Africans are metaphorically linked to slavery ("It's the triangle trade all over again"), so the Chinese criminals are slave traders. Murtaugh explains to Riggs why he rescued illegal immigrants, the Hong family, and is sheltering them in his home: "The way I see it, those are slave ships out there. And I'm freeing slaves. Like no one did for my ancestors, OK?" Although Mr. Hong and his brother are killed, the rest of the family in the end receives political asylum.

Lethal Weapon 4 concludes with a group snapshot. Two children have just been born—Riggs's child and Murtaugh's grandchild—and the white and black families gather in the hospital for a joint picture. The stranger taking the photo asks, "Are you friends?" They answer loudly, in unison, "No, we're family!" In this utopian conclusion, Americans are one big, happy interracial family, white and black together, with room also for Chinese boat people. It is reminiscent of the conclusion of *Guess Who's Coming to Dinner*. This is yet another example of contemporary, color-blind racism.

As Benjamin DeMott comments about such feel-good narratives, "Now playing nonstop in virtually every medium, our national, self-congratulating epic of amity provides the right-minded with unlimited occasions for contemplating their own sensitive, antiracist selves—and no occasion whatever for confronting objective race realities. It also supplies the majority culture with huge supplies of fantasy capital—fantasy moral capital."[21]

The Shawshank Redemption: True Romance

The Shawshank Redemption (1994), based on a story by Stephen King, is yet another fable of friendship and true love between a white man (Tim Robbins) and a black man (Morgan Freeman). In *The Defiant Ones,* a black and a white inmate help each other escape. Here the inmates help each other survive many years behind bars. Like most of the 1990s interracial buddy films, *The Shawshank Redemption* shows no hostility between the black and white heroes and never mentions race.

The white hero is Andy Dufresne, a young bank executive from Portland, Maine, sentenced to life in prison for the murder of his wife and her lover, a crime he did not commit. Andy survives nineteen years in Shawshank prison (from 1947 to 1966) by helping fellow inmates and by offering financial advice to the guards and the warden.

The warden needs Andy in jail, so he has a guard kill a young inmate who has evidence that Andy was innocent. At this point, Andy escapes through a tunnel he has been excavating for nineteen years. Using a fake identity, he withdraws the warden's laundered money from the banks, mails evidence to the local newspaper incriminating the warden and a vicious guard for corruption and murder, and flees to Mexico.

The Shawshank Redemption is a *Count of Monte Cristo* story of a strong, smart, and persistent hero who survives decades of unjust imprisonment and finally escapes, becomes rich, and gets his revenge on the villains who oppressed him. It is a tale of the triumph of the human spirit that one cannot help but applaud.

From this summary, it sounds like the film has nothing to do with interracial friendship. But the element that humanizes and enriches the story is the love between Andy and an African American, an older and wiser lifer named Ellis Boyd "Red" Redding, who narrates the story. Red helps Andy in prison and Andy gives Red the money to join him in Mexico in the end. The symbolic marriage between the two men, white and black, enables both to survive and ultimately to triumph.

Unlike other interracial buddy films, the story is told through a voice-over narrative by the black friend. Usually, if there is voice-over narrative in a Hollywood film, the white hero narrates and controls the point of view, as in *Glory, Little Big Man,* and *Dances with Wolves.* The effect of Red's narration, however, is not to heroize Red but rather to create admiration and sympathy for the white hero, like the voice-over narration of the white daughter in *To Kill a Mockingbird* or *The Long Walk Home.* Andy is the best of the white self: a natural leader, exceptionally smart, active, resourceful, patient, brave, compassionate, color-blind, and, above all, an innocent and good man who defeats injustice and evil.

By comparison, Red is kind and wily but a follower, not as resourceful or hopeful as Andy. After forty years behind bars, Red is a passive, self-proclaimed "institutional man." When he is finally paroled, he is scared and can't adapt to life on the outside. He contemplates suicide or a return to prison until Andy rescues him in the end. Thus, despite his voice-over narration, Red is simply a new version of the black sidekick who serves to glorify the white hero.

We also need Red's narration to explain at the end what has been going on, for Andy is something of a mystery, "a closed book," as his wife called him. Andy largely keeps to himself, concealing from everyone, including Red, his elaborate schemes to escape and to gain revenge. This lengthy concealment creates our pleased surprise at the denouement. Along with his disciple Red, we marvel at Andy's ingenuity.

As mentioned, race is not an overt issue in the film. All the prisoners in *The Shaw-shank Redemption,* both white and black, are slaves at the mercy of the warden and his brutal guards, which tends to erase distinctions between the races. However, American prisons are not utopias of racial harmony. On the contrary, they are often hotbeds of racial antagonism. It is far more common in American prisons for whites to associate with whites and blacks with blacks. Therefore, it is hard to believe that in an American prison during the period 1947 to 1966, a black inmate would be in the position of close friendship and equality with whites in which the movie shows Red. This is the contemporary strategy of color-blindness, which can also be called "color evasiveness" and "power evasiveness" because it is a way of asserting equality by ignoring reality.[22]

Class and Homosexuality in *The Shawshank Redemption*

The film tends to displace the issue of race, which is never mentioned, with issues of class and of homosexuality. First, Andy is differentiated from the other prisoners, both black and white, through his education and class privilege. They are working class and he was a bank executive. He uses his education to gain favor with the guards and the warden and privileges for himself and his fellow prisoners.

Second, as a tall, handsome young man, Andy is at risk from a group of white homosexual prisoners who repeatedly beat and gang rape him. These "bull queers" are set apart as the most violent and feared prisoners. Red even claims that they are not human, an argument often used by white racists against blacks.

The repeated homosexual rape of Andy also distracts us from the fact that the true romance in the film is between Andy and Red. There are no women in the film except Andy's wife, who is killed in the opening sequence. We also see a brief film clip of Rita Hayworth in *Gilda* (1946), playing a beautiful, adulterous woman parallel to Andy's wife. The other women are merely posters—first of Rita Hayworth, next of Marilyn Monroe, and finally of Raquel Welch—decorating the wall of Andy's cell. The posters attest to Andy's heterosexuality, show the passage of the decades, and also conceal the escape hole Andy is tunneling.

Homosexuality may also be unconsciously suggested by Andy's servitude to the warden and repeated images of excrement. Referring to the kickbacks the warden accepts, Andy tells Red, "There's a river of dirty money running through this prison." To escape, Andy crawls through the prison sewers. Says Red, "Andy crawled to his freedom through 500 yards of shit-smelling foulness I can't even imagine . . . crawled through a river of shit and came out clean on the other side." When he finally gets outside the prison, he celebrates his freedom as he stands in a creek and is cleansed by the pouring rain. Andy has been sodomized by the "bull queers" and, symbolically, by the warden as well. Prison has been a dirty experience for Andy, yet he escapes untainted. The ideal white self is miraculously still innocent and clean.

Compared with the adulterous wife, Red shows Andy true love. Andy rewards him by giving him directions, should Red be paroled, to uncover some treasure hidden beneath a rock in a New England field. The hidden treasure box contains money and a letter suggesting Red join him in Zihuatanejo, Mexico. The box is placed where Andy first made love to and proposed to his wife. By directing Red to the place where his marriage began, symbolically Andy is offering him marriage and a Mexican honeymoon. Like a

The Shawshank Redemption: *Prison has been a dirty experience, yet the ideal white self is miraculously still innocent and clean. Copyright 1994 Columbia Pictures Corporation.*

romance, the movie ends with the two embracing on a Pacific beach. The utopian scene—the open air, the white sand, and the green ocean—provide a final image of freedom, cleanliness, and purity. As in *The Defiant Ones,* the treacherous white woman is replaced by the hero's true love: his faithful black male companion.

The "Magical Negro"

It is worth briefly comparing *The Shawshank Redemption* to *The Green Mile* (2000). Both are directed by Frank Darabont from screenplays based on novels by Stephen King, relate a prison drama set in the American past, and feature a friendship between a white and a black man. Both mix brutal violence with sentimentality. In *The Green Mile,* the

The Green Mile: *A "magical Negro" at the service of the white hero. Copyright 2000 Warner Bros.*

black man and not the white is falsely accused of murder. Here the white hero is a kind prison guard who is helped by the prisoner and befriends him but cannot save him from the electric chair. The black character is particularly powerless: he seems feeble-minded, is black in the white South in the 1930s, and is a condemned man on death row. Yet at the same time, through the added element of supernatural fantasy, he is presented as extraordinarily powerful: a gentle giant of a man with magical healing powers. But in the course of the movie, he only heals white people. He is a kind of black Christ who goes willingly to his electrocution. The director Spike Lee objected to the fact that the character is another "magical Negro" at the service of the white hero, a phenomenon also seen in other recent movies like *The Family Man* (2000) and *The Legend of Bagger Vance* (2001).[23] Such movies demonstrate that, in Hollywood, the more things change, the more they remain the same.

Men in Black and the New Immigrants

If *48 Hours* and the *Lethal Weapon* series blended the white cop/black cop buddy movie with comedy, then *Men in Black* (1997) adds to this generic mix a droll, inventive spoof of science-fiction films about UFOs, "lashing together elements of sci-fi comic-book satire and 60s spy-television chic with enthusiasm and ease."[24] *Men in Black,* one of most popular films of 1997, led to commercial tie-ins including a music video and an animated TV series. A sequel was released in 2002.

The film concerns race not only because the partners are white and black but also because they police aliens. The "Men in Black" belong to a secret supragovernmental organization charged with protecting Earth from invasion or destruction by extraterrestrials. There are "good aliens," cosmic refugees granted political asylum and working on Earth disguised as human beings, and there are "illegal aliens," evil invaders from outer space, also wearing human disguise. It is the task of the MiB to keep the public blissfully unaware of the presence of either group. The movie's slogan is "Protecting the Earth from the Scum of the Universe."

The opening scene is intended to neutralize the notion that the movie is anti-immigrant. The U.S. Immigration and Naturalization Service halts a truck in the Southwestern desert and uncovers a group of Mexicans hiding in the back. The MiB arrive and take charge, taking aside one large Mexican man for questioning. He is exposed as a hideous extraterrestrial in disguise: in other words, one illegal alien is hiding inside another! Whereas the MiB agent K speaks Spanish and is kind to the Mexicans, whom he welcomes to the United States and tells the INS to release, he kills the evil extraterrestrial when it attacks.

The movie is thus an allegory about the new, "exotic" immigration to the United States from Latin America and Asia and our need to distinguish between "good" immigrants—those who can assimilate into American society—and "evil" ones—those who are supposedly inassimilable, criminals, or terrorists. It was also very popular in Europe, perhaps because the countries of Western Europe also currently face problems with xenophobia about immigrant workers. Like the supernatural comedy *Ghostbusters* (1984), *Men in Black* plays on somatic disgust to create horror and comedy. There is a lot of emphasis on *slime*; the evil aliens are exceptionally disgusting and repulsive. "Extraterrestrials today tend to be *wet,* the glycerine sheen variously suggesting evisceration, birth, mucus, dangerous bodily fluids, otherwordly goo."[25] The chief antagonist of the MiB resembles a giant cockroach that leaves a trail of bugs and slime and explodes at the end in a huge puddle of goo. But Mexican Americans in the Southwest United States are sometimes also contemptuously referred to as "cockroaches."

Men in Black: *Mexican Americans are sometimes contemptuously referred to as "cockroaches."* Copyright 1997 Columbia Pictures Corporation.

The Authoritarian Assumptions of *Men in Black*

Aside from its racial stereotyping, the movie takes for granted certain antidemocratic assumptions through which xenophobia can thrive, such as our need to be ruled and protected by a self-generating elite and the notion that "ignorance is bliss." The MiB are secret agents, members of a secret organization who operate behind the scenes, with all the powers of law-enforcement agents and more. They have contempt for the U.S. government, for they possess information and alien technology about which the government knows nothing. They are an elite, hierarchical order who carefully select their own members. Membership requires complete erasure of one's previous identity and severing all ties to the outside world, including friends and family. Like priests or monks, they dress in black, take solemn vows, assume a new identity and a new name, and cut themselves off from the world to serve it.

We could view the MiB as similar to the FBI (even the initials are similar), although Wendy Somerson reads the MiB as the epitome of the new multinational corporate liberalism, which recruits women and people of color, only to demand total loyalty to the organization and the elimination of difference in the name of profitability. "Structural racism and sexism are thus denied through visual inclusion within corporate culture."[26]

The transnational corporations have been called the new colonial powers. Certainly K and J are colonial agents par excellence. Like James Bond, they have superior knowledge and super technology and are licensed to kill.

K is the impersonal voice of authority, taking on "the white man's burden" to protect the public from dangerous aliens. J (Will Smith), the apprentice he recruits, is a young, brash, black cop, always ready with a smart quip. *Men in Black* thus reverses the partnership of the *Lethal Weapon* series: the white cop is older, more conservative, and ready for retirement, and the black cop is younger, hipper, funnier, and bolder than his partner.

The MiB see the people as a panicky mob that needs to be kept in ignorance for its own good. The movie "celebrates precisely the sort of clandestine guv'mint shenanigans [sic] we're all supposed to fear and loathe in waking life."[27] As another reviewer wrote, "The Men in Black aren't merry entrepreneurs, like the Ghostbusters. They're cold-blooded bureaucrats whose job is to control and suppress information."[28]

Their chief tool to control information is erasing memory through a high-tech device called a "neuralyzer." One flash, and the memories of any period from the past ten minutes to the past thirty years are obliterated. Individuals or groups can then be reprogrammed with any false memories the agents choose. Although the movie uses this effect mostly for comedy, the implications of such a device are dystopian. To control the public's memory is to control history; think of the "memory holes" in Orwell's novel *1984*.

Audiences probably fail to notice the movie's racial and antidemocratic assumptions because it is such an appealing power fantasy. Just as audiences identify with FBI agents in the movies or with James Bond saving the world from archvillains, so they can identify with the MiB. K is sympathetic because he is a lonely, battle-weary veteran who wants nothing more than to lay down the white man's burden and return to his wife, from whom he has been cut off for decades because of his job. It turns out in the end that he recruited J as his replacement. J is sympathetic because he is a bewildered newcomer who undergoes a rapid initiation into the MiB in which his physical strength, courage, resourcefulness, and quick wit are tested to the utmost. J is played by the likable Will Smith, who also played a fighter of extraterrestrials in *Independence Day* (1996).

Men in Black is also acceptable because it introduces apparently progressive elements, such as the white-black partnership. K chooses J as his apprentice simply because he is the best man for the job. At the end, the white agent retires and is replaced by the black man and a white woman, medical examiner Dr. Laurel Weaver, who is pulled into their adventures and becomes J's romantic interest and new partner. The feminist critic Marleen Barr celebrates the movie because supposedly "*Men in Black* transforms patriarchal constructions into the feminine and the feminist."[29]

But, this ignores the fact that at the end the MiB remains the same paternalistic, hierarchical, largely white male organization, still headed by the white man Zed. Wendy Somerson argues that J is simply the black man coopted to serve the organization: "*Men in Black* capitalizes on Will Smith's coolness that is inextricable from his race. By bringing him inside the organization, the film appeals to white audiences' desires to see Smith aligned with corporate law and order."[30]

Displaced Racism in *Men in Black*

Finally, the movie is popular with a large audience worldwide because the elements of science fiction and comedy seem to distance it from serious concerns. It is presented as tongue-in-cheek, an amusing science-fiction spoof. It even seems to make fun of typical science-fiction film xenophobia about extraterrestrials. As K tells J, most of the aliens are "decent enough . . . trying to make a living."

However, if the villains had been, for example, Iraqis, it would have been easy to recognize the stereotyping: there are good, hardworking, productive immigrants or aliens we welcome to America and evil ones who threaten us, and we can tell the difference, or at least the MiB can do that for us. As K tells J, "bugs thrive on carnage . . . they consume, infest, destroy, live off the death and destruction of other species." They resemble the locust-like invaders in *Independence Day* (1996). Such slimy monsters must be squashed like roaches. As J says to the Bug as he steps on a cockroach, "Oh, I'm sorry, was that your aunty? . . . You know y'all look alike." "Reversing the racist joke that all African Americans look alike, Smith becomes the quintessential U.S. citizen by situating the aliens as the representative Outsiders who do not deserve to live."[31] Even reversed, the joke is still racist.

In *Lethal Weapon 2,* racism is displaced onto cartoon South African villains who intrude into American society. In *Men in Black,* racism is displaced onto a cartoon interstellar cockroach who intrudes into American society. The effect in both movies is to glorify the heroes and to present racism as a foreign import, not something endemic to American institutions.

Conclusion: See No Color

We have seen the evolution of the black-white buddy movie over the course of almost forty years since the Civil Rights movement, from *The Defiant Ones* (1958) through *Men in Black* (1997). These films construct interracial utopias through black-white male bonding and consign women to the background. They also have in common a blend of violence and sentimentality, as well as a homosocial attraction between the buddies that is denied through bickering or jokes. Although the films begin by highlighting the initial racial hostility that the heroes must work through to bond as partners and friends, as in *The Defiant Ones, In the Heat of the Night,* and *48 Hours,* beginning with the *Lethal Weapon* series in 1987, racial difference has vanished as an issue. Although there are some exceptions to this pattern—in *Die Hard 3* (1995), a store owner from Harlem must overcome his hostility to whites when he is forced into temporary partnership with a New York City policeman—by and large the recent buddy films prefer to remain color-blind.

Color blindness is applied by whites to people of another color as a way of evading the continued significance of race in American society. "'Color-blindness' is a luxury that only those who are very secure in, and dysconscious of, their own racialized positions of whiteness and power can have."[32] Although color blindness has recently been adopted by some whites as a form of "political correctness," it is really a very old strategy. For example, in Ralph Ellison's novel *Invisible Man* (1952), the white political leader Jack is so high minded that he claims not to see race. He gets angry whenever the black hero analyzes situations in racial terms, telling him, "'You're riding 'race' again,'" to which the hero replies, "'I'm riding the race I'm forced to ride.'"[33]

The popularity of black-white buddy movies over the past 45 years testifies to the continuing crisis of whiteness the white American male has been undergoing since the Civil Rights movement, as white men struggle to find new ways to define themselves and to justify their privilege. "These race men of Hollywood dreams promise to annihilate what ails our nation and resolve our contemporary crisis of race, of nation, and of manhood."[34]

Notes

1. Shickel, Richard. 1987. Review of *Lethal Weapon*. *Time*, March 23, 87.

2. Willis, Sharon. 1997. *High Contrast: Race and Gender in Contemporary Hollywood Films*. Durham, N.C.: Duke University Press, p. 34.

3. Tasker, Yvonne. 1993. *Spectacular Bodies: Gender, Genre, and the Action Cinema*. New York: Routledge, p. 47.

4. Carby, Hazel V. 1998. *Race Men*. Cambridge, Mass.: Harvard University Press, p. 184.

5. Pfeil, Fred. 1995. *White Guys: Studies in Postmodern Domination and Difference*. London: Verso, p. 5.

6. Bogle, Donald. 1997. *Toms, Coons, Mulattoes, Mammies, and Bucks: An Interpretive History of Blacks in American Films*. New York: Continuum, p. 276.

7. Wiegman, Robyn. 1991. "Black Bodies/American Commodities: Gender, Race, and the Bourgeois Ideal in Contemporary Film," in *Unspeakable Images: Ethnicity and the American Cinema*, ed. Lester D. Friedman. Urbana: University of Illinois Press, pp. 308–28 (p. 322).

8. Pfeil, *White Guys*, p. 13.

9. Fiske, John. 1994. *Media Matters: Everyday Culture and Political Change*. Minneapolis: University of Minnesota Press, p. 256.

10. Carby, *Race Men*, p. 188.

11. Pfeil, *White Guys*, p. 12.

12. Carby, *Race Men*, p. 178.

13. Bogle, *Toms, Coons, Mulattoes, Mammies, and Bucks*, p. 276.

14. Ibid., p. 7.

15. Baldwin, James. 1963. *The Fire Next Time*. New York: Dial, p. 76.

16. Carby, *Race Men*, p. 187.

17. Baldwin, *The Fire Next Time*, pp. 8–9.

18. Willis, *High Contrast*, p. 31.

19. Tasker, *Spectacular Bodies*, p. 47.

20. Feagin, Joe R., and Hernán Vera. 1994. *White Racism: The Basics*. New York: Routledge, pp. 90–105.

21. DeMott, Benjamin. 1995. *The Trouble with Friendship: Why Americans Can't Think Straight about Race*. New York: Atlantic Monthly Press, p.186.

22. Frankenberg, Ruth. 1993. *White Women, Race Matters: The Social Construction of Whiteness*. Minneapolis: University of Minnesota Press, p. 14.

23. Lee, Spike, quoted in Kevin McDonough. 2001. "The Mortar of Predictability; Brickmaker Tale Gets Stuck in the Familiar," *Newsday*, September 20, B31.

24. Kermode, Mark. 1997. Review of *Men in Black*. *Sight and Sound*. August, 47.

25. Andersen, Kurt. 1997. "The Origin of Alien Species," *New Yorker*, July 14, 39.

26. Somerson, Wendy. 1999. "A Corporate Multicultural Universe: Replacing the Nation-State with Men in Black," *Narrative*, 7(2): 213–34 (p. 217).

27. Hoberman, J. 1997. Review of *Men in Black*. *Village Voice*, July 7, p. 69.

28. LaSalle, Mick. 1997. "*Men in Black*: Alienating Comedy." *The San Francisco Chronicle*, November 28, C18.

29. Barr, Marleen S., ed. 2000. *Future Females, The Next Generation: New Voices and Velocities in Feminist Science Fiction Criticism*. Lanham, Md.: Rowman & Littlefield, pp. 67–84.

30. Somerson, "A Corporate Multicultural Universe," p. 227.

31. Ibid., p. 223.

32. Rains, Frances V. 1998. "Is the Benign Really Harmless? Deconstructing Some 'Benign' Manifestations of Operationalized White Privilege," in *White Reign: Deploying Whiteness in America*, ed. Joe L. Kincheloe, et al. New York: St. Martin's Press, pp. 77–101 (p. 93).

33. Ellison, Ralph. 1952. *Invisible Man*. New York: Random House, p. 469.

34. Carby, *Race Men*, p. 191.

CHAPTER 12

Conclusion:
The Crisis of Whiteness

In our introduction we spoke of learning to be white through the movies. I (Hernán Vera) grew up in Chile and did not come to the United States until I was 31. My first awareness of the American Civil War came as a child in Chile from viewing *Gone with the Wind*. It was a war initiated by principled, cultured, handsome young Southern white men, the only ones with whom I could identify in the movie at that time. I learned that these heroes suffered greatly during the war: the men were wounded or killed and their cities burned while Union soldiers raped and looted. After the war the heroes were abused by unscrupulous, new rich black and white carpetbaggers. My first knowledge of the Civil Rights movement was based on *The Defiant Ones*, which I saw as a law student in Chile. I was astonished to realize from this movie that American blacks and whites hated each other so openly. Fortunately, once blacks were chained to whites, they would get to love and sacrifice for each other.

Surprisingly, I (Andrew Gordon), born and raised in the United States, discovered that my first knowledge of the American Civil War also came from *Gone with the Wind*, and my memories of the Civil Rights movement are mixed up with the drama of *The Defiant Ones* that was released in that epoch.

The Bubble That Is Culture

The movies, along with many other products of popular culture, such as television and music, provide us with the elements we use in our everyday life to think with and to function in an increasingly complex world. We live in the bubble of our stock of knowledge, that collection of ways of thinking, feeling, and acting we share with other members of our society. It is impossible to think, feel, or act outside this bubble, just as it is impossible to think and speak a language we do not know. In other words, we live using sincere fictions, those mental templates we use to relate to others. These templates of the mind are our "object relations," which we started learning in infancy and continue to acquire all our lives. "Film representations," writes Michael Ryan, "are one subset of wider systems of social representation (images, narratives, beliefs, etc.) that determine how people live."[1]

185

A traditional approach to the study of race relations has been to describe ethnic and racial groups by characteristics derived from empirical studies: African Americans, Latinos, Asian Americans, Native Americans, Jewish Americans, and so on. The problem with this approach is that it reifies the categories that society uses to stereotype, oppress, and exploit these groups.

In this book we have instead studied the fictionalizing of a set of images and types of relationships that we call race. Rather than looking at separate racial or ethnic groups, we look at the processes in the white mind as it creates representations of the white self and its relations with others. These processes, which include selective representation, rewriting of history, idealization, denial, projection, and displacement, guarantee the misrecognition of the sources of the racial divide in the United States. These images produced by white minds, disseminated through the Hollywood cinema, influence the entire American culture as well as the cultures of the rest of the world.

Whiteness in Crisis

We found that the image of the white self has remained essentially unchanged in American films across the twentieth century even as the images of the racial other have improved. At the same time, however, we claimed that the images of whites and others are intertwined, which seems contradictory. This is only an apparent contradiction. Despite the changes brought about by the Civil Rights revolution of the 1950s and 1960s, white privilege still dominates American society. The gains made by minorities were not granted by whites out of the goodness of their hearts but were won by African Americans and other minorities through struggle. In other words, the improved representation of racial others is a device to maintain the status quo of white privilege against the recognition earned by previously suppressed groups.

We noted that, over the decades, Hollywood appears to improve the representation of African Americans and Native Americans. The rabidly Negrophobic images of *Birth of a Nation* (1915) give way to the brilliant Dr. Prentice of *Guess Who's Coming to Dinner* (1967), the heroic African-American soldiers of *Glory* (1990), and the wise Cinqué of *Amistad* (1997). Nevertheless, these "improved" characters are as fantastic as the images in *Birth of a Nation*. In other words, one set of stereotypes is replaced by another. Minority figures in Hollywood movies remain projections of the white imagination intended to prop up the white self. A similar transformation can be observed in the image of Hollywood's Native Americans, whose early representation was based on nineteenth-century fiction, dime novels, and Wild West shows in which they were either bloodthirsty savages or noble savages. By 1970, in *Little Big Man,* the Indians are the heroes and the whites the savages. Images of Latinos have also apparently improved. The sweaty, dirty, mustachioed Mexican bandido of *Treasure of the Sierra Madre* (1948) gives way to the dedicated Chicano math teacher in *Stand and Deliver* (1988) and the high-achieving Chicano teenager who becomes a Navy pilot in *crazy/beautiful* (2001). These well-intentioned, improved images are no less fantasy projections than the images of African Americans in Hollywood films.

Robert M. Entman and Andrew Rojecki did a content analysis of top-grossing 1996 Hollywood movies and found that, despite greater representation in starring roles,

African American characters continue to be characterized as more violent, more sexual, and more profane and ungrammatical in speech. Their review of 1999 films suggests this to be a continuing trend. An interesting result of their analysis is that all the characters they coded as "criminal" turned out to be Latino. "Making Latinos the bad guys," they write, "may expose filmmakers to less danger of criticism for stereotyping than would their choosing Blacks."[2]

By contrast, the heroic, brave, kind white Americans in *Birth of a Nation* recur to this day in Hollywood movies such as *Glory, Amistad,* and *Men in Black.* In the Hollywood imagination, white heroes are natural-born leaders who continue to deserve the loyalty and admiration of racial others. These images have survived across the twentieth century despite all the changes and the gains made by minority groups. The resilience of the image of the white self in Hollywood cinema is remarkable.

Howard Winant claims that whiteness is in crisis since the arguments for the biological superiority of whites have been demolished. "Whiteness," he proposes, "has been deeply fissured by the racial conflicts of the post-civil rights period . . . Therefore it has been forced into *re*articulations, *re*presentations, *re*interpretations, of the meaning of race and, perforce, of whiteness."[3] These rearticulations, paradoxically, can only be achieved by conceding dramatic changes in the image of African Americans and other minorities but still reproducing the old image of the heroic white self. The changing representations are political in the sense that they are related to the distribution of power and privilege in the United States. The new images apparently recognize the humanity of minority groups but actually misrecognize the true relations between minorities and whites. White hegemony has to remain hidden at all costs. Whites, who have the power and cultural capital to implement racist practices, also array considerable resources to deny its existence.

Like Winant, Kelly Madison proposes that, in the last forty years of the twentieth century, whiteness faced a "legitimation crisis" provoked by the painstaking "illustration of the illegitimacy of the structure of white 'racial' oppression."[4] One way of resolving the crisis was by reconstructing collective memory through the "anti-racist/white-hero" film. Since 1987, many films, including *Mississippi Burning, The Long Walk Home,* and *Amistad,* focus on the heroism of white characters struggling for African American equality. By defining white supremacy only as a particularly brutal form of oppression that was practiced solely in the past in the American South, and by focusing primarily on the raised consciousness of the white heroes, these films suggest that whites have resolved the problem and that no further action needs to be taken. African Americans in these films are represented largely from the outside and as helpless victims.

We agree with Winant and with Madison, but we also find symptoms of a legitimation crisis as early as *Birth of Nation.* This film, too, attempts to revise collective memory. In *Birth of a Nation* we see whites whose consciousness is raised about racial matters and who take decisive action. In this case, the action is not to liberate African Americans, as in the anti-racist/white-hero films, but to justify the terrorist violence of the Ku Klux Klan against them. Although the representational extremes of *Birth of a Nation* did not continue, the film paved the way for the nostalgia films of the 1930s, such as *The Littlest Rebel,* and *Gone With the Wind,* which, like *Birth of a Nation,* promoted the Confederate version of the Civil War.

The black-white buddy films that we analyzed can also be seen as attempts to contain the crisis of legitimacy of the white self. These films emerge with the beginning of the Civil Rights movement, starting with the *Defiant Ones* (1958), and they especially proliferate in the past twenty years. Such films present a utopian view of American race relations in which all difference can be overcome through the male bonding of black and white heroes. Like the "anti-racist/white-hero" films, the *Lethal Weapon* series also attempts to revise history, although in this case it is more recent history. A critical characteristic of the movies in this series is the enormous destruction that takes place as the two cops bond. It is as if the violence between the races in the United States has been displaced by external threats. The films are so filled with violence that they are essentially war films, with the pair foiling international evil, acting more as global policemen—agents of American foreign policy—than as LAPD cops. For example, the first film of the series rewrites the collective memory of the Vietnam War as the newly bonded partners, one black LAPD cop and one white, both Vietnam vets, win a war against drug-dealing mercenaries.[5] In *Lethal Weapon 2,* the black and white buddies defeat evil, racist South African diplomats, thus helping to dismantle apartheid. In *Lethal Weapon 4,* the heroes fight Chinese gangsters who abused the partners' girl friend and daughter. The warring races may have changed, but the defense of the purity of innocent women against racial others is the same as in *Birth of a Nation.*

The *Lethal Weapon* series ends with the creation of a multiracial extended family, the ultimate denial of American racism. So much for segregated schools, white flight to the suburbs, enormous wealth differences, racial profiling, attempts to end affirmative action, and the disproportionate number of minority members in prison.

The main teaching of the *Lethal Weapon* series, like the majority of Hollywood films with a racial theme in the past 20 years, is that the color line can be easily crossed. However, this teaching does not advance equality in the United States. Films such as *Dances with Wolves,* according to the Native American writer David Seals, "neutralize real action, the possibility for social or political reform that might arise from truly stimulating literature or drama." He calls attention to "the New Custerism" of white liberals "torn between their cultural guilt and self-interest."[6]

The divided white self (see chapter 2) is torn between the ideals of equality and democracy and the reality of the violence on which white privilege rests. The division that Seals mentions is a psychological consequence of the split in the white self. For example, *Dances with Wolves* is self-congratulatory in presenting the nobility of the savage and the nobility of the white hero who can so easily go native and transform himself into a white Indian. This plot maneuver is a social therapy that simultaneously overcomes white guilt and promotes self-interest.

Racism Is a Project

Racism is a project (see chapter 6) that wants to preserve the privileges attached to being white in a democratic society. It wants to bring about a state of affairs where racial justice is impossible. Howard Winant describes five white racial projects that attempt to deal with the contemporary crisis of whiteness across the political spectrum: far right, new right, neoconservative, neoliberal, and new abolitionist.

The far right racial project is biologically grounded in "ineluctable, unalterable racialized difference between whites and non whites."[7] Winant identifies fascist features in this project: a belief in the biologic superiority of whites and an insurrectionary posture toward the state. Some of the groups in the far right openly admire the racial ideals of the Nazis. The Ku Klux Klan and the Christian Identity Movement are two among a plethora of such far-right organizations. Even though it was made in 1915, *Birth of a Nation* is the most representative film of this project. In fact, to this day white supremacist groups use this film as recruiting tool.

Unlike the far right, what Winant calls the contemporary new right is a "national electorally oriented, reactionary social movement" that "seeks to present itself as the tribune of disenfranchised whites." It embraces mainstream political activity and provided the basis for the Reagan revolution. Although it does not espouse racial supremacy, it exploits it through code words such as "welfare," "affirmative action," and "immigration." "The new right," explains Winant, "understands perfectly well that its mass base is white, and that its political success depends on its ability to interpret white identity in positive terms."[8] It has employed racial fears and demagoguery to achieve its aims. The Willie Horton ad in George Bush's 1990 campaign[9] and Pete Wilson's attacks against immigrants in California are examples of this project. The current campaign against affirmative action shows the vitality of the new right racial ideology. The basic scheme of movies such as *Soul Man* (1986) and *Falling Down* (1993) belongs to this project.

Most of the films that we have analyzed fit in the middle of the political spectrum, which in Winant's terms is represented by neoconservatism and neoliberalism. Hollywood aims to please and to soothe the widest possible audience, aiming at the middle yet still offering something to both the left and the right. While the neoconservative racial project "seeks to *preserve* white advantages through denial of racial difference . . . neoliberal discourse seeks to *limit* white advantages through the denial of racial difference." In spite of the considerable overlap of these two projects, Winant notes significant differences between them. A central neoconservative argument is that "beyond the proscription of explicit racial discrimination, every invocation of racial significance manifests 'race thinking', and is thus suspect. . . . Yet a refusal to engage in 'race thinking' amounts to a defense of the racial status quo, in which systematic racial inequality, and, yes, discrimination as well, are omnipresent. . . . They suffer from bad faith."[10]

Neoliberals differ from neoconservatives, according to Winant, because they recognize "the cross-cutting and competitive dynamics of race- and class-based forms of subordination in the postindustrial, post civil-rights era." Neoliberals seek "to narrow the differences which divide working and middle class people as a strategy for improving the 'life-chances' of minorities, who are disproportionately poor."[11]

Two recent movies, *Finding Forrester* (2000) and *O* (2001), reveal the neoconservative and neoliberal projects, respectively. The movies have similar plot elements: in both, a bright, talented young black man is recruited on a basketball scholarship to an exclusive white prep school. Both become basketball stars and win white girlfriends, in both cases dean's daughters. Both heroes then fall from grace because of white villains: Jamal, the hero of *Forrester*, is falsely accused of plagiarism by an envious white teacher. Odin, the hero of *O*, is falsely led to believe that his girlfriend is unfaithful, owing to the slander of an envious white teammate. There the plots diverge. *Forrester* has a happy ending, with Jamal rescued by his mentor, the famous white writer Forrester, who testifies on his behalf. But *O*, based on Shakespeare's

Othello, ends tragically: Odin, crazed with jealousy, murders his girlfriend and kills himself.

Forrester could be considered the neoconservative version of the plot. It downplays race and tries to be color-blind. The difficulties Jamal gets into are not the result of racial discrimination. On the contrary, the film implies, for talented young men of color, there are no real barriers. Yet, at the same time, the moral of *Forrester* seems to be: meet a famous white writer and rise to the top. It took a white messiah to recognize and nurture the black boy's talent. And the boy also succeeds because he is like the characters played by Sidney Poitier in films of the 1960s such as *Guess Who's Coming to Dinner* (1967) and *In the Heat of the Night* (1967): a black superman. Jamal overcomes racial difference by being both a basketball star and a supremely talented writer, and by adopting the culture of his white mentor.

O is the neoliberal version of the same story. The envious white teammate plays the race card, relying on Odin's insecurity as the sole black student in a white school. Nevertheless, the system is not perceived as racist because his fellow students hero worship Odin for his success, his white girlfriend truly loves him, and the white coach publicly proclaims that he loves him like a son. The importance of racial difference, however, is downplayed by making jealousy, not racism, the dynamic element in the plot.

The last white racial project, according to Winant, is new abolitionism, which advocates a "historical reinterpretation which aims to see race—and more properly, the gestation and evolution of white supremacy—at the center of U.S. politics and culture." New abolitionists have produced a series of studies that have had a significant impact on the way we understand race and class dynamics in the United States. These studies, according to Winant, reveal "how crucial the construction of whiteness was, and remains, for the development and maintenance of capitalist class rule in the United States."[12]

The core of the new abolitionist project, as we can observe in *Little Big Man, The Watermelon Man, Bulworth, Lone Star* (1996), and a few other movies, "is the imperative repudiation of white identity and white privilege."[13] Winant notes that new abolitionists want to accomplish this repudiation through intellectual and practical measures. Roediger, for example, has argued that "it is not merely that whiteness is oppressive and false; it is that whiteness is *nothing but* oppressive and false. . . . It is the empty and terrifying attempt to build an identity based on what one isn't and on whom one can hold back."[14] On the practical level, new abolitionists argue that whites can become "race traitors," as, for example, Robert Elliot Fox writes: "Since whiteness is not an essence but a construct, it isn't given but has to be acquired; therefore, one can refuse to (seek to) acquire it. If whiteness must reproduce itself each generation, as Noel Ignatiev argues, then one can refuse to reproduce it. I can't become black, but I can become postwhite."[15]

Winant critiques the new abolitionists for not taking social construction sufficiently into account. "Is the social construction of whiteness so flimsy that it can be repudiated by a mere act of political will, or even by widespread and repeated acts aimed at rejecting white privilege? I think not. . . . Rather than trying to repudiate it, we shall have to rearticulate it." Because "race," as we have proposed, is a way of relating, rearticulating whiteness necessarily involves the construction of new social relations. In this task, a critical challenge is how to modify the social unconscious that the moving pictures and other products of popular culture shape on a daily basis.

To De-invent Racial Superiority

We have argued that films provide some of the templates we use to think with about ourselves, others, and how we relate and should relate to each other. Films are powerful weapons to maintain white privilege, and thus could serve equally well to produce new object relations to eliminate it. At present, Hollywood is not doing that. "When it comes to the treatment of race, Hollywood . . . now lags behind the rest of the country, trapped in a time warp of its own making, brandishing a mantle of tattered liberal sainthood that has never looked more like a chain."[16]

Only neo-abolitionism wants to eradicate white privilege. The other four white racial projects aim to make the white self look beautiful, and this is why Hollywood movies continue to glorify white heroes and to turn minority characters into symbols.

We wonder what constitutes entertainment in the United States today and what kind of progress has taken place in American film in the past century when we view a recent film like *Black Hawk Down* (2001), a technically astonishing, realistic depiction of combat, but nonetheless hollow. It is based on a true story about a firefight that took place in Mogadishu, Somalia, in 1993 and cost more American lives than any other American combat incident since Vietnam. A troop of American soldiers, all white except for one token black, are pinned down in enemy territory, surrounded by thousands of hostile Somali militia. It is a nonstop shoot-'em-up, reminiscent of old Hollywood Westerns in which the U.S. cavalry is outnumbered and encircled by bloodthirsty Indians or the English movie *Zulu* (1964) in which an outmanned British garrison is besieged by thousands of African warriors. The purpose of *Black Hawk Down* is not to criticize the misconceived mission, an abortive "surgical strike" that cost eighteen American and a thousand Somali lives, but to glorify the heroism of the white soldiers and the U.S. military policy of "leave no man behind." It is a "stark good-versus-evil story. The Americans are uniformly dedicated, likable, and brave. The Somalis are uniformly grasping, creepy and savage—dark-skinned anthropoids with submachine guns,"[17] a horde of swarming Africans, "scary blacks . . . turned into the bursting targets of a video game."[18] We recall that *Birth of a Nation* (1915) was also based on historical events, featured realistic war scenes that were technically amazing for its day, and glorified the heroism and sacrifice of white soldiers. And in *Birth of a Nation* as well the enemy at the end was a mob of swarming blacks. Eighty-six years after *Birth of a Nation*, we get *Black Hawk Down*.

Stuart Hall proposes that we think of identity "as a 'production,' which is never complete, always in process, and always constituted within, not outside, representation. . . . Cultural identity is not a fixed essence at all, lying unchanged outside history and culture."[19] Whiteness was invented during the rise of imperialism and colonialism; it should be de-invented in our post-colonial age. However, to end racism we need to attack not just its ideology but also the social conditions that make it possible. If race is the "political unconscious of American film" as Nick Browne suggests, then what needs to be changed is that unequal, unjust way of relating we call race.[20]

The agents in *Men in Black* use a gadget called a "neuralyzer": they simply flash its blinding light into the eyes of an unsuspecting individual and thereby erase your memories of the recent past or even of entire decades of history, so that they can then reprogram you with the fantasies they choose. This blinding light that erases and re-programs

Men in Black: *The Men in Black use the "neuralyzer" to erase and re-program memories. Copyright 1997 Columbia Pictures Corporation.*

could be taken as a metaphor for the power of the movies. As we have said, the movies attempt to overcome the crisis of legitimation of white identity—the fact that white people in the United States no longer know who they are or are supposed to be—by erasing and re-programming collective cultural memory. As we showed in chapter 5 on *The Mutiny on the Bounty,* movies respond to tensions of the social moment and redefine the templates of the audience's mind in regard to dominant myths.[21] And fiction may be far more important than non-fiction in forming public opinion.

Certain ideas are hammered into the public with such persistence and through so many channels that they are difficult to escape. They become the consensus. One of these is the idea of white supremacy. Yes, the reaction of any individual in the audience cannot be predicted. Many reject white supremacy, and others find the notion repugnant when it is crudely presented, as in the propaganda of far-right organizations. Yet for most Americans, of whatever color, white supremacy is a given, an institutionalized notion, an automatic assumption that requires constant, conscious effort to resist.

Hollywood racial representations may change in the future as the result of demographic and market pressures. Blacks and Latinos already constitute a disproportionately large share of the U.S. movie audience. It is estimated that by 2010 one-third of the population of the United States will be non-white, and by 2030 there will be no majority group in the United States. In addition, more than half of Hollywood revenue comes from abroad. The growing American minority population and the non-white world will pressure Hollywood to be more inclusive and respectful in its racial and ethnic representations.[22]

However, for the present, we continue to live in a media-manipulated society, saturated in imagery of white supremacy. What exacerbates this situation is the fact that we rarely communicate actively about these images among ourselves. Instead, as in *The Matrix,* we exist each in a private womb, isolated, but all plugged into the same central program. In other words, we live today in a hegemonic totalitarianism in which our desires and necessities are determined by a few corporate authorities. Under such conditions, resistance is impossible without conversation and without solidarity.

We do not advocate censorship or codes of political correctness from the left or the right. Such a route is dangerous and does not work. Instead, we believe we need to educate ourselves and our children to view media critically so that we can move toward cultural democracy, toward a society that communicates actively and proactively. This can be done in part through group discussion. All schools of education should train future teachers on how to conduct discussions of film and other media with their students. Not just in schools, but in other social organizations as well it is vital to create forums to foster in all citizens a critical consciousness of media. More radically, some educators have called for a "media-based pedagogy" that would inform all school learning. The use of film and video would empower students to rewrite Hollywood scripts from different perspectives.[23]

We have taught thousands of American college students who at first resist the critical analysis of popular culture. For example, some laugh at the attempt to see the animated feature *The Lion King* (1994)—the highest grossing film in Disney's history—as anything more than light entertainment. Only after a group discussion of the elements of the movie do students begin to react against the implicitly racist assumptions of the movie, such as the lions as natural-born leaders and the hyenas as natural followers. We wish we could share with you the epiphany in our students' eyes when they realize that they have gained, through critical discussion, a deeper understanding of media and its role in their thinking, feeling, and acting.

Films and other media products should be the object of the same curiosity that has led humans to overcome the barriers of ignorance in other fields. As Paulo Freire puts is, this should be "a curiosity that is critical, bold and adventurous."[24]

Notes

1. Ryan, Michael. 1988. "The Politics of Film Discourse, Psychoanalysis, Ideology," in *Marxism and the Interpretation of Culture,* eds. Cary Nelson and Lawrence Grossberg. Urbana: University of Illinois Press, pp. 477–86 (p. 480).

2. Entman, Robert M., and Andrew Rojecki. 2000. *The Black Image in the White Mind: Media and Race in America.* Chicago: University of Chicago Press, pp. 195, 203.

3. Winant, Howard. 1997. "Behind Blue Eyes: Whiteness and Contemporary U.S. Racial Politics," in *Off White: Readings on Race, Power, and Society,* ed. Michelle Fine. New York: Routledge, pp. 40–53 (pp. 40–41).

4. Madison, Kelley J. 1999. "Legitimation Crisis and Containment: The 'Anti-Racist-White-Hero' Film." *Critical Studies in Mass Communication,* December, 399–416 (p. 400).

5. Carby, Hazel V. 1998. *Race Men.* Cambridge, Mass.: Harvard University Press, p. 183.

6. Seals, David. 2000. *Cinema Nation: The Best Writing on Film from The Nation, 1913–2000,* ed. Carl Bromley. Emeryville, Calif.: Thunder Mouth Press/Nation Books, p. 283.

7. Winant, "Behind Blue Eyes," p. 43.

8. Ibid., p. 44.

9. Feagin, Joe R., and Hernán Vera. 1994. *White Racism: The Basics.* New York: Routledge, pp. 114–22.

10. Winant, "Behind Blue Eyes," p. 45.

11. Ibid., p. 46.

12. Ibid., p. 47.

13. Ibid.

14. Ibid.

15. Fox, Robert Elliot. 1997. "Becoming Post-White," in *MultiAmerica: Essays on Cultural Wars and Cultural Peace,* ed. Ishmael Reed. New York: Viking, pp 6–17 (p. 12).

16. Gleiberman, Owen, 2002. Review of *Hart's War. Entertainment Weekly,* February 15, 43.

17. Massing, Michael. 2002. "Black Hawk Downer." *The Nation,* February 25, 5–6, 23 (p. 6).

18. Rothkopf, Joshua. 2002. "Heroes and Survivors." *In These Times,* February 18, 59–60 (p. 60).

19. Hall, Stuart. 1989. "Cultural Identity and Cinematic Representation." *Framework,* 36: 68–81 (p. 71).

20. Browne, Nick. 1992. "Race: The Political Unconscious of American Film." *East-West Film Journal,* 6 (January 1992): 5–16.

21. Lipsitz, George. 1990. *Time Passages: Collective Memory and American Popular Culture.* Minneapolis: University of Minnesota Press, p. 169.

22. Entman and Rojecki, *The Black Image in the White Mind,* p. 204.

23. Shohat, Ella, and Robert Stam. 1994. *Unthinking Eurocentrism: Multiculturalism and the Media.* New York: Routledge, pp. 357–58.

24. Freire, Paulo. 1998. *Pedagogy of Freedom: Ethics, Democracy, and Civic Courage.* Boulder, Colo.: Rowman & Littlefield, p. 38.

Index

Note: Page references to photographs are indicated by italic type.

About the Authors

Hernán Vera was born and grew up in Santiago, Chile, where he practiced law until, at the age of 31, he came to the United States to teach political institutions of Latin America at the University of Notre Dame. In 1974 he obtained a Ph.D. in sociology from the University of Kansas and joined the faculty at the University of Florida, where he is now Professor of Sociology. He has taught at the State University of Utrecht, in the Netherlands, and at the Universidad de Chile in Santiago, Chile. He is author of six books, among which are *White Racism: The Basics*, and *Liberation Sociology* (both with Joe R. Feagin), and *The Agony of Education: Black Students at Predominantly White Universities* (with Joe R. Feagin and Nikitah Imani). Hernán Vera is married to María I. Vera, and they have three children and three grandchildren. He teaches Sociology of Knowledge, Sociological Theory, and courses in race relations. His current project is the creation of a Latin American film collection at the University of Florida.

Andrew M. Gordon was born in Miami and raised in New York City, where he attended Stuyvesant High School. After receiving a B.A. in English from Rutgers University and a Ph.D. in English from the University of California, Berkeley, from 1973 to 1975 he was a Fulbright Junior Lecturer in American Literature at the Universidad de Barcelona and the Universidad de Valencia, Spain. Since 1975, he has taught at the University of Florida, where he is now Associate Professor of English and Director of the Institute for the Psychological Study of the Arts. He has taught contemporary American fiction, Jewish-American fiction, science fiction, and film. He organizes the annual International Conference on Literature and Psychology. He has also been a Fulbright Junior Lecturer in American Literature at the Universidade do Porto, Portugal, and a Fulbright Senior Lecturer in American Literature at the University of Niš, Yugoslavia. In addition, he has been Visiting Professor in American Literature at Janus Pannonius University in Pécs, Hungary, at the Universidad de Alcalá de Henares, Spain, and at the Linguistic University of Nizhny Novgorod, Russia. He is the author of *An American Dreamer: A Psychoanalytic Study of the Fiction of Norman Mailer* and of many essays on fiction and film, and co-editor (with Peter L. Rudnytsky) of *Psychoanalyses/Feminisms*. His current project is a book on the films of Steven Spielberg. He is the father of Daniel T. Gordon.